Philosophy of the Performing Arts

Foundations of the Philosophy of the Arts

Series Editor: Philip Alperson, Temple University

The Foundations of the Philosophy of the Arts series is designed to provide a comprehensive but flexible series of concise texts addressing both fundamental general questions about art as well as questions about the several arts (literature, film, music, painting, etc.) and the various kinds and dimensions of artistic practice.

A consistent approach across the series provides a crisp, contemporary introduction to the main topics in each area of the arts, written in a clear and accessible style that provides a responsible, comprehensive, and informative account of the relevant issues, reflecting classic and recent work in the field. Books in the series are written by a truly distinguished roster of philosophers with international renown.

1. The Philosophy of Art   *Stephen Davies*
2. The Philosophy of Motion Pictures   *Noël Carroll*
3. The Philosophy of Literature   *Peter Lamarque*
4. Philosophy of the Performing Arts   *David Davies*

Philosophy of the Performing Arts

David Davies

WILEY-BLACKWELL

A John Wiley & Sons, Ltd., Publication

This edition first published 2011
© 2011 David Davies

Blackwell Publishing was acquired by John Wiley & Sons in February 2007. Blackwell's
publishing program has been merged with Wiley's global Scientific, Technical, and Medical
business to form Wiley-Blackwell.

Registered Office
John Wiley & Sons Ltd, The Atrium, Southern Gate, Chichester, West Sussex, PO19 8SQ,
United Kingdom

Editorial Offices
350 Main Street, Malden, MA 02148-5020, USA
9600 Garsington Road, Oxford, OX4 2DQ, UK
The Atrium, Southern Gate, Chichester, West Sussex, PO19 8SQ, UK

For details of our global editorial offices, for customer services, and for information about how
to apply for permission to reuse the copyright material in this book please see our website at
www.wiley.com/wiley-blackwell.

The right of David Davies to be identified as the author of this work has been asserted in
accordance with the UK Copyright, Designs and Patents Act 1988.

Library of Congress Cataloging-in-Publication Data

Davies, David, 1949–
Philosophy of the performing arts / David Davies.
      p.   cm. – (Foundations of the philosophy of the arts)
   Includes bibliographical references and index.
   ISBN 978-1-4051-8802-9 (hardback : alk. paper) – ISBN 978-1-4051-8803-6
(pbk. : alk. paper)
1. Performing arts–Philosophy.   I. Title.
   PN1584.D38 2011
   790.2–dc22

                                                  2010049296

A catalogue record for this book is available from the British Library.

This book is published in the following electronic formats: ePDFs 9781444343472;
Wiley Online Library 9781444343458; ePub 9781444343441

Set in 11.5/13pt Perpetua by SPi Publisher Services, Pondicherry, India
Printed in Malaysia by Ho Printing (M) Sdn Bhd

1   2011

Contents

Preface and Acknowledgments   viii

Part One   Performance and the Classical Paradigm   1

1   The Nature of Artistic Performance   3
   1   Introduction   3
   2   What is a Performance?   4
   3   Institutional Theories of Artistic Performance   7
   4   Aesthetic Theories of Artistic Performance   10
   5   Artistic Performance and Artistic Regard   14
   6   Overview   17

2   The Classical Paradigm I: The Nature of the Performable Work   23
   1   Introduction: Berthold and Magda Go to the Symphony   23
   2   The Multiple Nature of Performable Works   24
   3   Performable Works as Types   29
   4   Varieties of Type Theories: Sonicism, Instrumentalism,
      and Contextualism   32
   5   Other Theories of the Performable Work   38

3   The Classical Paradigm II: Appreciating Performable Works
  in Performance   51
   1   Introduction: Talking Appreciatively about
      Performable Works   51
   2   Can Performable Works Share Artistic Properties
      with Their Performances?   53
   3   The Goodman Argument   57
   4   Answering the Goodman Argument   62

4   Authenticity in Musical Performance   71
   1   Introduction   71
   2   Authenticity in the Arts   72
   3   Three Notions of Historically Authentic Performance   74

5 Challenges to the Classical Paradigm in Music 87
  1 Introduction: The Classical Paradigm in the
    Performing Arts 87
  2 The Scope of the Paradigm in Classical Music 90
  3 Jazz, Rock, and the Classical Paradigm 94
  4 Non-Western Music and the Classical Paradigm 101

6 The Scope of the Classical Paradigm: Theater, Dance,
  and Literature 103
  1 Introduction: Berthold and Magda Go to the Theater 103
  2 Theatrical Performances and Performable Works 105
  3 Challenges to the Classical Paradigm in Theater 112
  4 Dance and the Classical Paradigm 120
  5 The Novel as Performable Work? 128

Part Two   Performance as Art 133

7 Performances as Artworks 135
  1 Introduction: Spontaneous Performance in the Arts 135
  2 The Artistic Status of Performances Outside the
    Classical Paradigm 138
  3 The Artistic Status of Performances Within the
    Classical Paradigm 143

8 Elements of Performance I: Improvisation and Rehearsal 149
  1 Introduction 149
  2 The Nature of Improvisation 150
  3 Improvisation and Performable Works: Three Models 154
  4 Improvisation and Recording 160
  5 The Place of Rehearsal in the Performing Arts 164

9 Elements of Performance II: Audience and Embodiment 172
  1 Can There Be Artistic Performance Without an Audience? 172
  2 Audience Response 181
  3 The Embodied Performer and the Mirroring Receiver 189

10 Performance Art and the Performing Arts 200
  1 Introduction 200
  2 Some Puzzling Cases 201
  3 What is Performance Art? 206
  4 When Do Works of Performance Art Involve Artistic
    Performances? 209
  5 Performance as Art: A Final Case 216

References 219
Index 226

For Ann

Preface and Acknowledgments

In philosophical aesthetics, there has been a recent turn towards what is called "philosophy of the arts." The assumption underlying this development is that, if we want to acquire philosophical insight into the arts, we must do justice not merely to the ways in which they resemble one another but also to the ways in which they differ. This is not to say that there is no longer a place for general theorizing about what artworks in general are or what their appreciation involves. But we must also be sensitive to the different ways in which such issues are inflected in different art forms. As we move away from general theory, however, we need to determine which ways of grouping the arts are likely to prove most fruitful if our explorations of similarity and difference are to prove illuminating. To take one example, photography is in one sense a sister art of cinema – we have moving and still images that rely on the same general technology. But in another sense it is a sister art of painting – they both present the eye with a still image, share an interest in portraiture and have histories that intersect in complex ways.

The place of the performing arts in this new philosophical landscape is interesting, for the very notion of "the performing arts" already imposes a structure on the arts. The things usually grouped under this label – music, dance, and drama – are in some ways strikingly different. For example, they seem to appeal to different cognitive capacities and different senses. We think of music as primarily a heard art, dance as primarily a seen art, and drama, at least as traditionally viewed, as the visual presentation of a narrative that speaks more to the understanding than to the senses. What, then, links these arts? Most obviously, it is the activities of performers through which works are realized for our appreciation. It is not surprising, then, that it is the notion of artistic performance that poses the most distinctive philosophical questions about the performing arts.

What is surprising, however, is that few attempts have been made to systematically study these questions as they apply to the performing arts as a whole. Rather, most philosophical inquiry bearing on the performing arts has concerned itself exclusively or primarily with music. There has been a widespread assumption that classical music provides us with a model for the performing arts as a whole. This model, which we may term the "classical paradigm," provides the framework for our explorations in the first part of this book. We look at what the model involves, the questions that it raises in the musical case, and the plausibility of thinking that it extends to other musical genres, to theater, and to dance.

In bringing out certain disanalogies between performances of classical music and other kinds of artistic performances, we establish the framework for our explorations in the second part of the book. We begin by looking at performances conceived as artworks in their own right. We then examine certain dimensions of artistic performance – improvisation, rehearsal, the role of the audience, and the embodied nature of the artistic performer – and note interesting similarities and differences between the performing arts. In the final chapter, we bring our general way of thinking about the *performing* arts to bear upon some of the most puzzling cases in contemporary art usually classified as "*performance* art."

In a couple of places in this book, I draw, with permission, on material that has appeared elsewhere or is forthcoming. The general framework for thinking about the performing arts set out in Chapter 1 was first sketched in chapter 9 of my *Art as Performance* (Blackwell, 2004), where I also looked at some of the examples discussed in Chapter 10. The notion of "artistic regard" defended in Chapter 1 is spelled out in more detail in "Pornography, Art, and the Intended Eye of the Beholder," due to appear in a forthcoming collection on *Aesthetics and Pornography* edited by Jerrold Levinson and Hans Maes (Oxford University Press, Oxford). In Chapters 6 and 8, I draw on "Rehearsal and Hamilton's 'Ingredients Model' of Theatrical Performance," *Journal of Aesthetic Education* 43 (3) (2009), 23–36. A slightly modified version of the discussion of embodiment in Chapter 9 is forthcoming as "'I'll be your mirror'? Embodied Agency, Dance, and Neuroscience," in Elisabeth Schellekens and Peter Goldie (eds), *Aesthetic Psychology* (Oxford University Press, Oxford). And in Chapter 10 I draw on "Telling Pictures: The Place of Narrative in Late-Modern Visual Art," in Peter Goldie and Elisabeth Schellekens (eds), *Philosophy and Conceptual Art* (Oxford University Press, Oxford, 2007), and on "Performance Art," in Stephen Davies et al (eds), *A Companion to Aesthetics*, 2nd edn (Wiley-Blackwell, Oxford, 2009), 462–465.

I would like to acknowledge the support and encouragement I have received in pursuing this project from Philip Alperson, the series editor, and from Jeff Dean and Tiffany Mok at Wiley-Blackwell. Jeff gave valuable feedback on early drafts of some chapters, and Jeff and Tiffany provided a very helpful framework that helped me to complete the first draft of the manuscript. I would also like to acknowledge the assistance I have received from all those people who have critically responded to some of the ideas in this book over the past couple of years, either through raising questions at presentations or less formally in discussions at conferences. I owe a particularly large debt of thanks to three of those people who also acted as reviewers for the press – Stephen Davies, James Hamilton, and Andrew Kania. Each read an entire draft of the manuscript and provided me with a wealth of critical comments and suggestions that made the process of revision both stimulating and productive. This book would have been much poorer without their input, although responsibility for the flaws that remain is of course entirely my own. I would also like to acknowledge the continuing support of the Social Sciences and Humanities Research Council of Canada whose funding has been of great help in the research for and writing of this book. Finally I would like to thank my partner Ann for her love, tolerance, and support over the past two summers when I worked on this book while more traditional summertime activities beckoned!

Part One

Performance and the Classical Paradigm

1

The Nature of Artistic Performance

1 Introduction

The aim of this book is to identify, explore, clarify, and perhaps even answer a range of philosophical questions that arise when we reflect upon the nature of the performing arts and our involvements with them. Most of us have participated in different ways in broadly artistic performances. Indeed, preparation for such participation begins early in life. Few of us manage to pass through primary school without finding ourselves on a stage trying to master a primitive instrument or struggling to remember our lines, under the nervously expectant eyes of our parents and friends. Some who emerge unscathed from such experiences pursue these kinds of activities in a more accomplished and self-assured manner not only in later schooling and university but also in adult life. They become professional or amateur singers or musicians, or participants in theatrical or dance productions, or orchestrators of the performative efforts of others. For most of us, however, our subsequent encounters with artistic performances are in the less heady role of spectator. We sit reverently at a performance by a string quartet or a theatrical troupe, or shiver under blankets at an open-air festival, or peer through lorgnettes at the posing of a diva, or pause in our evening meanderings to watch a street mime.

As you reflect upon your own encounters with the performing arts, it may seem strange to talk, as I did a few sentences ago, of the "philosophical questions" that arise when we reflect on such experiences. For our involvements with artistic performances hardly seem to generate such questions, apart from the ruminations inspired by the *content* of some performances we have attended – dark existential meditations inspired by a performance of *Hamlet*, for example. What I hope to show in the following chapters, however,

Philosophy of the Performing Arts, First Edition. David Davies.
© 2011 David Davies. Published 2011 by Blackwell Publishing Ltd.

is that our experiences of the performing arts, whether as performers or as spectators, already implicate us in questions about the very nature of artistic performances, independent of their particular content.

But before we take up these matters, we must look more critically at some notions that I have thus far taken for granted. I have spoken of "the performing arts" and of "artistic performances," and I have given some content to my use of these expressions by providing examples of familiar activities that might fall under these descriptions. But, we might ask, in virtue of what are these activities rightly brought under these descriptions? What makes a particular practice a performing art, or a particular event an artistic performance?

Consider the following response: a performing art is a practice whose primary purpose is to prepare and present artistic performances. This may be true as far as it goes, but we need to explain what it is for something to be an artistic performance. To answer that an artistic performance is the kind of event in which we actively participate or which we receptively encounter in the context of the performing arts is hardly illuminating. For we are simply moving in a narrow definitional circle. How should we try to break out of this circle? Since the circle involves two terms, we might try to give an independent account of one of them and then use this to explain the other. Suppose we take the notion of an artistic performance as our first term. Then we might characterize artistic performances in terms of some manifest properties that distinguish them from performances of other kinds. Given this analysis of artistic performance, we could define the performing arts as those practices designed to enable the presentation and appreciation of artistic performances so construed. We find something like this approach in Monroe Beardsley's (1982) attempt to characterize the movements that make up artistic performances in dance in terms of their distinctively "aesthetic" qualities. Suppose, on the other hand, we take the notion of a performing art as our first term. Then we might characterize those practices we commonly think of as performing arts – theater, music, and dance, for example – in terms of "institutional" features that do not presuppose the nature of the performances presented within them. And we could define artistic performances as those that are presented within the context of such institutionally characterized practices. We find something like this approach in George Dickie's "institutional" theory of what it is that makes something a theatrical performance.[1] After some preliminary remarks about the nature of performance in general, I shall explore this second kind of approach before considering the former alternative.

2   What is a Performance?

Since we are interested in the nature of artistic performances, and not simply in whether they are properly classified as theater or dance, we should start by asking, in the most general way, what leads us to talk of a particular event as a *performance*. All performances, in the sense that interests us, are actions, whether individual or collective. In a collective performance, different individuals not only act but do so in a way that aims at some kind of coordination of their individual efforts. As actions, performances involve behavior that falls under at least one description specifying a purpose governing that behavior and, implicitly or explicitly, a result at which it aims. This is how the action of shutting the window differs from those bodily movements described in purely physical terms through which that action is accomplished. In so characterizing the sense of "performance" that interests us, we distinguish it from the use of the term to assess the behavior of things that may be incapable of action. We can mark this distinction by talking, in the latter case, of performance "in the merely evaluative sense," and in the former case of performance "in the full sense." When I describe to a garage mechanic my car's erratic performance when I drive it in the rain, for example, I am not attributing actions to my car, but merely characterizing what it does in a context where this is a subject of evaluation. My car is in no sense a *performer*, even though what it does is indeed its performance in the merely evaluative sense.

But, if all performances in the full sense are actions, not all actions are performances in the full sense. It is unlikely that brushing one's teeth in the morning, or walking to one's place of work or study, would normally qualify as performances in the full sense, for example. We rightly describe an action as a performance in the full sense only if it meets certain further conditions. Suppose, for example, that Basil regularly carries an umbrella when he travels to work, and that he twirls it ostentatiously as he walks to and from the station. This could just be a nervous tic, but suppose that the twirling becomes more stylized and daring when he passes through neighborhoods where his actions are likely to be observed. It now starts to seem natural to describe what Basil does not merely as an action but as a performance in the full sense. Part of our evidence for characterizing what Basil does in this way is the patterns that we observe in his behavior, the actions that are repeated from one occasion to another. But a performance in the full sense need not be an instance of a type of behavior that is repeated in this way. Young Ben who stomps from the room slamming the door after being told that he can't play his new video game on the family television may also rightly be described as giving "quite a performance" even if this is (happily) an isolated punctuation of the domestic calm.

What then are the features that distinguish those actions we are inclined to call performances in the full sense from other actions? First, as our examples indicate, performances in the full sense not only involve actions aimed at achieving some result, but are also open, at least in principle, to public scrutiny and assessment. But this by itself obviously fails to distinguish performances from mere actions. Ben's mother may comment that he is getting better at brushing his teeth properly, but we would resist saying, on these grounds, that Ben's tooth-brushing behavior is a performance in the full sense. We might talk of it as a performance in the merely evaluative sense, since it is a regularity in Ben's behavior that we are evaluating relative to some standard. In this sense, parents worry about the performance of their children in school. But the worry would be different if it was reported that their children were "performers" in school, that their actions were performances in the full sense. To see why, it will be helpful to use a different example.

Consider how one might talk about one's local football team after watching them slump to yet another ignominious defeat. One might bemoan the performance of the team while also singling out the performances of certain players for particular vilification. But, as with Ben and my car, to talk about performance here is to talk in the merely evaluative sense about what someone or something does. It does not entail that the persons or things evaluated are *performers* in the sense that Basil can be described as a performer. But consider the footballer Edwin who "showboats" because he believes a scout from a big team is in the crowd. Confronted by the somewhat agricultural fullback of the opposing team whom he could easily outpace, Edwin makes a point of executing a smart "step-over" routine that leaves the fullback floundering in his wake. Here, as with the pupil who deliberately acts up in class, it seems right to talk not just of his performance, but also of him as *performing*. To perform is to act in certain ways *for* the attention of those who are or may be observing one's actions. The football player normally chooses to act in the way he does because of what his opponent is doing. His actions are guided by, and are responses to, the actions or expected actions of the other players. In the case of Edwin, on the other hand, his actions are guided not merely by what the other player does but by his expectations as to how the scout will evaluate these actions. He is acting *for* the scout, and it is these expectations that explain why he makes the particular moves that he does.

Thus the performer differs from the mere agent whose behavior is subject to evaluation in that she *intends* for her actions to be appreciated and evaluated, and thus is consciously *guided* in what she does by the expected eye or ear of an intended qualified audience. It is because we take Basil and Edwin to be so guided in their actions that we think of them as performing and of what they do as performances in the full sense. This is not to say that such performances require an *actual* audience – a point to which we shall return in Chapter 9. Basil's expectation that his umbrella twirling will be admired by startled neighbors interrupted in their breakfasting by the sight of his astonishing manual dexterity may be ill-founded. No one may observe him, but it still makes sense to say that he is performing. Similarly, if Ben's behavior becomes more common, his parents may become immune to his tantrums, so that none of the expressive nuances of his stomping are registered, but he will still be performing. In fact, even the execution of ordinary mundane tasks can qualify as performances in the full sense. For example, if Ben brushes his teeth with special vigor and care on the assumption that his mother is watching him, in order to impress her, it seems reasonable to describe him as performing and what he does as a performance in the full sense. (In future, I shall speak here simply of "performances," and use the term "performance in the merely evaluative sense" to talk of the other sense in which some behavior can be rightly described as a performance.)

None of the actions just described will strike us as "artistic performances" of the sorts to which I alluded in the opening paragraph. But the kinds of things done on stage by actors, dancers, and musicians are certainly *performances* in the sense just characterized. The musician's manipulation of her instrument, the actor's delivery of his line, or the dancer's execution of a pirouette, have the form that they do at least partly in virtue of conscious expectations as to how these actions will affect and be evaluated by members of an intended audience, even if that audience is sometimes the performers themselves. This, however, brings us back to our earlier question: what is it that distinguishes *artistic* performances from the performances of Basil, Ben, and Edwin?

3   Institutional Theories of Artistic Performance

The second approach canvassed earlier holds that an artistic performance is one that takes place in the context of those established practices that we think of as "performing arts." These practices, we might say, embody norms prescribing specific kinds of conduct for performers and for receivers of performances. We find such a conception of what makes something a *theatrical* performance in George Dickie's argument for an "institutional" theory of art. Dickie proposes that to be an artwork is to have acquired a particular kind of status within what he terms "the artworld." The artworld is "the broad social institution in which works of art have their place" (1974, 31). This institution comprises a set of systems of "established practices" which correspond to the different art forms. Each such system functions as a framework for the *presenting* of works of art. To be an artwork, according to Dickie, is to be an artifact a set of whose aspects has acquired, through the agency of some person or persons acting on behalf of the artworld, the status of "candidate for appreciation." To be a "candidate for appreciation" is to be eligible for presentation within the appropriate system of the artworld, the aim being that receivers appreciate – find some value in – what is presented.

The theater is Dickie's primary example of a system of the artworld. In the theater, "the roles of the actors and the audience are defined by the traditions of the theater. What the author, management, and players present … is art because it is presented within the theaterworld framework. Plays are written to have a place within the theater system and they exist as plays, that is, as art, within that system" (Dickie 1974, 30).[2]

An analogous account might be given of works and performances in those other artworld "systems" that we intuitively view as belonging to the performing arts. A musical work or a work of dance, we might say, is something composed to be performed within the "musicworld" or the "danceworld." Dickie's concern is with defining what it is to be a work of art, rather than with the notion of an artistic *performance*, and we shall inquire shortly about the relationship between artistic performances and artworks. But we can offer a tentative "institutional" definition of artistic performance in line with the strategy canvassed above. An artistic performance, it might be said, is a performance that has had conferred upon it, by a person or persons acting on behalf of the artworld, the status of candidate for appreciation in the theaterworld, or the musicworld, or the danceworld. We can add additional artworld systems to our definition if we want it to cover events that fall within the rather eclectic category of "performance art" but that fit uneasily into the artworld systems listed so far. For example, Vito Acconci's *Following Piece* (1969) involved following unwitting citizens through the streets of New York over a period of a couple of weeks, and Stelarc grafted an ear onto his forearm with the intention that it incorporate a microphone capable of transmitting to receivers what the "ear" was hearing.

Our tentative Dickiean institutional account of artistic performance began by characterizing the performing arts "extensionally" through listing the relevant conventions definitive of the artworld systems in question. We then defined an "artistic performance" as a performance having the status of "candidate for appreciation" in one of the performing arts so construed. But this account faces some serious objections grounded in a feature upon which Dickie insists. It should not be thought, he maintains, that there is a distinctive *kind* of appreciation for which artworks or artistic performances are candidates. Appreciation, in his definition of "artwork," is just what it is more generally outside the arts: "All that is meant by 'appreciation' in the definition is something like 'in experiencing the qualities of a thing one finds them worthy or valuable,' and this meaning applies quite generally both inside and outside the domain of art" (Dickie 1974, 40–41). He is motivated here by the concern that, if our definition specifies a more narrowly "aesthetic" kind of appreciation, we will be unable to accommodate many late modern artworks that deliberately eschew the aesthetic as traditionally conceived. But while Dickie is right to think that such works must be accommodated, he is wrong, as we shall now see, to think that the institutional theorist can do so by simply denying that there is anything distinctive about the kind of appreciation for which artworks, and artistic performances, call.

The first difficulty arises if we ask how the presentational systems that make up the artworld differ from other practices that serve to present things as candidates for appreciation. In the context of our proposed institutional definition of artistic performance, the difficulty lies in identifying in a principled way the systems to be included in our extensional definition of the "performing arts." The performances of university lecturers, for example, are presented in a context where there are norms that prescribe certain kinds of behaviors on the part of both participants and receivers. Given these norms, the performances clearly have conferred upon them by their performers the status of "candidates for appreciation," if appreciation is simply a matter of the receiver's finding value in experiencing those performances. As we saw above, we need a measure of flexibility in our conception of the presentational systems making up the artworld if we are to accommodate radical innovations in artistic performance. But what principled reasons are there for extending this conception to include the activities of Acconci and Stelarc while refusing to extend it to include the activities of university lecturers? If we deny ourselves any recourse to a distinctive kind of appreciation or attention appropriate to artworks, this challenge is difficult to answer.

It might be replied, of course, that it is simply a brute fact, admitting of a sociological but not of a rationally principled explanation, that we group some of these systems under the concept of art while excluding others. But this response leaves us unable to justify in any principled way our willingness or unwillingness to classify as artistic performances that occur outside our own immediate cultural context. Various kinds of dance, music-making, and role-playing as they occur in non-Western cultures, for example, will count as artistic performances, on the proposed account, only if they take place within presentational systems of the artworld. But, to the extent that the presentational practices of these cultures differ from our own, how are we to determine whether these practices are rightly seen as constitutive of artworld systems? We might appeal to obvious observable "similarities" between the performances licensed by the practices in question and practices in recognized performing arts. But this strategy quickly founders when we note, for example, that, in spite of Dickie's insistence on the ancient ancestry of the theaterworld, much Greek dramatic performance resembled what goes on in our "sportsworld" in being presented competitively.[3] If the institutional theorist is to meet these kinds of objections, she needs to bring into play something more fundamental that unites the systems within which artistic performances can take place. I shall explore below the suggestion that the presentational systems characteristic of artistic performance are designed to foster a particular kind of appreciation. But this appreciation cannot be "aesthetic" in the traditional sense that associates the latter with the experience of something as beautiful.

A further difficulty arises even if we can identify in a principled and projectable way the presentational systems that enable artistic performances. How are we to delimit the relevant conventions in such systems so as to include performances of avant-garde theater and exclude stage hands who ham it up while rearranging props between scenes? It might be said that this distinction is embodied in one of the relevant conventions constitutive of the theaterworld system. One of the things that qualified theatergoers know, it might be claimed, is that the movement of props on stage by people who have not figured in the dramatic action is not part of the artistic performance. But of course this is not universally true. Certain modern plays – for example, Robert Wilson's 1981 production of *Medea* – deliberately integrate such activities into the piece. This is why there is a problem in accounting for avant-garde theater, where "stagehands" may not in fact be stagehands but, rather, participants in the artistic performance itself. It is not, it seems, the conventions in themselves that exclude certain things going on onstage from the artistic performance, but the spectators' independent ability to work out which things are part of the play and call, therefore, for a particular kind of attention.

4   Aesthetic Theories of Artistic Performance

This point is, I think, of great significance, and we shall return to it after considering the other approach canvassed earlier. This approach, it will be recalled, aims to give an independent account of artistic performances in terms of manifest features distinctive of such performances. It can then define the performing arts as those presentational systems designed to present artistic performances so conceived. This clearly avoids the kinds of difficulties seen to beset the institutional approach. For, if we have an independent account of the nature of artistic performance, we also have a principled way of determining which presentational systems are rightly included in the performing arts. But, as we shall see, this approach faces difficulties of its own.

I shall take as a model here Monroe Beardsley's (1982) attempts to clarify the distinctive nature of those performances that we encounter in artistic presentations of dance. Like Dickie, Beardsley brings a more general theory about artworks to bear in his analysis. An artwork, for Beardsley, is an ordering of elements with the intention that they afford a markedly aesthetic experience, or an ordering of a type that is generally produced with such an intention.

Beardsley's conception of "aesthetic experience" underwent a number of changes. He increasingly stressed the phenomenal nature of such experience, which requires that we imaginatively attend to an object in an emotionally detached way. Pleasure in such experience arises from the discovery of relations between the elements of which the object is composed and from the formal and expressive qualities thereby apprehended.[4] In his account of those dance performances that qualify as artistic, Beardsley makes two distinct claims: (1) a claim about the elements of which such dance performances are composed, and (2) a claim about how these elements are realized through the movements of the dancers and thereby made accessible to an audience.

In elaborating the first claim, he distinguishes between two senses in which a "medium" is involved in the creation and constitution of a work of art. The "physical medium" employed in a given artwork is the "stuff" of which the artist makes use in order to articulate some kind of aesthetic or artistic content. The "artistic medium," on the other hand, is what links manipulation of the physical medium to the articulation of particular meanings – to the expression of a particular emotional quality, for example. In the case of a painting, we can think of paint and canvas as the physical medium, and such things as brushstrokes and impasto as elements in the "artistic medium." To characterize a painting in terms of its artistic medium – as we standardly do in describing such a work and explaining our responses to it – is to see it as the realization in the physical medium of the expressive activity of the artist. We talk here about the brushstrokes and design, rather than the pattern of paint, and we see particular designs or arrangements of brushstrokes as articulating particular contents.

Beardsley draws an analogous distinction between the physical medium of dance – bodily movements – and its artistic medium – what he terms "movings" and "posings." The claim is that, in attending to a dance, we see what is going on in terms of movings and posings, and we interpret such movings and posings as representing or expressing or exemplifying certain qualities. One question, here, is how the movings and posings that make up the dance are related to the bodily movements performed by the dancers. Beardsley distinguishes two ways in which actions can be built out of one another, such that one act "generates" another. First, *causal* generation occurs when the performance of one action causally brings about some result in terms of which we can describe the second action. For example, I drive in the nail by hitting it with the hammer. In the case of *sortal* generation, however, doing one thing counts as doing another thing in virtue not of causal relations but of shared understandings in the cultural context in which one acts. The clearest examples of sortal generation involve social conventions. For example, if I raise my hand during the bidding at a public auction, I thereby make a bid for whatever is being sold.

Beardsley claims that the movings and posings constitutive of dance are sortally generated by the bodily motions of the dancer. But we must then specify the "generating conditions" in virtue of which certain bodily motions count as movings and posings and thus as elements in an artistic dance performance. This brings us to his second claim. He maintains that what counts are certain manifest properties of the bodily movements – what he terms "regional qualities" – the consequent "expressiveness" of which we take to be willed by the agent. This allows that even *practical* movements that have a certain social function, such as the North American pueblo corn dance, can count as artistic performances insofar as they have an expressiveness that goes beyond the execution of the motions necessary for the social function to be fulfilled. In the case of such a practically motivated ritual, "if … there is more zest, vigor, fluency, expansiveness, or stateliness than appears necessary for practical purposes, there is an overflow or superfluity of expressiveness to mark it as belonging to its own domain of dance" (Beardsley 1982, 249).

The problems with any such attempt to delimit artistic performances in terms of manifest properties of the sort cited by Beardsley are well brought out in a critical response by Noël Carroll and Sally Banes (1982). They argue that the "superfluity of expressiveness" which he seems to regard as the distinguishing feature of artistic dance performance is neither necessary nor sufficient for the latter. It is not *sufficient*, because there are obvious instances of movements that manifest such superfluity yet which fail to be examples of dance performance. They cite the evident enthusiasm that might characterize the behavior of members of a group of socialist volunteers participating in the harvest. But, given our earlier remarks on what is distinctive of performance in general, it seems open to Beardsley to question whether what we have in this case is a performance at all. For it is not apparent that the behavior is consciously guided by expectations concerning the evaluating eye of an intended audience. If we take dance in the performing arts to involve a kind of performance, then it seems that Beardsley's condition will apply only to performances and not to mere actions. Thus the socialist volunteers are not a counter-example to Beardsley's account of artistic performance. But suppose the actions of the volunteers *did* qualify as a performance because they were performed for the anticipated eye of the party chairman. It seems very strange to say that the superfluity of expressiveness would make it a performance of artistic dance, so Carroll and Banes's general point still stands.

More significantly for our purposes, they argue that "superfluity of expressiveness" is not a *necessary* condition for artistic dance performance, because there are incontestable examples of the latter that fail to meet this condition. They cite *Room Service*, a piece by Yvonne Rainer that falls within the more general category of "task dances." The dancers perform a series of ordinary movements that involve, among other things, the moving, arranging, and rearranging of objects such as mattresses and ladders. Carroll and Banes, who attended a performance of the piece, remark that one of the central elements in the performance is "the activity of two dancers carrying a mattress up an aisle in the theater, out one exit, and back in through another." Crucially, the movements of the dancers were in no obvious way intensified so as to differentiate them from ordinary activities such as – indeed – moving a mattress around in a sequence of rooms. Carroll and Banes comment on the piece as follows:

> The point of the dance is to make ordinary movement qua ordinary movement perceptible. The audience observes the performers navigating a cumbersome object, noting how the working bodies adjust their muscles, weights, and angles … The *raison d'être* of the piece is to display the practical intelligence of the body in pursuit of a mundane goal-oriented type of action – moving a mattress. (Carroll and Banes 1982, 251)

It is obviously essential for the successful performance of this dance work that it *not* manifest a superfluity of expressiveness which would make it observably different from the movements involved in the ordinary execution of the tasks in question. For the point of the work is to make those movements as such perceptible.[5]

If our characterization of artistic performance is to accommodate such contemporary works in the performing arts, therefore, we cannot appeal to manifest features of the sort cited by Beardsley. But what lesson should we draw from such cases? Commenting on the possibility that a choreographer might transform the activity of the socialist volunteers into a dance by placing them on a proscenium stage, Carroll and Banes assert that

> in such a case, it seems to us that it is the choreographer's act of framing, or recontextualizing, rather than an intrinsic quality of the movement, that is decisive. In general, whether one is speaking about art dance or social dance, the context of the event in which the movement is situated is more salient than the nature of the movement itself in determining whether the action is dance. (Carroll and Banes 1982, 250)

On perhaps the most natural reading of this passage, the act of "framing" or "recontextualizing" just is the act of presenting the movements of the volunteers on a proscenium stage. So read, Carroll and Banes are endorsing something like the institutional theory of artistic performance we had reason to question above. But the role they ascribe to the choreographer, or to the performers themselves, in constituting something as an artistic performance also admits of a non-institutional reading – or, at least, of a reading that makes the role of institutions more oblique. In the following section, I shall develop an account based on such a reading, thereby weaving into a more textured account two threads introduced earlier. First, difficulties with Dickie's institutional theory were traced to his refusal to countenance a distinctive kind of appreciation for which artworks and artistic performances call. And, second, I suggested that the distinction between performances and mere actions lies primarily in the way in which a performer is consciously guided in her actions by the anticipated evaluative attention of an intended audience for whom she performs. The account I shall develop brings these threads together by taking the attention solicited by artistic performances to be of a distinctive kind, in virtue not of their manifest properties per se, but of the way in which their manifest properties are used by performers to articulate the content of their performances. Artworks in general, and artistic performances in particular, call for a distinctive kind of "regard" from receivers in virtue of how they are intended to work. Like Dickie and Beardsley, I shall draw on a more general view about artworks in developing this account of the distinctive features of artistic performances. I shall conclude this chapter by fulfilling the earlier promise to address the relationship between artworks and artistic performances. This will establish the framework for our inquiries in the remainder of this book.

5   Artistic Performance and Artistic Regard

Let us return to Rainer's *Room Service*. Richard Wollheim, himself arguing that there is a distinctive kind of regard for which artworks call, suggests that if we want to test any hypothesis about the spectator's attitude to artworks, "it would be instructive to take cases where there is something that is a work of art which is habitually not regarded as one, and which we then at a certain moment come to see as one" (Wollheim 1980, 120). He offers familiar works of architecture as such a test case. But it is more illuminating for our purposes to focus on the kind of case that has been a mainstay of recent work in the ontology of art. I refer here to the *indistinguishable counterpart*, something that shares all of the perceptible qualities of the vehicle of a given artwork without itself being a vehicle of that work.[6] Our interest here is not, as in most of the literature, in what makes one entity the vehicle for a particular artwork where another perceptually indistinguishable entity is either the vehicle for a different artwork or a mere "real thing." Our interest, rather, is in how our manner of regarding – attending to – something that we take to be an artistic vehicle differs from our manner of attending to a perceptually indistinguishable mere real thing. Rainer's piece offers a case of this sort. The sequence of movements presented to the audience in a performance of her piece is not perceptibly different in any essential respects from the sequence of movements we might observe in a furniture warehouse. Her piece is nonetheless a work of dance because of how she wants her intended audience – people familiar with the more general traditions of the dance – to respond to an execution of that sequence. She wants the audience to attend to the movements with the same sort of care and intensity, and the same kind of "artistic" interest in grasping the *point* of the movements, as they would do if they were watching a performance of a more traditional work of dance.

We can note a couple of features of this attention. First, many details of the movements to which we would pay no regard if observing two people moving a mattress in a furniture warehouse are significant if we attend to those movements as a work of dance. In fact, every visible inflection of the bodies through which the act of moving the mattress is executed is significant in this way. We must therefore attend much more closely to the nuances of the movements than if we were observing perceptually indistinguishable movements executed in an ordinary setting. Second, as Carroll and Banes make clear, we are expected to look for a "point" to the sequence of movements performed. This is not merely the practical point of moving a mattress, but the point of presenting such a sequence of movements to us in a context where we are required to attend to those movements in the close and discriminating way just described. The actions of the dancers stand as *examples* of how the human body serves as an instrument of our desires and purposes. By being presented as such examples, they also serve as a comment on our embodiment as described by Carroll and Banes.

The difference between a sequence of movements that serves as the vehicle for an artistic performance and something, indistinguishable in terms of its manifest properties, that does not so serve, is, I claim, to be explained in terms of the kind of regard for which the first entity calls if we are to grasp the content being articulated through that sequence. "Content," here, includes what the performance represents, expresses, or exemplifies both at the most immediate level and at the more thematic level that gives the "point" of the performance's having the manifest features that it does. The artist prescribes or enacts a particular sequence of movements with the intention that it articulate a particular artistic content. She assumes that the audience will know that it is supposed to treat the sequence in particular kinds of ways, attending to it in what we may term an "interrogative" manner that seeks to make sense of the sequence in terms of reasons for it being ordered in the way that it is. Such an interrogative attention is informed by the belief that there is a more general "point" behind the sequence's manifest properties, and that this point is being made by means of the more obvious representational, expressive, and exemplificational properties that it articulates.

It is not merely that artistic performance in dance involves the articulation of a content by means of a sequence of movements, however. A crew of furniture movers could communicate to a new recruit something of the form "this is how to hold a mattress when you move it" by executing the same sequence of movements as is incorporated in Rainer's dance. But their execution of that sequence would not thereby be an artistic performance. What is also required is that the content is articulated in certain distinctive ways, and for this reason requires a distinctive kind of attention on the part of the viewer.[7] We have seen that *close attention* to the details of the artistic vehicle is necessary if we are to correctly determine the content articulated, that artistic vehicles often serve to *exemplify* some of their properties, that many *different properties* of the vehicle contribute to the articulation of content, and finally that the vehicle not only serves a number of distinct articulatory functions, but does so in a "*hierarchical*" manner, where "higher level" content is articulated through lower level content.[8]

The suggestion, then, is that what makes something an *artistic* performance is not, per se, the elements of which it is composed or the way in which those elements are put together, but how the assemblage of the elements that make up the artistic vehicle is intended to function in the articulation of content. It is in virtue of these distinctive ways of articulating content that artistic performances must be *regarded* in a distinctive way. "Counterpart" cases, where the artistic vehicle is not visually discriminable from something that does not serve as an artistic vehicle, serve to make this manifest. But, as we have seen, for something to be an artistic *performance*, the actions of the agent must be guided – either immediately or through the instruction of the choreographer or director – by the expectation that they will be the object of this distinctive kind of regard on the part of an intended audience. Something like an institutional setting of practices and conventions of the sort to which Dickie alludes may be a necessary *background* for forming the kinds of expectations that artistic performance requires. On the more obliquely institutional reading of Carroll and Banes that I am proposing, Rainer's act of "framing" or "recontextualizing" the movements executed by ordinary mattress movers is not merely an act of putting these movements on a stage, but also involves drawing upon institutionally grounded practices of attending to what is presented on stage in a particular way.

It is, I think, easy to see how the foregoing account of artistic performance as applied to a work like Rainer's *Room Service* might generalize to other kinds of dance and to other performing arts like music and theater. What will remain constant in such a generalization is a distinctive kind of regard for which an artistic performance calls in virtue of the ways in which its content is articulated. What will vary is the nature of the artistic vehicle that is the proper object of such a regard. In the case of classical ballet and much modern dance, the artistic vehicle will be a sequence of movements – grasped as "movings" and "posings" – executed in dialogue with a sequence of sounds. These sounds may issue from a live musical performance or from the playback of a recording of musical or more generally sonic material. In theater, the artistic vehicle will comprise not only the physical movements of the performers – grasped as represented or pretended actions – but also the sounds that they emit – grasped as represented or pretended speech acts such as statements, questions, commands, etc. In the case of music, the artistic vehicle will not be (or will not merely be) playings by the performers of their instruments but will be (or will also be) the sequence of sounds generated through these playings.

It is important to note one feature of the account of artistic performance that I have just sketched. In tying status as an artistic performance to being the intended object of a certain kind of regard, I have given an independent account, albeit somewhat schematic, of the distinctive features of that kind of regard, and have also related the necessity of such a regard to the manner in which the content of the performance is articulated. I have not identified it merely in terms of its being the kind of regard for which artistic performances, or artworks in general, call. The proposed account differs in this crucial respect from the kind of "historical-intentional" definition of art defended by Jerrold Levinson (1979). Simplifying a little, Levinson's claim is that something is an artwork if its creator, at a time t, intends it to be the object of a regard of the kind rightly accorded to things already established as artworks at t. This allows for a plurality of kinds of regard that at any given time are rightly accorded to things taken to be artworks at that time. For Levinson what links these kinds of regard is *not* some feature specifiable independently of their being accepted ways of regarding artworks at t. On the proposal defended above, however, different ways of regarding artistic performances will count as properly *artistic* only if they meet the more general requirements that I have set out and are mandated by the way in which those performances seek to articulate their artistic content. Because Levinson deliberately eschews any such attempt to provide a principled way of identifying the kinds of regard that are proper to artworks, other than their being or having been accorded to such works at a given time, his account is threatened by the same sorts of difficulties seen to beset the institutional theorist who refuses to place constraints on the kind of appreciation for which artworks call.[9]

6   Overview

In looking at the different ways in which we might try to characterize what is distinctive about artistic performances, or about the performing arts as the context in which such performances are presented, I have drawn freely on more general theories about artworks. But what is the relationship between artistic performances and works of art? In drawing upon more general views about the appreciation of artworks in characterizing the kind of regard required of one who views an artistic performance, I have implicitly assumed something like the following: an event counts as an "artistic performance" of the sort that is central to the performing arts if it manifests to receivers qualities that bear directly upon the appreciation of a work of art.[10] It is in virtue of this that the performance must be regarded in the manner distinctive of our appreciative engagement with artworks. There are two obvious ways in which this requirement might be satisfied.

(1)   The performance may *itself* be an artwork, what the performer does being the artistic vehicle whose observable features directly articulate, perhaps in association with contextual factors, the representational, expressive, and formal properties that make up the artistic content of the work.[11] Thus we might speak of Vito Acconci's enactment of *Following Piece* as a work of art whose artistic vehicle is the actions he performed in following his subjects. The performance event here plays a role analogous to that played by a particular painted surface in articulating the artistic content of a work in the visual arts. Or it might be claimed that the doing that is the artwork consists not merely in the actions performed but also in the sensible manifold that those actions generate, as in the case of an improvised performance by a jazz pianist.

(2)   The performance may play an essential part in the appreciation of *something else* that is an artwork through being one amongst a possible multiplicity of *instances* of that work. We speak here of a performance *of* an independent work. In this sense, the event attended by Carroll and Banes was a performance *of* Rainer's work *Room Service*.

In order to clearly distinguish between these two kinds of cases, it will be useful to introduce some terminology. First, where, as in situations of type (2), a performance is of an independent work and contributes to our appreciation of the latter, we can term the artwork appreciated a *performable work* – or, to use Stephen Davies's (2001) term, a *work for performance* – and the performance through which it is appreciated a *work-performance*. An artistic practice in which acknowledged artworks are designed to be performable works can be termed a *performed art*. In a performed art, our access to, and appreciation of, *works* (as receivers) is at least in part mediated by performances of those works, and thus by the activities of those in the *performing arts* such as conductors, directors, musicians, dancers, and actors. This is because certain qualities of those works, relevant to their being appreciated as the particular works that they are, are realizable, and thereby made available to receivers, only in those performances. For example, at least part of what we appreciate in a symphonic work is various audible properties of the sequence of sounds prescribed by the composer. Only through the realization in a performance of what the composer prescribed can we experience those audible properties. The need to experience a performance of a performable work in order to properly appreciate that work is thus the analogue, in the performed arts, of the need to perceptually engage with a particular visible surface in order to properly appreciate a visual artwork. Drama, music, and dance are traditionally taken to be performed arts in this sense.

In a performed art, a performance can qualify as artistic in sense (2) insofar as it is a performance of a performable work. It is a further question whether such a performance may also be an artwork in its own right and thereby qualify as artistic in sense (1). Where, on the other hand, there is no performable work that a performance can plausibly be taken to be of – as, for example, with free improvisations in jazz – the performance, if artistic, must be so in sense (1) – that is, it must itself be a work of art, or so I shall argue. In such a case, we have what may be termed a *performance-work*.

Work-performances and performance-works are two conceptually distinct kinds of artistic performances. Furthermore, as we shall see, they raise distinct kinds of philosophical questions: in the first case, questions about the nature of performances *of* works, and, in the second case, questions about the nature of performances *as* works. While at least some artistic performances arguably raise both kinds of questions – performances of works that are also proper objects of artistic appreciation in their own right – it will be helpful to use the distinction between the two kinds of questions to structure our explorations in the rest of this book. Let me briefly sketch the itinerary for these explorations.

Performances of works: As we have seen, some performances in the performing arts are artistic in virtue of being performances of independent artworks. A number of important questions arise when we try to understand such performances. Most of them pertain to the work–performance relationship that obtains in the performed arts. I shall take classical music as the model for a performed art – I term this the "classical paradigm." In Chapters 2, 3, and 4, I shall look at the philosophical questions that arise for this paradigm, both ontological (e.g., what is a performable work and what is the work–performance relation?) and epistemological (e.g., how do performances contribute to the appreciation of performable works?). A further question that requires serious investigation is the scope of the classical paradigm, and thus the extent to which the performing arts fall within the domain of the performed arts. Traditionally, the performed arts have been taken to parallel, and provide the material for, the canonical performing arts – music in general, theater, and dance. In Chapters 5 and 6, I shall examine some recent challenges to this view.

Performances as works: Some artistic performances which are not plausibly viewed as performances of independent artworks seem themselves to be objects of artistic appreciation and evaluation. We can ask whether, in virtue of this, they are themselves properly viewed as artworks, and, if so, whether, by the same reasoning, we can view at least some performances of performable works as artworks. In Chapter 7, I argue for a positive answer to both of these questions. Performances of performable works may, then, be artistic in both senses distinguished above, whereas performances that are not plausibly seen as performances of performable works can be artistic in sense (1) but not in sense (2). In Chapters 8 and 9, I examine other elements that enter into performances in the performing arts viewed as works in their own right – improvisation, rehearsal, audience response, and the use of the body in performance.

Performances in works: Some activities that we encounter in the arts and that seem to be "artistic" are not artistic in sense (1) – they are not themselves objects of artistic appreciation and evaluation. But nor do they seem to be instances of independent works that contribute to the appreciation and evaluation of those works, thus they are not obviously artistic in sense (2) either. This, I shall suggest, holds for some performances or prescriptions for performances that we encounter in our engagement with late modern and "conceptual" art. In the final chapter, I shall look at the more general tradition of "performance art" and its relation to the performing arts.

Notes

1. Dickie's "institutional theory" of art has undergone various refinements. For present purposes, we can focus on the canonical early version of the theory set out in Dickie 1974.
2. See also Thom 1993, 6: "True artistic performances [are distinguished] by the context in which they are given. In the case of true performances, there is an implicit social agreement that the performance will be given at a particular time and place and that both performers and audience will behave by mutual consent in more-or-less expected ways."
3. See Storey and Allan 2005. For a different example, see S. Davies 2007, 24–25.

4. See, for example, Beardsley's essays collected in parts I and IV of Wreen and Callen 1982. For a good overview of Beardsley's evolving conception of aesthetic experience and its place in his definition of art, see S. Davies 1991, 52–57.

5. The Rainer piece counts against Beardsley only if it is rightly treated as a work of *dance*, and this, it seems, is something Beardsley might challenge. He argues elsewhere (1983) that Duchamp's "readymades" are not in fact visual art-works but unorthodox critical comments on visual art itself. So he might argue here that Rainer's *Room Service* isn't a work of dance but a theatrical work about dance. This kind of move is not completely ad hoc. As we shall see in Chapter 10, Stephen Davies has offered a similar analysis of John Cage's *4′ 33″*. But there are good reasons to resist such a claim about *Room Service*. First, as we noted, the work belongs to the genre of "task dances," and is one of a number of works, by Rainer and other artists, that raise the same problems for Beardsley's account. They are treated in critical practice as interestingly different works, but if they are merely theatrical works about dance, it seems they are all making substantially the same point. Relatedly, the performers of *Room Service* and other "task dances" are trained as dancers, not as actors, and the works are presented in dance venues and reviewed by dance critics. These kinds of "institutional" considerations, while not themselves conclusive, place the burden of proof very much on Beardsley. Thanks to Andrew Kania for rais-ing this issue.

6. See, for example, Levinson 1980; Danto 1981; Currie 1989.

7. Wollheim himself characterizes the kind of regard required to grasp the artistic statement articulated through an artistic vehicle as one which makes the vehicle "the object of an ever-increasing or deepening attention" (1980, 122–123).

8. These distinctive ways of articulating content resemble in certain respects what Nelson Goodman described as "symptoms of the aesthetic" (see Goodman 1976, 252–255; 1978, 67–70). They can be roughly correlated with what Goodman characterizes in more technical terms as the "syntactic" and "semantic" density of the symbol system to which the artistic vehicle belongs, the use of exemplification, the relative "repleteness" of the artistic symbol, and the serving of multiple and complexly interrelated referential functions.

9. I have suggested that what is distinctive of an artistic performance is that the performers intend that their audience accord the performance's artistic vehicle a distinctive kind of regard, a kind of regard necessary if the audi-ence is to grasp the performance's artistic content and its "point." I have not claimed that they must also intend that their audience take an interest in the manner whereby this content is articulated *for its own sake*. We may think such an interest is necessary for a properly artistic appreciation of that performance – this is arguably a "dogma" of modernism – but that is a different matter.

10. I say "bear *directly*" in order to exclude from the domain of artistic perform-ances events whose manifest qualities bear *indirectly* upon the appreciation of

artworks by providing information germane to the appreciation of those works – for example, a talk given by a curator about a painting in a gallery.

11. Throughout this book, I shall for convenience follow the general consensus in taking an artwork to be the *product* of the generative activity of the artist(s). What the artist produces, on this view, is an artistic vehicle that articulates an artistic content in virtue of those shared understandings we have termed an artistic medium. In the case of a work like Vermeer's *View of Delft*, for example, the artwork is the physical canvas understood as possessing certain representational, expressive, and formal properties. In adopting for convenience this view of artworks, I bracket my own view, for which I argued in my 2004, that artworks are properly identified not with the products of artistic activity, but with the activity itself as completed by those products. Nothing in this book, I think, turns on whether I am right in this, with one exception addressed near the end of Chapter 2.

I should also perhaps note that, while, in my 2004, I characterized the artistic activities that are, on my view, artworks as "performances," I was not claiming that they are performances in the sense spelled out in this chapter. Artists are indeed guided by their expectations concerning the evaluative eye or ear of receivers, but it is the *product* of their activity, rather than the activity itself, that they expect to be evaluated in a certain way. See further my clarifications of what it is to act "for an audience" in section 1 of Chapter 9.

2

The Classical Paradigm I: The Nature of the Performable Work

1 Introduction: Berthold and Magda Go to the Symphony

Berthold and Magda sit expectantly in their well-appointed seats at the Royal Festival Hall, immersed in the low babble of the chattering classes and looking up at the stage where the musicians make final adjustments to their instruments. The conductor briskly scans the score, baton twitching in his hand. Berthold is particularly excited. He loves Sibelius, as Magda well knows – it was she who purchased the tickets as a surprise for her partner – and the piece that is to be performed this evening – Sibelius's Second Symphony – is a particular favorite of his. As the conductor addresses the musicians, baton poised in the air, the auditorium falls silent. An almost imperceptible flexing of the conductor's wrist coaxes the opening phrases of the piece, suitably *sotto*, from the violins. Berthold inhales deeply, closes his eyes, and prepares to scale the cold white peaks of art.[1] It was, he will opine later as they stroll along the South Bank, a sublime, almost transcendent, rendition of the piece.

Whether or not we empathize with the particular rapture experienced by Berthold, the general scenario is certainly a familiar one – a performance by a musical ensemble of a given piece of music attended by admirers who know it well yet, as lovers do, still find exquisite pleasure in the novel inflection of familiar routines. For, of course, what we have described is a particular listening to a particular performance of a musical work that has enjoyed

Philosophy of the Performing Arts, First Edition. David Davies.
© 2011 David Davies. Published 2011 by Blackwell Publishing Ltd.

many realizations by different musical ensembles. As Berthold's enthusiastic appraisal after the concert illustrates, the lover of a musical work not only seeks out novel opportunities to experience it in performance. He or she also hopes that each performance will reveal new possibilities of the work, and assesses a performance on this basis relative to others he or she has attended. In this way, the experience of those who attend different performances of a performable work differs crucially from the experience of those who attend different screenings of a film. In the latter case, we hope that repeated viewings will enable us to better see things that were already there to be seen in earlier screenings but that we failed to register. In the former case, on the other hand, we hope to deepen our appreciation of the performable work in virtue of differences in the way the work is performed. The performance of a performable work calls for interpretation on the part of the performers, and one goal of interpretation is to reveal new artistic values in a work.

All this, as I say, should seem very familiar. We might term this conception of artistic performance – as the interpretation and rendering of a performable work – the "classical paradigm." Let me, however, begin to defamiliarize the familiar. We customarily take for granted that there are things like Sibelius's Second Symphony that are rightly described as musical works. We also take for granted that two or more performances advertised as playings of a given work can indeed be performances of the same work, in spite of differences in the way they sound. Nor, it seems, is what we have described peculiar to performances of traditional works of Western classical music. We naturally extend this way of thinking to performances in different musical genres like rock and jazz, and to performances in the other performing arts. There are, we assume, many different productions and performances of a play like *King Lear*, or performances of a dance work like *Room Service*. In all such cases we assume that, in spite of sometimes radical differences between performances classified as being *of* a given work, there are certain essential features of that work that they share. But what are these essential features? And – to deepen the mystery – what kind of thing is a performable work such that it can allow of both repetition and difference in this way?

2   The Multiple Nature of Performable Works

It is a lot easier to say what performable works cannot be than to say what they are. There is, as we shall see, a fair measure of agreement over the first matter and an equally fair measure of disagreement over the second. The puzzling features of performable works stem for the most part from the relationships that obtain between such works and their performances or realizations. First, as we have seen, it is part of the very concept of a performable work that it can be properly or fully *appreciated* through, and only through, performances. A work of art whose proper appreciation was not constrained in this way would thereby fail to be a performable work. This suggests that the relationship between performable works and the performances through which they are appreciated is in some ways a very intimate one. But this should not lead us to think that such works can somehow be *identified* with their performances. On the one hand, it seems obvious that a performable work cannot be identified with a *particular* performance, since work and performance may differ in their properties. Sibelius's Second Symphony is a stirring work that may have limply disappointing performances, for example. And if we try to identify the work with an *ideal* performance that shares such artistic values with the work, the work will still differ from the performance in that the former, but not the latter, *might* be performed in a limply disappointing manner.

This rests upon a more fundamental difference between performable works and individual performances. The former, as we have seen, are at least in principle *repeatable* in the sense that they can be performed on more than one occasion. But to say that a performable work *can be* multiply performed is not to say that it is *in fact* multiply performed – indeed, it is not even to say that it is performed at all. Imagine if we were to discover a score by Sibelius for what was announced on attached papers to be his Eighth Symphony, something written late in his life which, as we learn from the papers, would have been performed had not an untimely demise prevented him from making his intentions known to anyone. We have surely discovered a hitherto unknown and unperformed performable work, a work that might never have been discovered. It would sound very strange to say that the work came into existence only when it was performed, or that, had we not discovered the score, there would have been no work to discover. Furthermore, it seems equally clear that a performable work that has been multiply performed could have had fewer or more performances than it actually has. For example, the performance attended by Berthold and Magda might have been cancelled because a misfortune befell the conductor without thereby affecting the identity of Sibelius's work. Thus we cannot identify a musical work with the *collection* of its actual performances, since it may have none, and may have had a different set of performances from the ones that actually take place.[2]

Thus, if there is an intimate link between being a performable work and being open to performance, the work must also be somehow independent of its actual performances. The performances themselves seem unproblematic – they are just events of a particular kind, no different in this respect from other kinds of events that fit easily into our ordinary conception of what there is in the world. But the performable work begins to look much more mysterious. Again we may ask, what sort of entity can have the kinds of properties just described? What sort of entity can be somehow tied to particular things in the world yet not identifiable with them taken either individually or collectively? What sort of entity can be repeatable in the way that performable works are repeatable? And, we may remind ourselves, we must also explain the diversity among performances, the manner in which the "repetitions," while somehow repeating the *work*, can fail in significant respects to repeat *one another*.

The repeatability of musical works is, however, only one example of a broader phenomenon that we encounter in the arts. A musical work is repeatable because different events can qualify as performances of that work. But in the cinema we have a parallel phenomenon. A film like *Citizen Kane* is also "repeatable" in the sense that different events can qualify as *screenings* of the work. Indeed, just as two performances of Sibelius's Second Symphony may occur in different locations at the very same time, one in London and the other in Oslo, so two screenings of the same film frequently occur at the same time, not just in – say – Los Angeles and San Antonio, but even in the same cineplex. And, once we are alerted to these kinds of possibilities, we will also be impressed by a parallel with other art forms where we have something analogous to repeatability, but in respect of *objects* rather than events. Many people own copies of Jane Austen's literary work *Pride and Prejudice*, for example, and many art galleries boast copies of prints of Stieglitz's photographic work *The Steerage*. And more than 20 casts of Rodin's *The Thinker*, all treated as casts of the work, exist in addition to the original cast exhibited at the Musée Rodin in Paris. In these cases, different objects can qualify as copies, prints, or casts of a given work.

We might want to speak a bit more precisely about such matters, however. For example, it seems natural to say that some performances of musical works fail to contain all and only the notes specified in the score, some screenings of films involve damaged copies of the film, and some copies of novels contain typographical errors. We might, therefore, wish to talk not merely in the loose sense of different things that "qualify" as performances, copies, etc., but also, in a stronger sense, of things that "fully qualify" as renditions of a given artwork in virtue of not being flawed in these ways. What such entities "fully qualify" *for* is a particular kind of role in the appreciation of that artwork. To properly appreciate an artwork, whether it be a musical work, a film, or whatever, requires a particular kind of experiential engagement with the work. Someone who lacks the relevant kind of experience of a work cannot be credited with a true appreciation of it. You can't judge a book, for example, without reading what lies between its covers, and you can't judge a film or a painting or a play unless you've seen it. We hold claims to appreciate artworks answerable to such experiences because many qualities of a work bearing on its proper appreciation can be fully grasped only *through* an experiential engagement with something that can enable us to grasp those qualities. We may talk here of an entity playing "the experiential role" in the appreciation of an artwork.

In the sense in which I shall use this term, something *fully qualifies* to play this experiential role in the appreciation of a given artwork X just in case it possesses *all* those experienceable properties that are *necessary*, according to the practices of the art form in question, to fully play this role. Where something fully qualifies in this sense, we may term it a *work-instance* of X. The latter is a technical term to be understood in the manner just specified. To say, then, that *different* events or objects may fully qualify to play the experiential role for a given artwork is to say that the work admits of a plurality of work-instances. Where this is the case, we have what can be termed a "multiple" art form. Classical music, film, literature, and cast sculpture are treated as multiple art forms in this sense. Not all art forms are treated as multiple, however. It is our practice to require, for the proper appreciation of paintings and works of carved sculpture, for example, that one experientially engage with a unique object. We assume that, to properly appreciate a work like Vermeer's *View of Delft*, one needs to visually engage with the very canvas painted by Vermeer. Only the original canvas, it is generally assumed, can possess all of the properties necessary in something capable of fully playing the experiential role in the appreciation of the work. While a good reproduction may provide us with a measure of experiential access to the work, it doesn't fully qualify for the experiential role and thus is not a work-instance. Where, as here, we treat works belonging to a given art form as capable of having only a single work-instance, we can speak of a "singular" art form.[3]

In those art forms generally viewed as singular, like painting, there is little mystery as to how an artist establishes the status of a particular entity as the unique work-instance of a given work. The work-instance here is just the entity, or some set of properties of the entity, that the artist brings into existence through manipulating the relevant physical medium – for example, through applying oil paint to a prepared surface. In the case of multiple works, however, the story is more complicated. In fact, as a number of writers have pointed out,[4] there seem to be at least three different ways in which an artist can make specific the conditions to be met by work-instances of a multiple work – that is, the conditions that must be met to fully qualify for the experiential role in the appreciation of the work. These different modes of specification correspond to different kinds of multiple art forms.

Take, first, literature. Here the author's activity in writing a literary work itself characteristically brings into existence a work-instance which then serves as an *exemplar*. I say "characteristically" because, to obtain the exemplar, it may be necessary to make minor revisions to rectify errors in spelling, etc. Further work-instances are then generated through successful attempts to emulate the exemplar in those respects determined to be relevant by artistic conventions in place. These conventions require that other work-instances conform to the exemplar in specific respects. We don't require, for example, that all work-instances of a literary work employ the same *font*. But we do require sameness of spelling and word order in anything that fully qualifies to play the experiential role in the appreciation of a literary work.

In other arts such as cast sculpture, however, the artist makes use of a different strategy to pick out a work's work-instances. He or she produces an artifact which, when employed in prescribed ways, generates work-instances. Following Nicholas Wolterstorff (1980), we may term this a *production-artifact*.[5] As in the case of exemplars, conventions in place in the relevant art form determine how this artifact must be used if a work-instance, in our sense, is to result. Only those entities having the properties that would result from the right use of this artifact will be work-instances of the work. Photography and film clearly fall into this category. In the case of an analog photograph, for example, the production artifact is the negative, and images generated from the production artifact by appropriate means count as work-instances of the work. Films, on the other hand, have as their production artifacts those entities used, in various cinematic media, to generate screenings of those films – film prints, videotapes, digital files, etc., which either are, or stand in a "copy" relation to, master encodings of the film. Because the right use of a production artifact in such cases may result in entities that differ in some of their qualities – for example, photographic prints from the same negative may differ in tone – work-instances of such works may differ in these respects.

Neither of these models seems appropriate for performable works, however. The composer of a traditional Western classical musical work only rarely produces an exemplar and makes no use of a production artifact. Rather, the artist responsible for a performable work provides *instructions* that serve as "recipes" for generating work-instances if properly followed by performers who are aware of the relevant conventions and practices. Such instructions call for interpretation on the performers' part, and it is only in these cases that we characterize work-instances of multiple artworks as *performances*. In the case of performable works of Western classical music, the score plays the most significant part in preserving and transmitting the composer's instructions for generating performances of the work, although, as we shall see, other considerations may also come into play. If the classical paradigm extends to the other performing arts, an analogous role will be played by instructions transmitted to performers by playwrights or choreographers.

Performable works, then, are multiple artworks the requirements for whose work-instances are specified by means of instructions issued by those responsible for the work. This suggests how we should go about answering one of the questions about performable works raised above. We asked how we could explain the degree of diversity in the things that provide such works with their repeatability. The answer, presumably, is that it is in virtue of the interpretive freedom conceded by the composer to the performer that performances of a given performable work can vary in the ways that they do. Furthermore, the interpretive freedom given to the performer allows different performers to make manifest different qualities of the performable work, different aesthetic possibilities that exist within the "envelope" furnished by the composer's performative directives. And this explains why we can hope to discover in a given performance of a performable work qualities that were not there to be discovered in earlier performances, whereas this is not the case with a cinematic work. Also, because of the role accorded to interpretation in the performance of performable works, two performances that fully qualify, in our sense, to play the experiential role in the appreciation of a performable work – they both meet all the requirements for correct performance established by the composer – may not be equally capable of illuminating the artistic values of the work. A fully qualified performance may be unimaginative in interpretation, for example. Indeed, we might prefer a performance that is technically flawed to one that is fully qualified on just these sorts of grounds. Thus performable works may not always be best appreciated through their work-instances in our sense. We shall return to this point in the following section.

3   Performable Works as Types

This still leaves us with our initial puzzle. What sort of thing *is* a performable work, so conceived, given that it somehow exists independently of actual performances? There is a widely endorsed answer to this question. Performable works, it is claimed, are *types*, and their work-instances are, or are among, the tokens of those types. Indeed, it is widely believed that all multiple works are types. In order to assess this proposal, we need to say something about the notion of a type.

The distinction between types and tokens is familiar in everyday contexts where we distinguish between, say, the letters in the alphabet and particular uses of those letters. If asked, "How many letters are there in the word 'sheep'?" we can correctly answer both five (there are five occurrences of letter-*tokens* in the word) and four (there are occurrences of four different *types* of letters). Types are *generic* entities[6] which can have other entities falling under them. If performable works are types with performances as their tokens, this explains how, as already noted, a performable work like Sibelius's Second Symphony could have had more or fewer performances than it actually has. For the identity and nature of a type does not change as the number of its tokens changes. The word-type "sheep" remains the same no matter how many or how few tokens of it appear on this page, and the identity of the currency type "English ten pound note" is unaffected by the enactment of economic policies that increase the number of its tokens in circulation.

But if performable works, or multiple works more generally, are types, they are types of a distinctive kind. Take our last example of a type, the English ten pound note. Something qualifies as a token of this type if it has a certain distinctive appearance in virtue of having a particular history of making. Something that looked like an English ten pound note but was the result of a skillful act of forgery wouldn't *be* an English ten pound note. Nor would something that, as a result of a mistake at the Royal Mint, lacked the customary watermark. More generally, the type "English ten pound note" is associated with a condition that picks out, as its tokens, those things that satisfy this condition. There are no tokens of this type that only partly satisfy this condition yet are tokens nonetheless. The condition has the form: "Something is an X just in case it meets conditions C." There can, of course, be uncertainty over whether C are actually satisfied in a given case, or a measure of vagueness in the terms employed in characterizing C. But, among the things taken to satisfy C, there is no distinction between "correct" and "incorrect" Xs, and something which fails to satisfy C is not an X at all.

In the case of multiple artworks, however, we at least in practice allow that they can have examples that are *imperfect* in relevant respects yet still qualify as genuine examples of the work. For example, on our ordinary way of thinking about such things, the performances of a musical work include not only playings that meet all the requirements for right performance of the work, but also playings containing at least some incorrect notes.[7] If Berthold were to demand a refund on the grounds that one of the musicians misplayed one of the notes prescribed in Sibelius's score and that he therefore did not hear, as promised, a performance of the Second Symphony, he would receive short shrift from the house manager. Similarly, it would seem, a damaged print of Renoir's *La règle du jeu* can still provide an audience with a screening of the film, albeit one that is flawed in certain respects. Types that admit in this way of both correct and incorrect examples can be termed "norm-types."[8] Whereas ordinary types like the English ten pound note are associated with a condition that must be satisfied by their tokens, norm-types are associated with a condition that must be satisfied by their *correct or properly formed* tokens. This condition is of the form: "Something is a well-formed X just in case it meets condition C." As Nicholas Wolstertorff points out, norm-types are familiar to us from other contexts. When we say that the grizzly bear growls, for example, what we mean is that this is a property of well-formed grizzlies. We don't think that a creature that is incapable of growling cannot count as a grizzly at all. Similarly, when we say that T. S. Eliot's *The Waste Land* starts with the words "April is the cruelest month," we mean that well-formed, or correct, copies of the poem start with these words. If I have a copy of a text that departs from the standard text of the poem only in beginning with the words "April is the cruelest moth," I still have a copy of *The Waste Land*, albeit an incorrect one, if this textual feature is the result of problems arising in an attempt to print out Eliot's poem. (Matters would be different if this were a feature of a correct printing of a work by a previously unknown lepidopterist-poet who happened independently upon a verbal structure differing from Eliot's only in this respect ...)

Let us take stock of what we have established thus far. Performable works, by definition, are fully appreciable only through their performances. There may be many different performances that fully qualify for the appreciation of such works – the works may have multiple work-instances, as we have defined that term. As we have now seen, if performed works are taken to be norm-types, they also by their very nature admit of *incorrect* performances. Incorrect performances fail, by definition, to fully qualify for the experiential role in the appreciation of the performable work of which they are performances, and will not count as work-instances in our technical sense. Thus not all performances of a performable work will be among its work-instances. *Which* features of a performance bear upon its status as a work-instance of a performable work, however, depends upon which kinds of features are prescribed by the performable work for its correct performance – which features enter into the condition *C* that defines what it is for something to be a correct performance of the work. And this is a matter concerning which there is significant disagreement amongst those writers who take performable works to be norm-types.

This disagreement has a deeper significance if, as seems plausible,[9] we *individuate* types according to the conditions they prescribe for their tokens, or, in the case of norm-types, for their well-formed tokens. The American five dollar bill and the Canadian five dollar bill are arguably *different* note-types in virtue of the different conditions that their tokens must satisfy. The same would apply to the American five dollar bill and the American one dollar bill. In the case of norm-types, it seems reasonable to assume that we have different norm-types when we have different requirements for being a well-formed token. And, in the case of both ordinary types and norm-types, it also seems reasonable to think that if there is *no* difference in the conditions associated with what might appear to be two different types, there is in fact only a *single* type for which we have two different labels. This would apply to the type "Canadian one dollar coin" and the type "Canadian 'loonie,'" for example. If this is correct, then, if performable works are norm-types, we will have different performable works just in case we have different prescriptions for the correctness of performances of those works. A survey of the literature on performable works of classical music will give us a good sense of the range of positions taken on this question.

4   Varieties of Type Theories: Sonicism, Instrumentalism, and Contextualism

Our question, then, is the following: What sorts of features do performable works of music prescribe for their well-formed performances? The simplest and most conservative answer to this question is some form of what is termed *sonicism*.[10] The distinctive claim of the sonicist is that "whether a sound-event counts as a properly formed token of [a performable work] *W* is determined purely by its acoustic qualitative appearance" (Dodd 2007, 201), that is to say, purely by the way the performance sounds. That a performance sounds a certain way is at least a necessary condition for its being a properly formed token of a performable musical work. For, minimally, the composer of such a work prescribes that performers produce a sequence of sounds meeting certain acoustic conditions. The nature of these conditions is at least partly identifiable, in standard cases, by reference to the characters inscribed in the piece's score. The score prescribes at least that notes of specified pitches and durations be produced, either simultaneously or consecutively, in a given order, usually to a given rhythm.

We need to draw a further distinction, however, between *pure* sonicists and *timbral* sonicists. *Pure* sonicists hold that *only* these kinds of features enter into the features prescribed for correct performance of a musical work.[11] The pure sonicist maintains that (perhaps with very rare exceptions) to hear sounds as music is to attend only to their structural or "organizational" properties – pitch, rhythm, harmony, and melody (Scruton 1997, 20). The pure sonicist does not require that the sound sequence specified by the composer be performed on, or even sound as if it were performed on, any particular instruments, even if, as in most Western classical music after the mid eighteenth century, the composer specifies in the score that particular instruments are to be used. The "color" properties consequent upon the use of, say, an oboe rather than a flute, are not (or are only very rarely) of musical interest, on this view. One argument offered for pure sonicism is that many early composers did not specify particular instruments to be used in the performance of their pieces. But this cannot be decisive for later works where instrumentation is specified. And, even in the case of earlier works, there is evidence that many works were intended to be performed on particular instruments or kinds of instruments, even if this is not made explicit in their scores (see S. Davies 2001, 60–63). A second argument for pure sonicism is that we have no difficulty recognizing musical works when they are played on non-standard instruments. But this, again, is inconclusive. Our interest, recall, is in determining which kinds of properties are prescribed for *correct* performances of musical works. Unless we have a separate argument to show that performances on non-standard instruments are correct performances, nothing of interest follows from our ability to associate such performances with particular performable works (see Dodd 2007, 216).

Timbral sonicists, on the other hand, maintain that the *timbre* of the notes produced, which will vary according to the instruments used in generating those notes, is an essential part of what the composer prescribes for well-formed performances of the work.[12] Thus timbral properties are partly constitutive of the norm-type with which the performable work is to be identified. The case for timbral sonicism seems particularly strong if we consider a work such as Sibelius's Second Symphony. As we shall see at the beginning of Chapter 3, the expressive qualities of this work seem to depend crucially upon the contrasting sonorities of the passages ascribed to the brass and string sections in the score. More generally, the timbral sonicist can appeal to considerations raised by Jerrold Levinson. Levinson argues that many of the artistic and aesthetic properties of musical works depend upon the use of particular instrumentation (e.g., 1980, 73–78). Some of his examples will be outlined below in the discussion of "instrumentalism." Levinson also argues that pure sonicism makes it utterly mysterious why composers do specify particular instruments in most cases (1990b, 244). Again, this seems to support timbral sonicism over pure sonicism.

The timbral sonicist makes the timbral qualities of a sound sequence partly constitutive of the performable work. But he doesn't require that, in well-formed performances of a work, this sound sequence is actually *produced* on the instruments with which we naturally associate those timbral qualities. This is what makes him a *sonicist* in the specified sense. Suppose, for example, that we had a "perfect timbral synthesizer" (PTS) capable of simulating the timbral qualities of any standard instrument – for example, the piano or the trumpet. Suppose, further, that a composer prescribes that a given sound sequence be performed on certain standard instruments and that, so performed, the sequence would have certain timbral properties. Then, the timbral sonicist maintains, a performance of this sound sequence on a PTS that simulates these timbral properties would be just as well formed as a performance on the prescribed instruments themselves.

Instrumentalists reject this conclusion. They insist that a correct performance of a performable work must not only have the prescribed timbral qualities, but must also be performed on the prescribed instruments.

Instrumentalists maintain that, where different instruments are prescribed for producing a particular type of sound event, performances that respect those prescriptions are performances of different *works*. Levinson, for example, argues that specific "performance means," as he terms it, have been integral to the performable work of classical music since the mid eighteenth century. The aesthetic attributes of such works "always depend … in part on the performing forces understood to belong to them" (Levinson 1980, 77). He cites, as a particularly dramatic example, Beethoven's *Hammerklavier* Sonata whose "sublime, craggy, and barn-storming" qualities "depend in part on the strain that its sound structure imposes on the sonic capabilities of the piano" (76–77). Such qualities would be lacking in a performance on a PTS that duplicates the timbral properties of the piece, Levinson claims. If this is correct, then part of what a musical work of this sort prescribes must be the use of certain instruments to realize a given sound sequence.[13]

The instrumentalist, as characterized above, agrees with the sonicist that a performable musical work is a norm-type, but insists that what is prescribed for correct performance is not merely a certain sound sequence but also the production of that sound sequence on the instruments specified or intended by the composer. But Levinson offers reasons to question whether performable musical works are norm-types of either a sonicist or an instrumentalist stripe.[14] He argues that such accounts fail in two crucial respects: (1) they don't allow for the creation of musical works by their composers, and (2) they don't account for those properties of a work that depend upon the context in which the composer establishes the prescriptions for its correct performance. Some of the issues raised by the first point are too technical for us to explore in detail here, but we can get a sense of Levinson's concerns and then assess our options in light of them.

It is natural for us to speak of artists as creators of the works that we ascribe to them. We think of a painter, for example, as someone whose inspired activity in the studio brings into being the particular pigment-covered canvas that we later contemplate in a gallery, and we naturally identify the work with that canvas. In a similar way, we credit the poet with authoring her poems and the novelist with bringing into existence his novel. Such a conception of artistic activity seems equally appropriate in the performed arts. While Shakespeare drew on various cultural resources in writing *King Lear*, the play we see being performed at the New Globe in London was, we will insist, created by the bard. And Sibelius, we may also insist, was the creator of his Second Symphony. But if performable works – and perhaps multiple works in general – are norm-types, can these common beliefs be right? How does one create – bring into being – a norm-type? It is not difficult to understand how one can bring into being the first inscription of the *score* of a performable work, and Sibelius certainly did this. But the norm-type is no more identifiable with a particular inscription of the score than it is with a particular performance that conforms with the score. And, for reasons already rehearsed, we do no better if we try to identify the performable work, as norm-type, with the *collection* of inscriptions of the score. Norm-types are types, and types don't seem to be the sorts of entities that can exist in some determinate region of space. Where, for example, might we find the word "sheep" – as opposed to some particular token of the word "sheep"? Types are what philosophers term *abstract* objects, and only *concrete* objects have determinate spatial locations at the times when they exist. So now our question becomes, what is it for an abstract object like a type to exist, and can such a thing be brought into existence by the activity of an artist, or by human activity more generally conceived?

There is some disagreement over the answer to the first of these questions. One suggestion – term this *ET1*[15] – is that a type exists at a given time just in case it is possible for it to have tokens at that time. Since, for any type of sound sequence prescribed by the composer of a musical work, an occurrence of just that sound sequence could presumably have occurred before the composition of the work, *ET1* commits the sonicist to saying that performable musical works pre-exist their composition, But if they pre-exist their composition, they are discovered, not created, by the composer. The norm-type instrumentalist is only marginally better off. She might argue that a performance of a musical work is possible only when the musical instruments specified by the composer themselves exist. But since the instruments pre-exist the act of composition, *ET1* also commits the instrumentalist to the possibility, at least in principle, of occurrences of the work prior to its composition. She too, therefore, must view the performable work, qua norm-type, as discovered rather than created by the composer. So on *ET1*, it seems that both the sonicist and the instrumentalist must say that composition is not creation but discovery.

The same conclusion follows if we adopt an alternative account of the conditions under which an abstract entity like a norm-type exists. What we may term *ET2*[16] first identifies, for each type, an associated property the possession of which is the condition that must be met by a token (or, in the case of norm-types, a well-formed token) of the type. Then it is further claimed that types exist at a time just in case their associated properties exist at that time. This is combined with the view that properties exist eternally as long as there is at least one time – past, present, or future – at which they have, or at which they could have, an instance.[17] It follows from this that properties (and thus types) exist eternally if they exist at all. So if performable works are norm-types, then they exist eternally if at all. If a performable work exists, therefore, it must exist eternally and be discovered, not created, by the artist to whom we ascribe it.

It might be argued that there is nothing wrong with this conclusion. Composers, it might be said, are esteemed not for their ability to *create de novo* the performable works we ascribe to them, but for the *creativity* they display in discovering those works, something that parallels the creativity of mathematicians in discovering novel proofs of theorems, for example (see, for example, Dodd 2007, 112–121). But, if we do want to preserve the idea that the artists to whom we ascribe performable works are their creators, and not merely their creative discovers, then we cannot accept the identification of performable works with norm-types on either a sonicist or an instrumentalist construal of the latter.

Levinson raises a second problem for the sonicist and instrumentalist norm-type accounts. He claims that they fail to take account of the significance, for the identity of a performable work, of the art-historical context in which the artist was working. He defends a form of *contextualism* about the identity of musical works. In so doing, he sides with philosophers who have defended contextualist accounts of works in other arts such as literature and painting.[18] Contextualists hold that at least some of the properties that must be grasped to properly appreciate an artwork do not depend only upon *manifest* properties of the artistic product – the perceptible properties of a painting, for example, or of a sound sequence that complies with a composer's prescriptions. Nor are they dependent only upon these properties suitably *supplemented* by consideration of the medium employed in their production – the kind of pigment used in a painting, or the kinds of instruments used to generate a sound sequence, for example. Rather, they also depend upon features of the art-historical *context* in which the artist was working. Such features include the body of existing artworks upon which an artist draws, the intellectual resources available in her culture, and her own developing *oeuvre* taken as manifesting more general artistic projects. It is in virtue of these contextual variables that the artistic product serves as the articulation of certain specific artistic contents and possesses certain specific kinds of artistic value.

The most common kind of argument for contextualism asks us to consider situations where artistic products indistinguishable in terms of their (supplemented) manifest properties are generated in markedly different art-historical contexts. We very rarely encounter such situations in our actual artistic practice, although certain monochromatic paintings offer perhaps the closest approximation.[19] But contextualists offer us thought experiments in which we are asked to imagine a situation where there *are* such doppelgängers. Levinson (1980), for example, offers us five hypothetical cases where we have dopplegängers for actual musical works, where work and dopplegänger prescribe the same things for their correct performances. He argues that, in each case, the actual work and its doppelgänger differ in their aesthetic or artistic properties. They do so because of differences in the musico-historical contexts in which they were composed. However, if A and B differ in their properties, they must be different entities.[20] So if, in the hypothetical cases, there is a difference between the appreciable properties of the actual work and those of its doppelgänger, then the doppelgänger must be a distinct work. But, *ex hypothesi*, the actual work and its doppelgänger share a norm-type, whether the latter is construed in a sonicist or an instrumentalist fashion. Thus the norm-type sonicist or instrumentalist must view them as two occurrences of the same work. So, the contextualist concludes, performable musical works cannot be types or norm-types of either the sonicist or the instrumentalist sort.

The properties that Levinson cites in differentiating between an actual work and its doppelgänger are of two kinds: *aesthetic* properties – properties that the work is properly experienced as having in abstraction from comparisons with other works; and *artistic* properties – properties that relate the work more explicitly to its art-historical context. The aesthetic properties in question pertain to what a work is taken to express or how it is appropriate for us to respond to it. The artistic properties pertain to the ways in which a work should be appreciated in light of other works – its originality, for example, or its deliberate allusions to the works of other composers. To cite one example, Levinson asks us to consider a work by Beethoven identical in its sonicist and pure instrumentalist properties to Brahms's Second Piano Sonata. In listening to Brahms's piece, we rightly note how it reflects the influence of Liszt. But this would be anachronistic if applied to the hypothetical piece by Beethoven. Similarly, we would rightly ascribe a visionary quality to the Beethoven piece but not to the piece by Brahms. The individuation of performable musical works must therefore take into account not only what is prescribed for correct performances, but also the context in which the prescription occurs.

These contextualist arguments can be challenged, however. For example, it can be argued that "artistic" qualities such as originality or influence pertain not to the proper evaluation of musical artworks as aesthetic objects, but to our assessment of their place in art history.[21] Contextualists will respond that to properly evaluate something as an artwork *is* in part to evaluate its place in art history and not merely to assess it in terms of its aesthetic properties.[22] A further proposal[23] is that contextually based properties of musical works are *relativized* properties of the form: being-x-as-produced-in-art-historical-context-y. A work can quite consistently possess both this property and the property: not-being-x-as-produced-in-art-historical-context-z. So, in the case of Levinson's Brahms–Beethoven thought experiment, the sonicist or instrumentalist can insist that there is a single work that is a norm-type while also allowing that this work possesses such properties as being-Liszt-influenced-as-composed-by-Brahms, and not-being-Liszt-influenced-as-composed-by-Beethoven. The contextualist may object, however, that this fails to correspond to the way we talk about works. We take a work to be Liszt-influenced *simpliciter*.

5   Other Theories of the Performable Work

Rather than pursue these matters further, we should consider what other possibilities remain open if we don't accept the norm-type theory of performable works in the forms considered thus far. I shall briefly examine four proposals to be found in the literature:

1 Performable works are indeed types, but they are "indicated" types that are by their very nature contextualized and, as a consequence, creatable.
2 Performable works are not types that exist independently of their realizations, but are "continuants."
3 Performable works are not types, pure or indicated, but are *indicatings* of types, actions performed by the composer.
4 There are in fact no such things as performable works. Talk of such things is just a useful "fiction" that helps keep track of the ways in which we group performances.

Performable works as "indicated" types

The initial attraction of the idea that performable works are types is that it provides the most natural explanation of their repeatability. Types are by their very nature repeatable because they can have multiple tokens.[24] But, as we have seen, if the type-token theory is understood in the way that sonicists and instrumentalists understand it, we cannot easily account for either the creatability of performable works or their possession of properties that depend upon their contexts of creation. This suggests the following compromise: performable works, we might say, are indeed types, but they are types that are by their very nature contextualized and, as a consequence, creatable. This is Levinson's own strategy (see Levinson 1980). He proposes that we think of performable works as what he terms "initiated types." These are to be understood in something like the following way: a musical work is a sound/performance-means-structure-as-indicated-by-X-at-t, where X is a variable ranging over persons and t is a variable ranging over times. Thus, if we assume that Sibelius's Second Symphony prescribes the sound sequence $S2$ to be performed on instruments I, then the performed work is identical to $S2/I$-as-indicated-by-Sibelius-in-1902.[25] "Indication," here, is a matter of prescribing certain things for correct performance of the work one is creating (see Levinson 1990b, 260). To indicate a structure is thus to specify what is prescribed by one's work, qua norm-type. The work is not the norm-type per se, but rather the norm-type-as-specified-by-X-at-t. The norm-type itself is what Levinson terms an "implicit type," which exists in virtue of the possibilities for generating sequences of sounds in various ways. As such, the norm-type pre-exists the compositional activity of the composer. The norm-type-as-indicated, on the other hand, is an "initiated type" that comes into existence only through an intentional human act of the appropriate kind. Thus performable works, as initiated types, are creatable. Furthermore, in virtue of the contextual elements intrinsic to them, they are finely individuated in the manner that the contextualist requires. In addition, since performable works, as initiated types, are *types*, they are repeatable through those performances that are their tokens. More specifically, according to Levinson, the work-instances of a performable musical work are events that comply with everything prescribed through the work's S/PM structure and that stand in the right causal/intentional relation to the composer's act of indicating that structure. As we saw earlier, a performable work may have performances that fail to qualify as work-instances. Such performances, for Levinson, stand in the right kind of causal-intentional relation to the composition of the work, but fall short of *full* compliance with the work's prescriptions while still succeeding to a reasonable degree.

This option is very attractive if we are persuaded by the arguments for contextualism or believe that performable works are the creations of their authors. However, some have found the idea of initiated types, as entities, puzzling (see, for example, Currie 1989, 57–61; Dodd 2000). More significantly, it has been suggested that, to the extent that initiated types are still *types*, they must exist eternally and therefore cannot be created. In arguing for the creatability of performable works qua initiated types, Levinson relies on the criterion of type existence we characterized earlier as *ET1* according to which a type exists at a given time just in case it is possible for it to have tokens at that time. He reasons that an initiated type cannot have tokens until it is initiated, which in this case is when the relevant norm-kind is indicated by the composer. If, however, it is *ET2* and not *ET1* that provides the correct criterion for the existence of a type, then it seems that even initiated types will not be creatable. *ET2*, we may recall, identifies, for each type, an associated property that sets out the condition that must be met by (well-formed) tokens of that type. It then claims that types exist at a time just in case their associated properties exist at that time, and that properties exist eternally as long as there is at least one time – past, present, or future – at which they have, or could have, an instance. It follows that properties (and thus types) exist eternally if they exist at all. If this is the right account of type existence, then Levinson's proposed conditions under which we have a work-instance of a performable work qua initiated type will furnish us with our "associated property" for the initiated type. If works are taken to be norm-*types*, whether indicated or not, they will still be individuated in terms of a condition for correct instantiation that can be expressed as a property.[26] This property (and, by

ET2, the "initiated type" with which it is associated) will exist eternally if at all. So we have not shown multiple works, as norm-types, to be creatable, if *ET2* is the correct account of the existence conditions for types.

Performable works as "continuants"

The standard "type" theorist, as we have seen, asks us to surrender our intuitions about the creatability of performable works in the interests of accounting for their repeatability. What other than a type, after all, could be repeatable in the way that performable works are repeatable? "Continuants," some philosophers reply. Since the notion of a continuant is not one with which most of us are familiar, we need to ask two questions: First, what are continuants? And, second, how do they manage to be both creatable and repeatable? While different "continuant" theories of performable works have been proposed, I shall focus here on one developed by Guy Rohrbaugh (2003).[27]

Rohrbaugh invites us to consider the nature of words.[28] Words, we may recall, were our initial example of types. But words change and evolve over time, and could have evolved differently, whereas types are supposed to be fixed and unchanging. Furthermore, words enter into and go out of the languages in which they have their places. These properties of words, Rohrbaugh claims, are characteristic of continuants, which are essentially historical individuals that depend for their existence on those concrete entities that are their *embodiments*. He identifies three properties that differentiate continuants from types. The first is "modal flexibility." Something is modally flexible if it could have differed in its "intrinsic" non-relational properties. Houses are modally flexible, for example, in that a particular house could have had more or fewer rooms than it actually has, or could have been constructed of different material than it actually was. The second property is "temporal flexibility." Something is temporally flexible if its "intrinsic" non-relational properties are changeable over time. Houses are temporally flexible in that something remains the same house even if it is internally remodeled, or has its roof replaced. The final property is "temporality." Something possesses this property if it comes into and goes out of existence. Individual buildings are obviously temporal, being erected and demolished at particular times.

Continuants have these three properties because of the relationship in which they stand to their embodiments. An embodiment of a continuant is a spatio-temporally locatable object or event, and the continuant itself is a "higher level" object that depends for its existence upon its embodiments. Take again our example of the house. A particular house comes into existence only when someone produces a particular ordered arrangement of physical matter. This is its first embodiment. It continues to exist as long as it has an embodiment of this kind suitably causally related to earlier embodiments, and it goes out of existence when no such embodiment exists. The existence of a particular house at a given time depends upon its being embodied in some arrangement of physical stuff at that time, but over time the physical stuff in which it is embodied will change. The house survives changes in the physical stuff in which it is embodied, and could indeed have been made of different stuff in certain counterfactual circumstances.

Continuants, then, are temporal, modally flexible, and temporally flexible. Types, on the other hand, arguably possess none of these properties.[29] And artworks in general, Rohrbaugh claims, are like continuants and unlike types in this respect. He argues first with respect to paintings, and then extends this account to multiple artworks like photographs. However, he intends his argument to apply to multiple artworks in general, including performable works. As continuants, artworks are creatable, and are embodied in various particulars. A traditional photograph's embodiments, for example, include the negative, but they also include what Rohrbaugh terms "occurrences," which are distinctive in that they display those qualities of the artwork that bear upon its appreciation and criticism. In terms of our own terminology, a photograph's occurrences include both work-instances and flawed prints of the work. A photograph is repeatable, then, because it can have multiple occurrences – and multiple work-instances – among the embodiments upon which its existence depends. The same applies, according to Rohrbaugh, to other kinds of multiple artworks, including performable works. The embodiments of a performable musical work will include its scores, and also those events that are its correct and flawed occurrences – its performances. This preserves the independence of a performable work from its actual performances. An artwork comes into existence when the artist produces an embodiment of that work, but that embodiment need not be an occurrence. Since a score of a performable work counts as an embodiment, the work, qua continuant, can exist unperformed.

Rohrbaugh's theory of performable artworks as historical individuals promises to deliver on both the creatability and the repeatablity of such works. But critics have raised doubts about both the intelligibility of the notion of "continuant" and the claim that artworks are continuants. In the first place, there are two ways of understanding the essentially historical nature of continuants and the relationship in which they stand to particular objects and events. For the *perdurantist*, continuants are *constituted* by their embodiments, which are taken to be their temporal parts just as a football field is constituted by those areas of the playing surface that are its spatial parts. The idea that performable works are perduring entities of this sort is not without its defenders (Caplan and Matheson 2006, for example), but it faces some serious objections. For example, it seems that, on this view, only part of a performable work is ever present in a performance, and it needs to be explained how something that is a "fusion" of temporal parts could have had *different* temporal parts in the way that a performable work might have had different performances.[30] Rohrbaugh espouses an alternative understanding of continuants, according to which they are *enduring*, rather than perduring, entities that depend upon, but are not constituted by, their embodiments. So construed, continuants are higher order entities that are always present in their entirety in their embodiments, thereby evading the first objection to perdurantism, and that could have been dependent on different embodiments, thereby evading the second objection. But it needs to be explained just what kinds of things continuants, so conceived, are, what the relation of "dependence" involves, and what it is for this relation to obtain in those cases where continuants are claimed to exist.

Even if these challenges can be met, there is a further problem with the claim that *artworks* are continuants of the sort proposed by Rohrbaugh. For this claim rests upon the assumption that artworks are modally and temporally flexible, something that is open to dispute both generally and in the case of performable works. Dodd, for example, argues that there are no good reasons to think of musical works as either modally or temporally flexible. Any locutions that might tempt us to think otherwise are, he claims, most plausibly understood in terms of suitable paraphrases. Where a work W^* differs in its intrinsic properties, either modally or through time, from a work W, or from a work W at a time t, then we should view W^* and W as distinct works, albeit distinct works that closely resemble one another, he maintains (Dodd 2007, ch. 2). While Dodd's arguments don't by themselves show that at least some multiple artworks *are* modally and temporally inflexible, they raise questions as to the force of Rohrbaugh's claims to the contrary.

Performable works as indicatings of types

Let us take stock. We have found reason to question the idea that performable works are eternally existing entities that are discovered rather than created by those to whom we attribute them. If types, including norm-types, are eternal existents, then we have reason to resist the idea that performable works are types. To counter that *initiated* types are indeed creatable seems to fall foul of at least one plausible account of the existence conditions of types. An alternative account of the repeatability of multiple artworks takes them to be continuants some of whose embodiments are occurrences. But we found the notion of a continuant to which Rohrbaugh appeals somewhat murky, and his argument for viewing multiple artworks as continuants rests on the contested assumption that they are modally and temporally flexible.

The challenge then is to find an account of performable works that allows them to be (1) repeatable and (2) creatable. We should also prefer an account that does not rest upon contestable claims about the modal and temporal flexibility of works. Indeed, claims about such matters should arguably be resolved *on the basis of* an otherwise adequate account of the nature of performable works, rather than serve as premises in formulating such an account. One option is to try to rework Levinson's proposal in such a way that it does not appeal to the notion of type. Dodd comments on Levinson's notion of an "indicated structure" that it contains a reference to a time and thus seems more like an event than a type (Dodd 2000, 440). While Dodd intends this as a *reductio*, we might view it rather as a suggestion as to how we might amend Levinson's view to evade the objections brought against it. Suppose, instead of holding that a performable work is an indicated structure and thereby a kind of type, we hold that it is the *indicating* of a structure, and thereby an event. More specifically, we might say that a performable work is the action of prescribing certain things for correct performance. Performable works are then repeatable because different performances on the part of others can count as fulfilling those prescriptions. This can be generalized to multiple artworks whose instances are specified in other ways – for example, by the production of an exemplar or of a production-artifact. In each case, we might say, the artwork consists in what is done in order to define a class of entities as work-instances. To appreciate the work is to appreciate what has been done. This crucially requires that we determine what artistic content is rightly ascribable to the work-instances defined by the work, qua action, and thus to the work itself.[31] Thus Sibelius's Second Symphony differs from his First Symphony in two crucial respects: (1) what Sibelius did in coming up with the sets of prescriptions for the former work was a very different – arguably a much greater and more original – artistic achievement than what he did in coming up with the set of prescriptions for the latter, and (2) the aesthetic and artistic properties realizable in performances that conform to the set of prescriptions for the former work are very different from the aesthetic and artistic properties realizable in performances that conform to the set of prescriptions for the latter. And a parallel account might be given of different photographic works by Diane Arbus or Edward Weston. Indeed, if we are at all tempted by an account of multiple artworks as identical to the creative acts of their authors, why shouldn't we extend this approach to artworks in general? Artworks, it might be said, whether singular or multiple, just are the artistic acts of their authors that are generative of an artistic vehicle of some kind that articulates a particular artistic content.[32]

The advantages of such a view in the present context should be obvious. Since artists are responsible for initiating their generative actions, they are in this sense the creators of their works. We also have an explanation of the repeatability of multiple artworks that doesn't identify the works themselves with types. The challenge to explain how there can be multiple correct performances *of* particular performable works is answered if we can explain how we are able to group certain events as a given work's correct performances, and such groupings can be explained in terms of the relationship in which such performances stand to the artist's generative activity. The "of" here need not be the "of" that relates generic entities like types to their elements. Rather, a performance can be "of" a work in something like the sense that a copy can be "of" today's *Times* because it stands in a certain causal-intentional relationship to the activity of journalists, editors, compositors, and printers. Indeed, by analogy, a print can be "of" a photograph by standing in a certain causal-intentional relationship to something done by a photographer. If there are nonetheless types elsewhere in the mix — types of sound sequences for example, as what the composer prescribes — this is not in itself an obvious difficulty. Levinson, for instance, is quite happy to grant that *implicit* types are eternally existing entities as long as artworks are not.

But of course there is a significant fly in the ointment here. For it sounds very odd to say that artworks are generative actions of artists productive of artistic vehicles. Surely, we want to protest, the artwork is the artistic vehicle itself together with the artistic contents articulated through it. While, like the contextualists, we may be eager to integrate the history of making of an artistic vehicle into the identity of the work, it seems much more plausible to do so by following Levinson in characterizing the work as the product-as-generated-in-a-context, rather than as the contextualized action of generating that product.

Fictionalism about performable works

The idea of performable works as indicatings of norm-kinds rather than as indicated norm-kinds clearly stands in need of further defense if it is to strike the reader as convincing, and this is not the place to attempt or to assess such a defense. There is, however, another approach that promises to free us from all of the difficulties in whose python-like grip we have found ourselves in the preceding pages. Our problem has been to explain the nature of the performable work. The latter, we have assumed, is the entity that is performed in traditional concerts of classical music, and, we might think, in traditional theatrical and dance performances as well. It is qualities of the performable work Sibelius's Second Symphony that sent Berthold into aesthetic raptures during the performance described in our opening paragraph, for example. From the austere conception of the performable work as an eternally existing abstract entity, we have moved first to the less esoteric idea of performable works as abstract entities initiated by composers, then to the promising if mysterious idea of performable works as particulars of a higher order somehow embodied in lower order particulars, and finally to the idea that performable works are simply the actions of artists that provide a way of grouping certain other events as performances or instances of the work.

But, now that we have acquired a taste for minimalism, why not go all the way? If the point of our talk of performable works is to explain the ways in which we group performances, why operate with such misleading talk of a "performable work" at all? Or, since we clearly do operate with such a locution, why not think of it as merely a useful *façon de parler*, a device that helps us to keep track of the kinds of groupings of performances that interest us. Why, in other words, shouldn't we be *fictionalists* about performable works, viewing them as simply useful fictions?

Fictionalism is a philosophical view that until quite recently was thought to have been definitively laid to rest. But philosophical views are the undead of the intellectual world, ever rising in a new guise to haunt our reflections. So it has been with fictionalism, which has enjoyed somewhat of a resurgence over the past few years, as a means of clearing what some have viewed as ontological slums without having to rehouse the occupants. Thus it is not surprising, in view of the difficulties we have encountered in wrestling with our theme, to find that the idea of a fictionalist view of musical works, and thereby of performable works more generally, has recently been canvassed in the literature.

Fictionalism is one way of denying that there "really are" the things to which we seem to be committed by the form of discourse that we employ in a given practice or domain of inquiry. It is thus a way of declining to be a *realist* about that form of discourse. Realism concerning a form of discourse D can be taken to involve the following claims: (1) sentences in D are to be taken at face value, rather than as disguised ways of saying something expressible in a different vocabulary; (2) taken at face value, they are genuine representations of a putative domain of fact, rather than, say, prescriptions as to how we should act; (3) acceptance of a sentence S in D is warranted in proportion to the grounds for thinking that S is true – D "aims at truth"; and (4) warranted sentences in D generally *are* true, or at least increasingly true.[33] The fictionalist about D accepts (1),[34] also accepts (2),[35] and may remain agnostic about (4).[36] The defining characteristic of fictionalism about D is the rejection of (3). What warrants the use of D in general, and what warrants the acceptance of individual sentences of D, is to be cashed out not in terms of the truth of those sentences but in terms of some other property that we value. And the attitude adopted to those sentences of D that we accept is not belief – for to believe something is to believe it to be true – but something more pragmatic – for example, a readiness to act *as if* we believed those sentences to be true, to defend them against criticism, etc.

The fictionalist may be making a *descriptive* claim about D as we actually use it, or a *prescriptive* claim as to how we should revise our use of D. It is the former kind of fictionalism – what is termed "hermeneutic fictionalism"[37] – that might be advocated in respect of our talk about performable works.[38] The fictionalist claims that, while there are actually no such things as musical works, we have shared ways of representing such things in our musical practice.[39] These shared representations play a valuable part in that practice, and this justifies continuing to talk as if there were such works even if the world contains no such things. The kinds of properties we have been assuming that musical works must have – creatability and repeatability, in particular – play an important part in sustaining different elements in our musical practice. But the tangled philosophical disagreements over the nature of musical works explored earlier in this chapter suggest to the fictionalist that there may in fact be no entities that correspond to our conceptions. Nonetheless, the fictionalist argues, "it would make no difference if there were no musical works, strictly speaking, as long as we all continued to behave as if there were" (Kania 2008, 440).

The fictionalist's claims raise deep philosophical issues that cannot be properly pursued here, but a few observations may at least give a whiff of the chasm from whose edge we strategically withdraw. In the first place, there seems no obvious reason to think that the fictionalist argument, if valid, holds only for musical works. Presumably the very same considerations would argue for a fictionalist view not just of other performable works but of multiple works in general, since, as we have seen, all multiples seem to raise the same general set of questions. Second, the fictionalist might deny that she is motivated by a more general resistance to abstract entities, and maintain that there is no reason to think that the arguments presented against musical works would also apply to other abstract objects such as numbers or properties. But then one wonders what kind of existence is being denied to multiple artworks yet extended to other abstract objects. What would it be for there to be something that corresponds to the conceptions of works that animate our artistic practice – in other words, what precisely is the fictionalist denying?

The fictionalist might respond that the difference between performable musical works, on the one hand, and numbers and properties, on the other, is that we do not need to posit the actual existence of the former in order to explain what is going on in our musical practice, whereas we do need to posit numbers and properties to explain what is going on in our mathematical and scientific practice.[40] To assess this response we would need to consider at least the following. First, to what model of explanation is the fictionalist appealing in claiming that abstract entities like numbers can "explain" our practice? If abstract entities of any kind are to explain our practices, it might seem that they must be capable of causing those practices to be one way rather than another, but the causal mechanisms in question are not clear. Second, if it be responded that the kind of explanation in question does not require such causal mechanisms, but involves our capacity to make sense of our mathematical and scientific practices, then the very role accorded by the fictionalist to our talk of musical works might seem to warrant ascribing a similar explanatory function to such works. Third, the assumption that our criterion for the existence of something is its ability to perform a particular kind of explanatory role itself stands in need of some clarification and defense.

We must leave these questions in the air, however, and turn to more pressing issues. We introduced the notion of the performable work at the beginning of this chapter when describing Berthold's attempts to deepen his appreciation of a particular performable work through attending one of its performances. This, indeed, is one of the principal ways in which the concept of the performable work animates our engagement with artistic performances. But we need to address more systematically an issue that has occasionally punctuated our discussion. How in fact are performable works to be appreciated through their performances? How are the properties of performable works that bear upon their appreciation made accessible to us in performance? And – a question to which we have already seen a number of answers, but which requires more thorough investigation – what features must a performance have if it is to play this mediatory role in the appreciation of performable works? These questions present themselves even if we accept the fictionalist's claim that talk of performable works is just shorthand for talk about the different groupings of performances that we effect in our musical practice. For we still need to understand how the qualities of individual performances bear upon what is rightly said about such groupings. It is to these matters that we turn in the following two chapters.

Notes

1. See Bell 1914, 33.
2. Could we meet these objections by identifying a performable work with the set of all its *possible* performances? This might seem attractive to someone who wants to avoid a "type" theory of performable works (see section 3 below) because they regard types as ontologically non-kosher. But, if performable works actually exist, then this option presumably commits us to the view that their possible performances themselves actually exist, which is itself a somewhat dubious ontological claim. And sets of *possibilia*, if they do indeed exist, don't seem to be the kinds of things that can be created, so we still face one of the more contentious implications of the "type" theory, as we shall see below.

3. Some writers have resisted this distinction, holding that, even in the case of painting or sculpture, it is at least theoretically possible for a work to have multiple work-instances: for, were we to have a *copy* of the "original" – the entity produced by the artist – that was guaranteed to be perceptually indistinguishable from the original, then this copy would also fully qualify to play the experiential role in the appreciation of the work. We need not pursue these issues here, but see D. Davies 2010.

4. See, for example, Wollheim 1980, 78–80; Wolterstorff 1980, 90–98; S. Davies 2003, 159–63. See also Carroll 1998, chapter 3, on film as a multiple art form.

5. Other terms used for the entity that plays this role in the specifying of work-instances in an art form like photography are "encoding" (S. Davies 2003) and "template" (Carroll 1998).

6. See Wollheim 1980, 75–84. Wollheim distinguishes types from other generic entities, such as sets, properties, and universals, and offers an account of how such generic entities differ from one another.

7. Nelson Goodman (1976) notoriously argues that we should insist that performances of a musical work conform to all of those prescriptions explicitly specified in musical notation in a work's score. See the discussion of the "Goodman argument" in Chapter 3.

8. See Dodd 2007. Dodd here follows Nicholas Wolterstorff, who uses the term "norm-kind" rather than "norm-type." See Wolterstorff 1975 and 1980. To avoid confusion, I shall use the term "norm-type" in discussing both Dodd's and Wolterstorff's views.

9. See Dodd 2000 and 2007, 9.

10. See S. Davies 2001, 60–65, for a critical discussion of sonicism, both "pure" and "timbral." See also Dodd 2007, 201–217.

11. Defenders of pure sonicism include Kivy 1983, 1988, and Scruton 1997.

12. Dodd 2007, 212–217. Timbral sonicists, like "instrumentalists" (see below), may restrict the scope of this claim to Western classical music composed after a certain date – see also Levinson 1980, 64–65.

13. The timbral sonicist might grant that a musical work's aesthetic properties depend upon its being *heard as* played on a particular instrument, but deny that correct performances of the work must actually be played on those instruments. See, for example, Dodd 2007, 230–235. This strategy, however, which separates the requirements for properly appreciating a musical work from the requirements for its correct performance, may be an unstable one for the timbral sonicist to adopt. For consider the following plausible principle: (AP) If W and W^* are artworks and if W and W^* have different properties that bear on their proper appreciation, then W and W^* are distinct artworks. The anti-instrumentalist strategy just canvassed seems to allow for works that share their timbral sonic properties but that have different properties bearing on their proper appreciation because they have to be *heard as* played on different instruments. Consider, for example, the *Hammerklavier Sonata* and a timbral sonic equivalent that is to be heard as played on a PTS. The timbral sonicist

must say that there is only a single work here, since both the *HS* and its doppelganger prescribe the same timbral sound sequence for correct performance. But, by AP, the *Hammerklavier Sonata* and its doppelgänger must be different works. For more on this, see D. Davies 2009b.

14. Levinson's target is the view that musical works are types rather than norm-types, but his arguments can be applied to the latter view as well as the former.

15. *ET1* is endorsed by Wolterstorff in his 1975, 335, and by Levinson in his 1980, 65. For arguments against *ET1*, see Dodd 2000; 2007, 104–106.

16. See Dodd 2000; Dodd 2007, 60–69.

17. Dodd's formulation of *ET2* in his 2000 differs from his formulation in his 2007. In the former, he holds that a property exists eternally as long as there is at least one time – past, present, or future – at which it *has* an instance. In the latter, what is required is that there is at least one time – past, present or future – at which it *could have* an instance. An obvious difficulty with the 2000 formulation is that, as applied to musical works as norm-kinds, it wouldn't allow for there to be unperformed works.

18. See, for example, Dutton 1979; Danto 1981; Currie 1989; D. Davies 2004, chs. 2 and 3.

19. Danto's "gallery of red rectangles" introduced at the beginning of his 1981 is a hypothetical example of this sort, but the white paintings of Kazimir Malevich, Yves Klein, and Robert Ryman are a real example of works whose differences cannot be reduced to the differences that exist in their (supplemented) manifest properties.

20. This follows from Leibniz's Law of the Indiscernibility of Identicals. This states that if *A* is identical to *B* – for example, if the morning star is identical to the evening star (they are two ways in which the Ancients picked out the planet Venus) – then *A* and *B* must have all their properties in common. It follows that, if there are any properties that they do not have in common, they cannot be identical.

21. See, for example, Dodd 2007, ch. 9.

22. A stronger but more controversial response is that in fact it is only through historical contextualization that we can properly assess a work's aesthetic properties. See, for example, Currie 1989, ch. 2; Baxandall 1985, 6–11.

23. See, for example, Wolterstorff 1991.

24. This is one of the reasons why Dodd treats the type-token theory of musical works as the default position. See Dodd 2007, ch. 1.

25. On an alternative formulation considered in Levinson 1980, pieces are indexed not to individuals and times but to musico-historical contexts. If we represent the musico-historical context in which Sibelius composed his Second Symphony as *MHC-S2/I*, then, on this alternative formulation, the performable work is identical to *S2/I-as-indicated-in-MHC-S2/I*. Since Levinson prefers the first formulation, and the alternative formulation seems to have counterintuitive implications for the modal properties of musical works, I shall focus on the first formulation in what follows.

26. The property in question will presumably be something like this: being correct if successfully complying with the performance specifications set out by

       B in context C and standing in an appropriate intentional-historical relation to that act of specification.

27. An alternative view of musical works as continuants is defended in Caplan and Matheson 2006. For criticisms of both accounts, see Dodd 2007, ch. 6.
28. He draws here on Kaplan 1990.
29. Dodd argues for this view of types in chs. 2 and 3 of his 2007.
30. See Dodd 2007, ch. 7, for these objections and Caplan and Matheson 2006 for attempts to answer them.
31. As we shall see in the next chapter, the content will be predicated of the work "analogically" rather than univocally.
32. See D. Davies 2004 for a defense of such a view. For critical responses to this view, see, among others, Dodd 2005; Kania 2005; Stecker and Dilworth 2005.
33. It might be thought that a realist about a given discourse D need only subscribe to the first three claims, and that realism about D is quite consistent with skepticism about the truth of statements in D. But to reject (4) is to advance an "error theory" with respect to D, and error theories, such as John Mackie's account (1977) of ethical discourse, are usually described as forms of non-realism. In any case, I shall use the term "realism" to encompass both a claim about the content of a given discourse (claims 1–3) and a claim about the general truth of statements in D (4).
34. Philosophers who reject (1) for a given discourse D may be described as having a "reductionist" view of D – they want to reduce the content of sentences in D to the content of sentences in another discourse.
35. Philosophers who reject (2) for a discourse D are described as "non-factualists" about D.
36. As just noted, philosophers who accept at least (1) and (2) but reject (4) for a form of discourse D are described as "error theorists" about D. Some fictionalists are error theorists, but think that, in spite of its falsity, we should still use D because of its other virtues.
37. This terminology derives from Burgess 1983. Kalderon 2005 contains a good collection of contemporary papers on fictionalism.
38. Kania 2008 explores without fully endorsing such a fictionalist option.
39. The idea is that we have shared ways of representing musical works just as we have shared ways of representing unicorns. In neither case does the existence of such representational practices require that the represented entities themselves actually exist.
40. I am grateful to Andrew Kania (private communication) for suggesting this response.

3

The Classical Paradigm II: Appreciating Performable Works in Performance

1 Introduction: Talking Appreciatively about Performable Works

In the notes that accompany the CD of Sibelius's complete symphonies played by the Vienna Philharmonic Orchestra conducted by Lorin Maazel, Timothy Day comments on the Second Symphony as follows:

> From his modest orchestral forces, Sibelius is able to conjure up astonishingly varied sonorities, eloquent and powerful in the Finale where he exploits the full range of the brass instruments, or harsh and forlorn, as in the slow movement, with thin textures and the dark colour of the lower registers of the orchestra. Sibelius is rarely serene: the pastoral quality of the opening *Allegretto* is tinged with melancholy and there is a solemnity in the triumph of the work's conclusion.
>
> The first movement is a sonata-form structure. Its themes give the impression of evolving from each other rather than presenting sharp contrasts, and indeed, in the recapitulation, material from the first and second groups of the exposition is contained without strain or distortion. This coherence adds great strength and inevitability to the movement's predominantly sunny and relaxed mood. The second movement is a more rhapsodic structure with a succession of beautiful themes. It begins, slightly menacingly, with a single melodic line played pizzicato by cellos and double basses, joined later by two bassoons in octaves intoning a modal lament, marked *lugubre*. A series of impassioned climaxes ensue and the movement ends in a solemn mood.

Philosophy of the Performing Arts, First Edition. David Davies.
© 2011 David Davies. Published 2011 by Blackwell Publishing Ltd.

The third movement is a scurrying *Scherzo* which erupts in fiery outbursts. Its lyrical trio, *lento e suave*, in which an oboe sings remote, plainsong-like phrases, is reintroduced before the movement surges into the Finale. The slower sections of the last movement recapture the pastoral quality of the first, but the dominant mood of the Finale is heroic, and its big tune undeniably stirring.[1]

Day's commentary conveys to us a number of different things about the Second Symphony, all of which arguably bear upon its appreciation. Some of these relate to broadly structural features of the work and the ways in which elements relate to one another. He talks here of such things as "sonata-form structure," "rhapsodic structure," "coherence," themes "evolving" out of one another, "exposition" and "recapitulation." These expressions characterize the sequence of sounds prescribed by the composer in terms of formal relationships that, if we had a trained eye and appropriate musical training, we might be able to grasp from a perusal of the score, where the composer's prescriptions are registered. Viewed as a pure structure having these features, it seems that the work could to some extent be appreciated without the need for a public performance, or even a private performance in the head of one perusing the score. Other features in Day's commentary concern the instrumentation prescribed for the execution of the sound sequence – brass, cello, bassoon, and oboe, for example. He thereby conveys to someone who is familiar with these instruments the kinds of timbral properties that would characterize a performance of the piece that complied with the composer's prescriptions. These are the "varied sonorities" to which he refers, including the "dark colour of the lower registers of the orchestra." His commentary provides support for the view, discussed in the preceding chapter, that timbral properties are integral to at least some works. For such properties seem crucial in the *oeuvre* of a composer like Sibelius who relies so much upon the "varied sonorities" to which Day refers. It also suggests that, to appreciate such works, we require more than the mere knowledge that certain instruments are prescribed. We must also be aware of the specific timbral qualities that might be realized through the collective execution, on those instruments, of the prescribed sequence of sounds. Indeed, it is difficult to imagine how the full timbral richness of a work like the Second Symphony could be gauged without hearing a public performance, even by the most skilled sight reader.[2]

However, the vast majority of Day's observations relate to what are broadly *expressive* properties of the prescribed sequence that depend at least in part upon its timbral richness. He speaks of passages in the work as "eloquent," "powerful," "harsh," "forlorn," "melancholy," "sunny," and "menacing," for example. He also anchors these expressive properties in prescriptions by the composer, referring to the markings of "*lugubre*" and "*lento e suave*" in the score. Given the nature of these kinds of qualities, we can appreciate them only through hearing the work performed. It might be thought that this is because we recognize expressive qualities in virtue of ourselves being put into the relevant emotional states. But we need not subscribe to such a view to see how hearing performances of a musical work matter for grasping its expressive qualities. Whether or not listening to the music puts us into a melancholy or sunny frame of mind, the melancholy or sunny nature of the music can be taken to be qualities of the music itself that relate by their very nature to what can be *heard in* it. If so, they can be given to us only in a hearing of the music, and this will be one reason why a performable work such as Sibelius's Second Symphony is properly appreciable only through its performances. It is in the hope of better understanding and appreciating these kinds of qualities in a work like the Second Symphony that aficionados like Berthold come to concerts like the one described at the opening of the previous chapter.

2   Can Performable Works Share Artistic Properties with Their Performances?

The nature of musical expression is a fascinating issue upon which much insightful work has been done.[3] But this is not the issue that concerns us here. Rather, our interest, at least initially, is in how the expressive and timbral qualities heard in a performance of a work like the Second Symphony can bear upon the appreciation of the work performed. This question may not have occurred to most of us in our appreciative engagement with musical works in performance. Indeed, in elaborating upon Day's critical analysis of the Second Symphony, we simply assumed that the expressive and timbral properties of a performance gave us appreciative access to the same properties of the work. But this assumption requires further defense in light of our discussion, in the previous chapter, of the nature of the performable musical work. Of the different accounts of the performable work that we examined, all but the fictionalist and the continuant accounts ascribe a role to *types* of some kind of which work-performances are the tokens. This is most apparent in the case of the sonicist and instrumentalist accounts, where the work itself just is a norm-type that prescribes the properties required in its correct performances. However, as we saw, Levinson's contextualist theory still identifies works with types – albeit initiated types – of which performances are tokens. And types also play an essential mediating role in the theory of performable works as the *indicatings* of norm-types, since it is through the indicated norm-type that we identify the class of performances that bear on our appreciation of *what was done*.

But types, as we have seen, are entities of a very different stripe from the performances that are claimed to be their tokens. They are, we are told, abstract entities that exist eternally, lack any determinate spatial location, and are arguably changeless in their intrinsic properties. If this is the case, we may ask what sorts of properties types can possess. More crucially, if performable works are types, we may wonder whether they can possess the same sorts of appreciable properties as the performances that are their tokens. If we ask what we appreciate in performances of performable works, what immediately come to mind are audible properties such as the ones cited by Day in his account of the Second Symphony – the "varied sonorities," and the expressive properties that we hear in those sonorities. These are properties of particular experienced events that take place at particular times. But how could such properties be possessed by something abstract and eternal? Indeed, if we accept some accounts of the nature of types,[4] they lack internal structure, and thus, it would seem, cannot possess even the structural properties to which Day refers. And lacking such structural properties, they cannot possess expressive properties that depend upon internal relations such as "recapitulation."[5]

It might be thought that there is really no problem here. Consider our initial linguistic example of types and their tokens. If I write the word "sheep," the word-token that I produce contains five letters, two of which are es. But surely the word-type "sheep" possesses exactly the same properties. And, indeed, these two facts seem to be intimately related. It is *because* the word-type "sheep" has these properties that its tokens have these properties, we might say: the type prescribes that its tokens possess certain of the properties that it possesses itself. Such a view is proposed by Richard Wollheim in his elucidation of the idea – discussed in Chapter 2 – that multiple works, including performable works, are types (1980, 74–84). Types, for Wollheim, are generic entities that can have other entities as elements "falling under" them. And generic entities, he maintains, may share properties with their elements. Sometimes this is merely a contingent matter. For example, the class of average-sized things may itself be average-sized. But sometimes a generic entity possesses a property *because* its elements possess that property, or vice versa. Where this is the case, Wollheim suggests, we can say that the property is *transmitted* between the generic entity and its elements. In the case of types, he claims, all, and only, properties of a specific kind are transmitted between a type and its tokens: namely, those shareable properties that its tokens must have in order to be tokens of that type. For example, the properties of being rectangular and bearing a particular design in red, white, and blue are transmitted between the Union Jack and its tokens.[6]

If types and their tokens transmit properties to one another in this way, then we can easily explain how both the word-type "sheep" and particular tokens of that word-type can possess the property of containing five letters. And, similarly, there is no problem explaining how the performable work

Sibelius's Second Symphony can possess those structural, timbral, and expressive properties characteristic of its correct performances that Day identifies in his commentary. Multiple artworks, then, simply inherit the expressive properties of their realizations through the standard relation of transmission between types and their tokens.

Unfortunately, however, things are not this simple. Reflect again on the word-type example. The word-token of "sheep" in this sentence has the property of containing five *occurrences* of letters, including two *occurrences* of the letter *e*, and these occurrences are particular strings of code in a computer file, or combinations of pixels on a computer screen, or (had I used a pen) particular characters inscribed in ink on a page. But *this* property cannot be a property of the word-type "sheep," since, qua type, it cannot contain such particular occurrences as parts. So, when we say that the word-type "sheep" contains five letters, we must be ascribing to the word-type a property different from the one that we ascribe, by means of the same predicate, to a token of the word-type. This insight is developed by Nicholas Wolterstorff in terms of what he terms "analogical predication" (1975, 326–328).

Wolterstorff argues that it is crucial to distinguish between the sharing of *predicates* and the sharing of *properties*. *A* and *B* share a predicate "*p*" just in case "*p*" is truly predicated of both *A* and *B*. On the other hand, *A* and *B* share a property *p* just in case they both have *p*. Usually, when we have a sharing of predicates, this is in virtue of a sharing of properties. For example, if Berthold and Magda share the predicate "lives in London," this is because they share the corresponding property of living in London. In such cases, we can say that the predicate is used *univocally*. On the other hand, it may be that Berthold and William share the predicate "lives near a bank" in virtue of possessing *different and unrelated* properties. Berthold may live near a financial institution while William lives near a river. Here the predicate is used *equivocally*. The interesting case, however, is where a predicate is shared in virtue of the possession of different properties, but there is a systematic relation between these properties such that one entity possesses one property *because* the other entity possesses the other. Here we can say that the predicate is used *analogically*. It is analogical predication, Wolterstorff claims, rather than the sharing of properties, that is really going on in the cases that Wollheim describes in terms of transmitted properties.

Consider, for example, what is going on when we truly predicate something like "contains a G sharp in the seventh measure" of both Bartok's First String Quartet and a performance of Bartok's First String Quartet. This, Wolterstorff would say, is a case of analogical predication, because different but related properties are being predicated in the two cases. What we are predicating of the performance is the property of containing an occurrence of a particular pitch at a given place in its temporal progression. But the performable work itself, if it is a type, cannot possess this property since it does not unfold in time. What property, then, are we predicating of the work? It cannot be the property of having only performances that contain an occurrence of a particular pitch (a G sharp) at a particular place (the seventh measure). For, we are assuming, performable works can have flawed performances and thus there could be a performance of Bartok's piece lacking such an occurrence. Rather, in line with his proposal that we think of works as norm-types, Wolterstorff suggests that the property ascribed to the work is that of having such an occurrence in all of its *correct* or well-formed performances.

The doctrine of analogical predication allows us to explain how performable works can be, or essentially involve, types yet still be properly appreciated in virtue of the experienced properties of their performances. The works themselves possess properties *analogically* related to appreciable properties of their correct performances – that is to say, properties of *requiring* certain appreciable properties in those performances. The appreciable qualities predicated of correct performances can then be referred analogically to the performable work in our appreciation of the latter. It is because the performable work makes the demands that it does on its correct performances that those performances have some of the qualities that we experience them as having. Thus, in appreciating how the orchestra uses the varied sonorities prescribed by Sibelius to such powerful expressive effect, Berthold is at the same time able to appreciate the performable work for the analogically related property it possesses – its *prescribing* (directly or indirectly) that its correct performances have these experienced qualities.[7]

We should note one interesting implication of the doctrine of analogical predication as it applies to performable works. We usually think of such works as things with which we can perceptually engage through our presence at their performances. This is surely right. But we also describe this in terms of having heard Sibelius's Second Symphony, or having seen *King Lear* or *Swan Lake*. But if performable works are, as many believe, pure or initiated types, or continuants, or artistic actions, then is it possible to hear or see *the works* in hearing or seeing *performances* of them? There are a couple of worries one might have here. First, it might seem plausible to say that one can perceive something visually or aurally only if one stands in an appropriate causal relation to the thing seen or heard. An appropriate causal relation here would involve some kind of direct or mediated relation to the visible or acoustic properties of the things seen or heard. For example, it is only if my visual experiences are appropriately caused by the cup in front of me that I can be said to perceive that cup in virtue of those experiences. But can we stand in this kind of causal relation to a type or a continuant? Some have argued that we are able to indirectly *refer* to abstract entities like types by directly referring to their tokens.[8] But perception seems to require a more intimate connection than reference.

There is, however, a deeper worry. As we have seen, the particular applications that we make of structural, sonic, timbral, and expressive predicates to musical works are to be understood analogically relative to the application of the same predicates to their performances. What we are thereby ascribing to the *work* is the property of prescribing the relevant structural, sonic, timbral, and expressive properties for its correct performances. A work's *performances* are certainly audible, and it is in virtue of this fact that we are able to appreciate the particular audible properties that they possess. But what of the predication of audibility of the musical work itself, as when Berthold says that he heard Sibelius's Second Symphony? How can something that possesses particular audible properties only analogically possess the general property of audibility in the *same sense* (that is, *non*-analogically) as its performances? If the doctrine of analogical predication applies to those particular audible properties of a work's tokens that they possess in virtue of being tokens of a given work – such as containing a G sharp in the seventh measure – why does it not also apply to audibility in general? These considerations acquire additional force if musical works, as types, lack the structure and temporal parts of their performances. For, it might seem, something that lacks temporal parts cannot possess the kinds of properties that any object of audition must possess – duration in time and temporal boundaries, not to mention particular acoustic or sonic properties. This suggests that, if (contra fictionalism) performable musical works exist and are any of the things canvassed in the previous chapter, they are only *analogically* perceivable. To say that we can hear Sibelius's Second Symphony is to say that we can hear its performances. To say that we have seen *King Lear* is to say that we have seen at least one of its performances. To this extent at least, our consideration in the previous chapter of the nature of the performable work may lead us to revise our understanding of at least some of the things we naturally say about such works.[9]

3   The Goodman Argument

We have seen that different views about the nature of the performable musical work go together with different views about what counts as a correct or incorrect performance of a work. This connection is most obvious when works are taken to be norm-types, since the work itself consists in a set of prescriptions for correct performance. But norm-types also play a role in the "contextualized type" and action-theoretic accounts considered in the previous chapter. And even the continuant theorist maintains that works conceived as continuants depend upon their occurrences in some way. This suggests that performable works, if there are such things, are inextricably linked to particular conceptions of their performances. Indeed, while from one perspective it is performable works that impose conditions on their performances, the arguments offered to clarify the nature of performable works generally run in the opposite direction. It is because we take certain features of performances, and certain kinds of differences between performances, to bear upon the appreciation of the works performed, that we are drawn to particular views about the nature of the performable works themselves. We have seen this in the kinds of arguments offered for the significance of timbral, instrumental, and contextual features of performances for the appreciation of such works.

Indeed, this is surely the way it should be. Performable works, assuming that they exist, are things that play a particular role in animating certain human practices. Our task, in asking about the nature of performable works, is to clarify both the nature of this role and the kinds of qualities that performable works must have in order to play it. Thus we must start with features of those practices themselves – the kinds of distinctions that we make both in our talk about and in our practical commerce with artistic performances, and the kinds of qualities that we seek out in our engagements with them. This is not to say that everything in our practice will stand up under rational scrutiny. There may be inconsistencies in that practice taken as a whole, and we may be moved to revise some features of that practice as a result of reflection. But rational reflection on the nature of the performable work must begin with practice, and must counsel revisions only in the interests of making better sense of our practice taken overall, given the goals that it is reasonably taken to serve.[10] In line with this general methodological directive, we have assumed a number of things in our discussion thus far. We have assumed, for example, that a work can have incorrect performances. Our discussion of Sibelius's symphonies also suggests that timbral qualities, and the use of particular instruments, bear upon the appreciation of at least some musical works through their performances. And, while our discussion of contextualism looked not at actual practice but at hypothetical cases, these were intended to mobilize intuitions that presumably guide our actual practice by asking us to consider how we would view such cases were they to be actualized.

But there is a famous argument that proceeds by reference not to our actual practice but to more general conditions to which, it is claimed, this practice must conform if we are to have a coherent conception of performable works. Here it is assumed that the demands of theory should regiment our practice rather than vice versa. Nelson Goodman's argument, in *Languages of Art* (1976), would, if accepted, compel us to accept a view of both the performable work and its performances that is strikingly different from the one suggested by our discussion thus far. We must therefore assess whether what may be termed the "Goodman argument" should lead us to revise the methodological assumptions that have guided us, at least implicitly, in our inquiries.[11]

Goodman begins by asking why we can have forgeries of existing works in painting and sculpture whereas we cannot have such forgeries in literature and the performed arts. This cannot be explained in terms of the singular nature of the former art forms. For we can have forgeries of existing works in printmaking and lithography, which are multiple arts. Rather, Goodman maintains, what matters is whether something's status as a work-instance of a given work can be divorced from that thing's *history of production*. The question is whether, given some entity *e*, it is possible to determine whether or not *e* is a work-instance of a work *W* without determining how *e* was produced or generated. A forgery of an artwork *W* is something that presents itself as having a history of making that it actually lacks, where having that history, so Goodman maintains, is a necessary condition for being a work-instance of *W*. We see this in the case of paintings. A forgery of the *Mona Lisa* presents itself as coming from the hand of Leonardo, and only if it does come from the hand of Leonardo can it be a work-instance (and indeed the solitary work-instance) of the work. In the case of painting, sculpture, prints, and lithography, according to Goodman, we cannot divorce status as a work-instance of a work from history of production. Thus the misrepresentation of that history in a forgery is possible.

However, Goodman argues, in literature and the performed arts, we *do* have a means of identifying work-instances of works without recourse to history of production. This is possible because there exist conventions or practices which specify, *without* making reference to history of production, the properties something must have in order to be a work-instance of a work. In order to specify the properties required in instances of a work without reference to their history of production, Goodman maintains, we need something that performs the function of a *notation*. In the case of literature, the notation in question is provided by the linguistic resources used in constructing the exemplar of the work:

> To verify the spelling or to spell correctly is all that is required to identify an instance of the work or to produce a new instance. In effect, the fact that a literary work is in a definite notation, consisting of certain signs or characters that are to be combined by concatenation, provides the means for distinguishing the properties constitutive of the work from all contingent properties – that is, for fixing the required features and the limits of permissible variation in each. (Goodman 1976, 116)

On the basis of this analysis, Goodman proposes that we identify literary works with *texts*, where texts are individuated in terms of the notational features just described. In the case of performable musical works, he gives the musical score the notational role accorded to the literary text. But since, as we have seen, many of the appreciable properties of musical works are given only in performance, he identifies the musical work not with the score itself but with the class of performances that "comply with" – satisfy the requirements set forth in – the score.

As we saw in Chapter 2, there are serious problems with the idea that a musical work can be identified with the class of its actual, or indeed of its possible, performances. But Goodman's insistence that the significance of the score lies in its ability to divorce status as an instance of a work from history of production merits further consideration. For a contextualist like Levinson, at least, does *not* allow status as a work-instance to be so divorced.[12] He requires that the performers of a work-instance stand in the right kind of intentional-historical relation to the prescriptive act of the composer.[13] As we shall now see, Goodman takes the role of the score in divorcing status as a work-instance of a work from history of production very seriously indeed.

The primary function of the musical score, Goodman maintains, is "the authoritative identification of a work from performance to performance." In order to fulfill this function, he claims, a score must do two things. First, it must "define a work" (Goodman 1976, 128), that is, it must sort performances into those that do and those that do not "belong to" the work. In this respect, a score functions like a traditional definition that provides necessary and sufficient conditions for falling under a concept. On the traditional definition of "bachelor," for example, we can tell whether or not someone is a bachelor by determining whether that person is male, adult, and unmarried. Similarly, according to Goodman, given the score for a work *W*, we can tell whether or not a given musical event is a performance of *W*. The second thing that a score must do, however, is much more demanding. The score, Goodman claims, must in turn be "uniquely determined" by each of its instances (130). What this means is that, given a musical event that is a correct performance of a work and given a system of scoring, there must be only one score in that system – that of the work in question – with which it complies. No analogous requirement obtains in the case of ordinary definitions. While the definition of "bachelor" in English allows us to tell if someone is a bachelor, a given bachelor may fall under a number of different English definitions – the definition of "accountant," for example.

If a score is to fulfill its primary function by doing both of these things, Goodman maintains, it must be a "character" in a "symbol system" that satisfies certain logical requirements. It is these requirements that qualify a symbol system to be what Goodman terms a "notation." We need not go into the technical details of these requirements here.[14] But it will be helpful to relate them to the kind of work that they do in ensuring that a score can fulfill its primary function. This will allow us to identify two significant implications of Goodman's account.

Some of the notational requirements for a score are necessary if the score is to fulfill the first part of its primary function by defining a work. If we are to determine whether a performance complies with the score of a work W, we must be able to tell, from the inscription used by the composer to prescribe certain things for correct performances of W, of which *particular* score it is an inscription. Only if we know this will we be able to tell *which* requirements W prescribes for its correct performances, and thus whether a particular performance meets those requirements. Goodman lays down certain conditions that must be met if a score is to define a work in this sense. For example, no inscription can belong to more than one score, and it must be possible at least in principle to determine *which* score an inscription belongs to.

Further notational requirements for a score pertain to the second thing a score of a musical work must do to fulfill its primary function, namely, be uniquely determined by each of the work's instances. What this means is that it must always be possible, at least in principle, to tell which score uniquely matches a given correct performance, and thus of which work it is a performance. If this is to be possible a performance cannot comply with two distinct scores.[15] Also, we must be able, at least in principle, to determine with which score a given performance complies.

These last two requirements, which are necessary if the score for W is to be uniquely determined by each correct performance of W, have some surprising consequences. First, Goodman argues that only some of the elements that we find on a standard musical score meet these requirements for notationality. There is no problem with the standard musical symbols – for example, the use of five-line staff and clef signs, the marks used to represent the pitch and duration of notes, time signatures and key signatures. Problems arise, however, when we consider the use of verbal elements. Take, for example, the use of words such as "*allegro*," "*allegro vivace*," "*allegro non troppo*," etc., to indicate tempo. A correct performance of W might fall under a number of different labels of this sort, since a score might verbally specify the tempo more or less precisely. For example, a performance that complies with a score that specifies "*allegro vivace*" might also be a particularly *vivace* performance of a work whose score specifies "*allegro*." Thus, if we include such verbal indications of tempo in the score, there may be no single right way of matching a score to a given performance, assuming that all we have to go on is the performance itself, without inquiring into its history of production. Thus, if the score is to enable us to divorce status as an instance of a work from history of production, and if the primary function of a score requires that a score for W be

uniquely determined by each correct performance of W, then verbal specifications of tempo cannot be viewed as part of the score. As a consequence,
they cannot play a part in defining the work, which is the first thing a score
has to do. This is precisely what Goodman concludes (1976, 184–185). And
what applies to verbal indications of tempo presumably also applies to verbal
expressions of mood, such as Sibelius's instruction "*lugubre*." In ruling that
verbal instructions on a score fail to meet the requirements for notationality
and therefore cannot play a part in defining a work, Goodman commits himself to the correctness of performances that we might regard as bizarre – for
example, a performance of the Second Symphony in which the standard temporal and expressive features of the work are freely interchanged between
and within the movements, and where, partly as a consequence, "melancholy"
and "sunny" passages exchange their expressive character.

But Goodman not only counts such bizarre examples as correct performances of a work. He also maintains that any performance that in the slightest
way departs from what is notated in the score of a work W is not a performance of W at all, however exemplary it may be in other respects. Again, it is the
requirement that we be able to uniquely identify the score of W, given a correct
performance of W, that leads to this conclusion. Goodman argues as follows:

> The innocent-seeming principle that performances differing by just one note
> are instances of the same work risks the consequence – in view of the transi-
> tivity of identity – that all performances whatever are of the same work. If we
> allow the least deviation, all assurance of work-preservation and score-
> preservation is lost, for by a series of one-note errors of omission, addition,
> and modification, we can go all the way from Beethoven's *Fifth Symphony* to
> *Three Blind Mice*. (1976, 187)[16]

The conclusion we are intended to draw from this argument – that there
cannot be performances of a performable work that depart even in the slightest way from what the work (through the score) prescribes – directly contradicts our assumption thus far that performable works are things that by their
very nature allow of both correct and incorrect performances. It also, thereby,
contradicts the idea that works are, or contain essentially, norm-types, since a
norm-type just is a type that can have both correct and incorrect examples.

4 Answering the Goodman Argument

Why does Goodman insist that, for a score to fulfill what he terms its "primary function," it must not only define a work – enable us to determine
whether or not something is a correct performance of the work – but also

be uniquely retrievable from performances of the work? What motivates this second requirement of unique retrievability? The idea, as noted earlier, is that we can explain why there are no forgeries of performable works by pointing to the role that the score plays in divorcing status as a work-instance of a performable work from history of production. It is the score alone, Goodman maintains, that preserves the performable work from performance to performance, and it can do this only if we deny any measure of indeterminacy in retrieval. Allow such indeterminacy and we get the dire consequences that he describes. But what should puzzle us is why the score should be assigned any role in retrieval at all. It is not as if it is part of our musical practice to construct scores on the basis of performances. Indeed, as we shall see in Chapter 6, it is because choreographic scripts for dance performances are often generated in this way that it is unclear whether dance fits the classical paradigm. Rather, in our practice scores only play the first of the two roles distinguished by Goodman, that of defining a work by enabling us to identify its performances. But they play this role by reference to the circumstances in which a performance takes place. We group performances as performances of a given work by reference to *the score from which the musicians are intending to play*. If, on two occasions of performance, we believe that the musicians are (with reasonable success) attempting to comply with the same set of requirements encoded in scores they take to have the same historical origins in a particular compositional act,[17] then we take the two performances to be of the same musical work, even if one of them is flawed in certain minor respects. This allows us to recognize genuine performances of a work that fail to be work-instances of that work. This doesn't pose a problem since we don't ascribe any role to the retrieval of score from performance in preserving the identity of the work. And it also allows us to assign a work-defining role to *verbal* instructions in the score, since, even if these instructions are imprecise or overlapping in the way described by Goodman, we can still determine which work is being performed on a given occasion by determining which score the musicians are attempting to comply with.

Of course, if this is indeed our practice, it requires that we attend to the circumstances and performative intentions of the performers in determining whether something is indeed a performance of a given work. Thus we have not divorced status as performance of a work, and therefore status as a correct performance of a work, from the conditions under which a performance takes place. We therefore cannot avail ourselves of Goodman's solution to the puzzle about forgeries with which he begins. But the puzzle itself allows of a much simpler answer. For the issue about forgeries is not merely whether we can tell whether something is a work-instance of a work independently of its history of production, but whether its having a particular history of production matters for its role in the appreciation of the work. In the case of paintings it does matter because we cannot determine whether an entity has the properties something must have in order to play the relevant experiential role in appreciation without knowing its history of making. Only if this canvas is from the hand of Leonardo can we have any confidence that it possesses the manifest properties necessary if it is to serve as a work-instance of the *Mona Lisa*. Even the greatest copyist may produce a canvas that differs from the original in subtle ways that bear upon the work's appreciation. In the case of literary works however, as Goodman points out, we assume that no such information about the history of making of a given text is necessary, once we have a canonical text with which to compare other texts. Any text that matches the canonical text in specifiable respects will provide equal access to those textual properties that bear upon the appreciation of the literary work.

It doesn't follow, however, that we can therefore identify literary works with texts. For factors other than the manifest properties of their texts – for example, contextual factors – can bear upon the appreciation of literary works. Philosophers of literature often point to a short story by Jorge Luis Borges about a fictional French writer Pierre Menard, at the turn of the twentieth century, who authors a text that is word-for-word identical to a fragment of Cervantes' *Don Quixote* (Borges 1970). The two texts, Borges' narrator argues, instantiate distinct works in virtue of the different contexts in which the texts were written. But since the two works *share* all their textual properties, it doesn't matter if, in trying to appreciate Menard's work, the text I am reading stands in an intentional-historical relationship to the writing activity of Cervantes or to that of Menard. In either case, the text is fully qualified to play the experiential role in the appreciation of the work. All that is necessary is that I locate the textual properties of what I am reading, whatever its own history of making, in the context of Menard's act of authorship. In fact, since we defined a work-instance of a work in terms of the experiential role that it plays in the *appreciation* of that work, the text, whatever its own history of making, can stand as an instance of both Cervantes' and Menard's distinct literary works so long as we have a prior guarantee that the works have identical texts.

The same line of reasoning can be applied to performable works of music. A performance of a work makes available to us certain audible qualities that bear upon the appreciation of the work performed. Suppose for the sake of argument that these qualities include the timbral properties that would be generated in realizing the prescribed sound sequence on the instruments prescribed by the composer. Since the *sound* of a correct performance of a work W on these instruments might, *ex hypothesi*, be duplicated by a performance of W's prescribed sound sequence on a PTS, exactly the same audible properties bearing upon the appreciation of W will be present in both performances.[18] So, in this respect at least, it doesn't matter, for our ability to appreciate the work performed, which kind of instrumentation has been used in generating the performance to which we listen. But, again, this doesn't show that the musical work W is to be identified with the sonic properties that these performances share, or with the class of performances having just these sonic properties. It may matter for the appreciation of W what instrumentation was intended, and it may also matter in what musico-historical context the prescriptions with which the performance complies were laid down. Appreciation of W, then, may require that we *hear* the audible properties common to the two performances *as* played on the prescribed instruments and *as* composed in a particular musico-historical context. But both performances will serve equally well as sources of the relevant sound qualities for the appreciation of the piece, if it is given that they are identical in their timbral sonic properties. And again, given that we have defined a work-instance in terms of the experiential role it plays in appreciation, both performances will count as work-instances of W, unless there is some other salient difference between them.[19]

This brings out the importance of distinguishing three questions concerning a performable work: (1) what properties does the work prescribe for its correct performances? (2) what properties are required in the work's work-instances, and (3) what properties of the work bear upon its proper appreciation?[20] Consider, first (1). Suppose we favor an instrumentalist construal of musical works. According to the instrumentalist, a composer prescribes the generation of a particular timbral sound sequence *on particular instruments*. If, as just suggested, something qualifies as a performance of a musical work W only if the performers attempt to follow the composer's prescriptions for W, a performance of W must be on the prescribed instruments. A sonically indistinguishable rendering of W's prescribed sound sequence on a PTS will not count as a performance of W. But, turning to (2), the defining condition for a work-instance of a work is epistemic: a work-instance is something that is fully qualified to play a particular experiential role in the appreciation of a work. The performance of W's prescribed sound sequence on a PTS, while not a performance of W, will, *ceteris paribus*, count as a work-instance of W. If we imagine another work W^* whose prescriptions are identical to those for W save that the prescribed instrumental means is a PTS that simulates the timbral qualities of the instruments prescribed in W, then, while W and W^* will share no performances, they will share work-instances. Turning finally to (3), while, as we have just seen, two distinct works can have work-instances in common, the properties that bear on their proper appreciation may differ for either instrumentalist or contextualist reasons.

Instrumentalists and contextualists sometimes fail to distinguish these questions. They assume that, if musical works are partly individuated in terms of the context in which they are created, or in terms of the instruments prescribed for their performance, and if two works *differ* in their contexts of creation or in their prescribed instrumentation, then they must also differ in their work-instances. Levinson (1980), for example, takes it to be a consequence of his instrumentalist and contextualist views on the nature of the musical work that instances of a musical work must be performed on the prescribed instruments and must also be performed by musicians who stand in the right kind of intentional-historical relation to the creative activity of the composer. We have seen that, while this is the case for performances, there is no general reason why it should also be so for work-instances.[21]

That a performance of one performable work can count as a work-instance of another such work is not as surprising as it may seem. It is possible because the notions of performance and work-instance do different kinds of jobs. The notion of performance helps us keep track of which playings are playings *of* a given work in a way that doesn't invest all authority in the score but accords a role to history of production. It allows us to evade the radically revisionary implications of accepting the Goodman argument. The notion of work-instance, on the other hand, is defined in terms of a particular role that something can play in the appreciation of an artwork. A work-instance of a work, in whatever artistic medium, is something that makes available to a receiver all of the manifest qualities of a work's artistic vehicle that bear necessarily upon the appreciation of the work.[22] It is possible for a performable work to have work-instances that are not performances because an event can play the relevant role in appreciation without standing in the relevant intentional-historical relation to the composition of the work.

Once we grasp the importance of this distinction, we might be attracted by the idea that it can obtain, at least in principle, in any art form.[23] A perfect forgery might indeed be a work-instance of a painting, contrary to Goodman's claims, without standing in the right intentional-historical relation to the painter's activity. But it is the intentional-historical relation in which the painter stands to the original that determines, at least for the contextualist, the kinds of considerations that need to be brought to bear in properly appreciating the artwork on the basis of the manifest properties that, *ex hypothesi*, the original and the perfect forgery share. But forgery matters, in the case of paintings, for the reasons Goodman cites. We are unable, in practice, to know whether a given entity *is* a work-instance of a work without referring to its history of making, since there is no other way of establishing that the entity possesses those properties required in order to fully qualify to play the experiential role in the appreciation of the work. We must not forget that the perfect forgery, if it is *guaranteed* to be perceptually identical to the original, is simply a device used to make a philosophical point about what is possible *in principle*.

Notes

1. *Jean Sibelius: The Symphonies.* Originally recorded in 1963, 1964, and 1968 and released on CD by Decca Records 1991. Released in the USA on London Records 430 778-2.

2. Or, indeed, by the composer himself. Andrew Kania has pointed out (private communication) that Sibelius made substantial revisions to his Violin Concerto after the first performance, although it is not clear whether he was responding to what he heard in the performance or to the suggestions of critics.

3. See, for example, S. Davies 1994; Matravers 1998, 99–187; Levinson 2005.

4. See, for example, Dodd 2007, ch. 2.

5. An amended form of this question might also be posed to the continuant theorist. Continuants, we are told, are higher level entities that depend upon but are not reducible to their embodiments. But, given that performances of works are among their embodiments, why should we think that the timbral and expressive properties that we encounter in a performance of the Second Symphony can also be possessed by the higher order entities that are continuants?

6. The restriction to "shareable" properties is to exclude properties that types by their very nature cannot possess, but that all tokens of certain types must possess in virtue of being particular things, for example, having a particular spatial location at any particular time.

7. This account will need to be more nuanced if we want to allow for performable works to manifest different and sometimes mutually incompatible properties in their correct performances. For the interpretive freedom of the performers – upon which composers depend for the realization of the timbral and expressive qualities of their works – may allow for different expressive qualities to be realized in performances that respect the prescriptions of a given work. In such cases, while we might appeal to other constraints in order to rule between such interpretations, we might also take the work to have a measure of expressive indeterminacy – or, to put a positive slant on this, expressive richness. Then, in describing the properties of the work analogically related to such expressive properties of its performances, we might talk of what the work *allows*, rather than of what it *requires*, in its correct performances.

8. See, for example, Quine 1969, 39–41.

9. For a fuller discussion of the significance of this point, see D. Davies 2009a.

10. For a general defense of this principle, see D. Davies 2004, ch.1; 2009b.

11. For a detailed critical examination of the Goodman argument, see S. Davies 2001, 154–158.

12. Will the instrumentalist also claim that status as a work-instance cannot be divorced from history of production? If the specification of instrumental

means is included in the score, can a performance's compliance with the score be determined independently its history of production? Goodman's reluctance to include verbal elements in the score (see below) suggests that he must reject the instrumentalist's claim that instrumental means are partly constitutive of the musical work. We don't need to resolve these matters here, however.

13. Here and in my earlier discussion in Chapter 2, I follow the consensus in the literature in taking the conditions for something to be a work-instance (in the technical sense) of a performable work to be identical to the conditions for correct performance established by the composer of that work, or, in Levinson's case, the latter conditions plus the requirement that the performers stand in the right kind of intentional-historical relation to the composer's act of establishing those conditions. But, given that we have defined the notion of work-instance in terms of fully qualifying to play the "experiential role" in the appreciation of a work, this consensus might be challenged. Suppose, for example, that we agree with the instrumentalist that it is part of a work's identity, qua norm-kind, that a correct performance must execute a given sound-sequence on specific instruments *I*. Might it not be enough, for something to fully qualify to play the experiential role in the appreciation of the work, and thus to be a work-instance, that it *sound the same* as a performance on *I* and be heard by the receiver *as if* it were a performance on *I*? In Chapter 2 note 13, we rejected such a strategy as a way of saving timbral sonicism. But the question here is whether adopting an *instrumentalist* conception of the identity of the musical work requires that one adopt an instrumentalist conception of work-instance. Similar remarks apply to Levinson's contextualist conception of work-instance. For further development of this theme, see my remarks at the end of section 4.

14. Goodman spells out these requirements in chapter 4 of his 1976. For critical discussion, see again S. Davies 2001, 135–150.

15. Goodman allows for a measure of redundancy, however. We might have two differently "spelled" scores that have exactly the same function in the symbol system. This is permissible because we can preserve identity of a work from performance to performance even if we don't preserve identity of score. A musical work, then, is to be identified with a class of performances that complies not with a score but with a class of semantically equivalent scores. This complication can be ignored, however, for our purposes.

16. Goodman moves freely here from talk of "instances" to talk of "performances," whereas we have restricted the term "work-instance" so that only *correct* performances can qualify. But in fact, as is clear from the passage, Goodman wants to deny that a work can have performances that are not work-instances — that is, he wants to deny that a work can have any incorrect performances.

The kind of reasoning that leads Goodman to the conclusion in the quoted passage can be spelled out as follows. Suppose we were to hold firm to the idea that the score of a work must be uniquely determined by each of its correct performances, but relaxed the "definitional" part of the primary function of the score to allow that performances departing from the notational requirements of the score may count as genuine, albeit incorrect, performances of the work. Consider a work W of which we have two performances: $P1$, which complies completely with the score for W, and $P2$, which departs from that score in a single note. Given a performance of $P2$, the score that is uniquely determined by that performance will be one that differs in respect of this single note from the score for W. Since works themselves are defined relative to what is prescribed for correct performance, and since the score derived from $P2$ differs from the score for W in what it prescribes, the score derived from $P2$ must be the score for a different work – term this W^*. Thus, $P2$ is not only an incorrect performance of W but also a correct performance of W^*. Now imagine $P3$, another performance of W^* which is flawed in departing from the score for W^* in respect of a single note other than the one in respect of which $P2$ differs from $P1$. The same reasoning that led us to conclude that $P2$ must be a correct performance of W^* as well as an incorrect performance of W will lead us to conclude that $P3$ must be a correct performance of another work W^{**} whose score differs from that of W^* in respect of a single note and from that of W in respect of two notes. W^{**} in turn will have an incorrect performance $P4$, and so on. Obviously we can extend this story to further performances and further works. Of all such cases something analogous to the following reasoning obtains: Since $P1$ is a performance of the same work as $P2$ (they are both performances of W), and $P2$ is a performance of the same work as $P3$ (they are both performances of W^*), and $P3$ is a performance of the same work as $P4$ (they are both performances of W^{**}), it follows that $P1$ is a performance of the same work as $P4$.

17.   The wording here reflects the intuition that what matters, in ascribing performances to works performed, is not the actual historical origins of the score from which the performers are playing but their beliefs about those origins insofar as this guides their interpretation of the score. Suppose we have two works from different composers, A and B, with identical scores. Suppose a group of performers intends to perform A's work, believes that the score in front of them is of that work, and is guided in its performance by knowledge of conventions for interpreting scores in the performing community to whom A's work was originally addressed. Suppose, however, that in fact the performers are playing from a score of B's work. Surely what we have is a performance of A's work – if someone switched the scores as a practical joke prior to the performance, this wouldn't change the identity of the work performed. What matters is the performers' intention to play a particular work whose prescriptions are contained in the score from which they are playing. So, if the only score available to them is one that they believe or know to be of B's work, they can still perform A's work as long as the scores of the two works explicitly prescribe the same things for correct performance.

18.   Note that we have not ruled here on whether the second of these performances is a performance *of the work*: timbral sonicists may say that it is and instrumentalists may say that it isn't.

19. An instrumentalist like Levinson, however, will insist that there *is* such a salient difference which excludes such performances from being work-instances. For, as noted in Chapter 2, Levinson argues that the expressive qualities that we ascribe to a piece of music may depend in part upon the physical nature of the activities we take to be involved in producing the sounds we hear. If so, such expressive qualities might not be graspable by those who attend a performance of a work, composed for string quartet, which is given a sonically indistinguishable rendering on a PTS. If we assume these expressive properties are properties of the work bearing on its proper appreciation, then the work will not be properly appreciable through such a performance. The latter, then, will not be a work-instance of the work. Its live instances must be restricted to performances on the prescribed instruments. See the discussion of Levinson's views on "authenticity" in Chapter 4.

20. For more on the significance of this distinction, see D. Davies 2009b.

21. No *general* reason, but see n, 19 above.

22. This would require a more nuanced formulation in the case of performable works, for the reasons noted in n. 7 above. I ignore this complication here.

23. For a defense of this thesis, see D. Davies 2010.

4
Authenticity in Musical Performance

1   Introduction

I suggested in the previous chapter that we have good reason to reject the Goodman argument and the premises on which it rests. But we must also ask what is required, more generally, for something to be a correct performance of a musical work over and above compliance with the notational elements in a score. We have already rehabilitated, as elements required in a correct performance, those temporal and expressive qualities that depend upon verbal prescriptions in the score. But what we count as a correct performance of a performable work does not depend solely upon what is *explicit* in the composer's prescriptions for that work, as represented by the score in standard cases. We have seen that the performed arts differ from other multiple art forms in the role accorded to *interpretation* in generating performances. Interpretation, here, is a matter of going beyond what the composer, playwright, or choreographer may have prescribed, and thereby realizing various artistic and aesthetic possibilities within the performative "envelope" furnished by these prescriptions. But performance of a performable work also requires interpretation in another sense. In the case of works within a written tradition, performers must interpret the inscriptions in which the artist recorded his or her prescriptions for the work. Before we can interpret within the performative "envelope" furnished by these prescriptions, we must determine what the prescriptions actually prescribe.[1]

Nicholas Wolterstorff raises these issues in the context of asking what it is to perform a musical work. It is, he maintains, not sufficient for correct performance that the performers succeed in their attempts to follow the directions explicit in the score. For composers seldom specify all the things that matter

Philosophy of the Performing Arts, First Edition. David Davies.
© 2011 David Davies. Published 2011 by Blackwell Publishing Ltd.

concerning correctness (Wolterstorff 1975, 332).[2] Often they simply assume that performers will translate what is specified in a score into a sound sequence having certain unspecified features because those features are required by the style or tradition that the composer shares with those expected to perform the work. This applies to such things as phrasing, dynamics, and the manner in which performers embellish what is prescribed.[3] In contrast to Goodman, Wolterstorff maintains that "if the performer limits himself to following the specifications of the score, not even attempting in other respects to produce a correct example of the work, it is at the very least doubtful that he has performed the work" (Wolterstorff 1975, 332). He holds that two things are necessary for something to count as the performance of a performable work. First, there must be an intention on the part of the performer(s) to produce a sound sequence that complies with both the score and the implicit performative expectations of the composer. Second, the performer(s) must be successful enough in realizing that intention to produce a recognizable, even if flawed, example of the work.

But why should performers of a work be guided by the performative expectations of the composer, or even, for that matter, by every detail that is made explicit in the score? To what extent does the value of a performance of a musical work depend upon the performance's compliance with musical understandings in place at the time of the work's composition? More generally, to what extent are the kinds of considerations educed thus far concerning what counts as a "correct" performance of a work normative for the actual practice of performers? Why should producing such a performance be an appropriate goal? Might not a performance that departs from those historically situated prescriptions and expectations better serve our appreciative interest in a performable work? If we reply that we must respect both the composer's explicit prescriptions and the period understanding of those prescriptions in order to present an *authentic* performance of the work, we enter one of the most contested areas in performance theory. In this chapter, we shall explore these issues as they relate to the performance of classical musical works. In the next two chapters, we shall consider how far the same considerations apply to artistic performances in other musical genres or in other performing arts. We shall also ask, relatedly, how far the classical paradigm itself – which provides the context in which questions about "historical authenticity" have traditionally arisen – can be extended to such performances.

2   Authenticity in the Arts

The notion of "historical authenticity" arises in the arts in respect of things that purport to be work-instances. In the visual arts, the authenticity of a canvas is a matter of its individual provenance. An authentic painting by

Leonardo is one from the hand of that artist (at least in its most artistically significant features). In the multiple arts, authenticity is sometimes understood in an analogous fashion. An authentic Dürer woodcut, for example, or an authentic print of Stieglitz's *The Steerage*, also owes its authenticity to its provenance, albeit in a more mediated way. Authenticity here is a matter of standing in the right kind of causal relation to a production artifact that was itself generated by the artist. In the performing arts, however, the authenticity of a performance, as this is usually understood, is not a matter of its standing in a *causal* relation to the activity of the artist. Rather, the relationship is a *normative* one, often characterized in terms of the performance's being "true to" the work. This highlights a necessary condition for the question of the historical authenticity of a performance to even arise: the performance must be *of* something to which it may be judged to be more or less true. This "something" is normally a performable work, although it might be an improvisational tradition if what is at issue is the historical authenticity of a jazz performance.

To ask about a performance's *historical* authenticity relative to a work, however, also assumes a historical context – the context of composition of the work – by reference to which we can define what it is for a performance to be true to that work. The idea of being true to a performable work is indeed usually linked in this way to historically authentic performance. But, more generally construed, a performance is true to a work just in case it meets the requirements for being a correct rendering of that work. What these requirements are, as we have seen, depends upon what we take the work itself to be. For the contextualist, for whom the work itself is partly *constituted* by its history of making, to be true to the work one must perform it in a way that takes proper account of that history. The contextualist therefore naturally associates the "truth to a work" of a performance with its historical authenticity in some sense. For the pure sonicist, on the other hand, truth to a musical work is simply a matter of compliance with the sequence of pitches, durations, etc., prescribed by the composer. Historical authenticity is unlikely to be a concern.

The nature and desirability of historical authenticity in musical performance is one of the most hotly contested philosophical issues in recent years concerning the performing arts.[4] The passionate nature of the debates surely owes much to the fact that the question is essentially a *practical* one: given a conception of what authentic performance would involve, should performers pursue authenticity in their practice? As such, it has implications for the kinds of performances one might wish or expect to see. Indeed, it is practical developments in the performing arts that have generated most of the recent philosophical interest in this topic. Prompted by research by historical musicologists on performance practices in early music, the "historical performance" movement has sought to present musical works in ways that are authentic given their provenance. As we shall see, there are different views as to what authenticity involves and the more general goals it is intended to serve. Among those who have questioned the coherence or the desirability of pursuing authenticity in these various senses, Peter Kivy has given the most extended critical treatment of these issues, and we shall consider a number of his arguments below. How we assess these arguments will depend, unsurprisingly, upon what we take to be the more general goals of performance in the performing arts.

While authenticity in musical performance is usually a matter of being true to the work, authenticity can also be construed in terms of the performer's performing the work in a way that is *true to herself*.[5] The kinds of constraints placed upon performers by the demand that they be true to the work might be thought to militate against "personal" authenticity in performance, and thereby to threaten a central value in our appreciation of performances of performable works. In considering this claim later in the chapter, I shall prefigure questions concerning the artistic value of performances considered in themselves, to which I shall return in Chapter 7.

3   Three Notions of Historically Authentic Performance

There are at least three ways in which we might understand the idea of a performance being historically true to a performable work.[6] First, we might think of the work as being tied in some essential way to its *composer*. A true performance of a work will then be one that presents it in the way that the composer intended it to be performed. Second, we might think of the work as tied in some essential way to a particular kind of historically situated *sound sequence*, whether construed in a pure or a timbral fashion. A true performance will then be one that reproduces the sound sequence of a performance of some kind. Finally, we might think of the work as tied in some essential way to the *performance practices* in place at the time the work was composed. A true performance will then be one that complies with those practices. This might involve not only respect for period ways of understanding the composer's explicit prescriptions, as just discussed, but also the use of period instruments or locations, or even replication of the dress or decorum of a period performance. These three ways of conceiving the historical authenticity of a performance are closely connected. A natural way to reproduce the sound of a period performance, for example, is to perform the work on period instruments in a location having the same acoustic properties as the performance spaces in which it would originally have been performed. Or, it might be said, in judging which period performances we should try to sonically replicate, we should appeal to the composer's intentions as to how and where her composition should be played.

Authenticity defined in terms of the composer's intentions

According to the first conception of authenticity, an authentic performance is one which performs a piece in the way in which its composer intended that it be performed. This prima facie plausible conception of authenticity is open to a number of serious objections, however. In the first place, if performers are to *act* on the exhortation to perform pieces authentically, we must anchor talk of the composer's performative intentions in accessible indicators of those intentions. The most obvious resource here is the score, where we have a scored work. We might also take the absence of any indication that the composer resisted the general performance practices of her time as evidence that she intended her score to be interpreted in light of those practices, or, at least, was happy for it to be so interpreted. And we might have other sources of evidence, in journals, letters, and other works by the composer, as to his or her intentions for the performance of a given work. The difficulty, however, set out by Randall Dipert (1980) in a much cited paper,[7] is that a composer has different kinds of intentions as to how a given work should be performed, and it may be impossible to realize all of those intentions at the same time in a modern "historically authentic" performance of the piece.

Dipert distinguishes three different levels of composer intentions regarding the realization of the score in performance. First, *low level* intentions relate to the manner in which the prescribed sound sequence should be produced – which instruments, played in which manner. Second, *medium level* intentions concern the qualities of the *sounds* to be produced, such as "temperament, timbre, attack, pitch, and vibrato." And third, *high level* intentions relate to the effects that the performance is to produce in the listener. The problem is that, when we attempt to perform the work for a modern audience in a manner that is authentic in relation to the composer's intentions, we may not be able to jointly satisfy the low level and the high level intentions. For the effect on a modern audience of the sounds produced by playing certain instruments in a certain manner may be very different from the effect of such sounds on a period audience. Dipert cites, as an example, the use of the clarinet by Gluck to startle an audience by its unfamiliar timbre. For a modern audience, fulfilling the lower level intention – that a clarinet be used – will not fulfill the higher level one – that the audience be startled – because we are familiar with the clarinet sound. Dipert maintains that a composer's high level intentions should trump his or her low level intentions, since the latter reflect only the means by which the composer intends to realize the former. But this means that historical authenticity understood in terms of satisfying the composer's intentions may support exactly the kind of performance to which proponents of historical performance are opposed – performance on modern instruments, unknown to the composer, that are still unfamiliar enough to us to provoke the intended response. Kivy develops Dipert's line of reasoning. He asks whether, on the "intentions" construal of authenticity, it is authentic to perform a piece on modern instruments capable of replicating the timbral or other properties of the instruments specified by the composer. Why shouldn't we say that, given the option of using such instruments to realize his middle or high level intentions, the composer would be happy for the piece to be played on the modern instruments? Another way in which this kind of point is sometimes put is that performers who wish to be true to the work should strive to be true to its *spirit* rather than to its letter (see, for example, Leppard 1988).

Aron Edidin offers an interesting response to this line of argument (1991, 413–415). He suggests that artists are interested not merely in producing a particular effect in their audience, but also in producing that effect by particular means – for example, startling the audience by the use of the clarinet, in the Gluck case. Indeed, this is itself a high level intention. But this high level intention would not be satisfied if the sought-after effect were produced by other means. This undermines the idea that a performance on modern instruments could be authentic in the sense of satisfying all of the composer's high level intentions. But it also raises the concern that an authentic performance conceived in these terms may in many cases not be possible. For the Gluck example supposedly demonstrates that the high level intention to produce a particular effect by specified means may not be satisfiable in a modern audience. This implication of the Gluck example might be questioned, however, if our ears can to some extent be trained to hear things in the way they were heard by contemporaries of the composer.[8]

There is a further objection to the idea that we should pursue authenticity defined in terms of satisfying the composer's intentions. Why, it might be asked, would a performance that complies with those intentions be desirable? In raising this worry, Kivy appeals to the general principle that we must evaluate any proposal as to how a work should be performed in terms of the "aesthetic payoff" of so performing it, that is, the aesthetically satisfying qualities that would be realized thereby (Kivy 1995, 152).[9] Why should we think that the aesthetic payoff of performing a work in accordance with the composer's intentions is likely to be higher than the aesthetic payoff of performing it in ways that depart from those intentions, even by ignoring the minimal requirement that the performers comply with the score?

Kivy suggests that even the greatest composers may not always know best how their pieces should be performed for maximal aesthetic payoff. This is particularly the case if we assume that performers learn over time the possibilities offered by a given piece and discover aesthetically rewarding ways of playing it that the composer could not have grasped.

Authenticity defined in terms of the sound of the work

One way of avoiding at least some of these difficulties is to define historical authenticity not in terms of the composer's more general intentions for performance, but in terms of the particular kind of sound sequence intended by the composer and prescribed through the score. This avoids worries about high level intentions that might be satisfied by other sound sequences. It also grants that low level intentions pertain only to the means whereby a particular sound sequence is to be realized. Stephen Davies (1987, 1988) has defended such a view.[10] An authentic performance of a performable musical work, he maintains, is one that aims to produce an *acoustic event* – a sound sequence – that stands in a particular relation to the provenance of the work performed. More specifically, the aim is to produce "the musical sound of a performance that might have been heard by the composer's contemporaries" (S. Davies 1987, 41). In order to determine what that sound is, we must be guided by what we take to be the composer's determinative intentions for the work as recorded in the score. But we must also take into account interpretive and performing conventions which would be known to the composer and the intended performers. In determining which notes should be played to correspond to the notes explicitly specified in the score for a work of early music, for example, we must take account of the fact that the pitches corresponding to those specified notes were lower. As a result, we face problems in producing the required sound if we play the piece at the modern pitch level – which will strain the voice and the wind sections – or tune down modern instruments – which will change the sound in various ways. We must therefore use period instruments or replicas of period instruments if we want to produce a sound sequence that is historically authentic.

Davies stresses that the aim is not to reproduce the musical sounds *actually heard* by the composer's contemporaries. Actual period performances might have been flawed owing to failings in the particular instruments or performers available. Rather, the aim is to produce an *ideal* performance relative to the piece created by the composer and the context in which that piece was intended to be performed. Since the composer's determinative intentions underdetermine the sound of an ideal performance, there will be a range of authentic performances of a work. Davies also argues that what matters is what the composer actually specified, not what the composer might have specified had other resources been available. The concern, in other words, is with the composer's realized intentions as represented by particular sound sequences. It is not with intentions more abstractly conceived that might be realized in different ways in different musico-historical contexts. He summarizes his view as follows:

> A performance will be more rather than less authentic if it successfully (re) creates the sound of a performance of the work in question as it could be given by good musicians playing good instruments under good conditions (of rehearsal time, etc.), where "good" is relativized to the best of what was known by the composer to be available at the time, whether or not those resources were available for the composer's use. (S. Davies 1987, 45)

Critics, however, have argued that there is an ambiguity in talk of "recreating the sound" of an ideal performance of the work. They have further maintained that, on either of two interpretations that we might give to such talk, it fails to provide a goal for performances of musical works that is both feasible and desirable. James Young (1988) expresses this in terms of a distinction between what is heard *objectively* and what is heard *subjectively*. The former is a matter of the acoustic information presented to the ear, the perturbations of air described in physical terms. The latter, on the other hand, is a matter of how we perceptually *experience* what is objectively there to be heard, what the latter is "heard as." It might be possible to recreate the sound of an ideal performance in the objective sense, given sufficient musicological research. But, Young maintains, it is unclear why this would be a desirable goal for performance. On the other hand, to recreate the sound of an ideal performance in the subjective sense is neither possible nor desirable. It isn't possible because how a listener hears (subjectively) an objectively characterized acoustic signal depends upon active interpretation of that signal by the brain, where this is a function of, inter alia, the listener's musical history. But our musical histories, which include hearing much music written after the composition of early musical works, differ radically from those of period listeners. So, as a consequence, our subjective hearings of what is, objectively, the same acoustic signal will also differ from how period listeners heard it. For example, we may differ in our judgments as to whether an interval is consonant or dissonant.[11] Or, to recall our earlier discussion, we may not share the period listener's experience of the sound of the clarinet in Gluck's piece as startling. Nor, Young claims, would it be desirable to hear musical works in the ways that period listeners would have heard them, since much great music is not understood by contemporaries of the composer.

Kivy draws a similar distinction between what he terms "sonic authenticity" and "sensible authenticity" (1995, 48–53). He argues that the rationale for the former must be that it is instrumental in bringing about the latter, and that the latter is neither a possible nor a desirable goal for musical performance. The quest for sensible authenticity – reproducing the subjective experience of a contemporary listener – involves what Kivy terms "the paradox of historical musicology" (1995, 71). Our ability to hear a performance of a musical work "historically" is a product of historical musicology. But it necessarily distinguishes our experience in listening to a sonically authentic performance of a period piece from the experience of period listeners, who heard the work ahistorically. He further argues, like Young, that eliciting what he terms "historicist listening," which replicates the experience of the period listener, is not a desirable goal of artistic performance, since period listeners were unable to properly appreciate the aesthetic value of the work performed. This is not to oppose "historical listening," listening that is informed by a knowledge of the history of the performed work. Kivy contrasts these two kinds of listening in respect of the introductory measures of Beethoven's Symphony No. 1 (1995, 205). In opening the piece on an active chord of the "wrong" key, Beethoven clearly intended to surprise or startle the audience. But the opening measures cannot have this effect on a modern listener. Thus historicist listening is not possible, and a fortiori not a feasible aim of sonically authentic performance. But, Kivy maintains, this is in no way to denigrate historical listening informed by the knowledge that the contemporary audience *was* surprised and shocked by the opening:

> that Beethoven intended to produce that effect, that he produced it by departing from the usual manner of Haydn and Mozart of strongly declaiming the tonic in the opening measures of slow introductions, that the departure consisted in starting on an active chord of the "wrong" key, and so on … This knowledge … can facilitate appreciation of *what* Beethoven was trying to do and *how* he was trying to do it. And *that* appreciation … is a kind of *aesthetic* appreciation of the work that is by no means contemptible. (Kivy 1995, 206)

None of this, however, Kivy stresses, involves historicist listening, and thus none of it is furthered by sonically authentic performances, assuming that the aim of the latter is to facilitate historicist listening.

The force of such objections to Davies's account of authenticity depends upon whether Young and Kivy are correct in saying that our modern ears cannot give us an experiential appreciation of period music as it was intended to be heard even if the performances to which we listen are sonically authentic. It also depends upon whether, to the extent that there are necessarily experiential differences between our listening and the listening of a period audience, this undermines the case for authentic performance understood in the way that Davies proposes. In his later defenses of his view, Davies answers both of these points negatively. First, he argues that Young and Kivy's objection "seriously underestimates our ability to control the way we listen to different kinds of music." While our ability to train ourselves to hear period music authentically in light of our knowledge of period ideals and practices will be tested in proportion to the discrepancies between the music of the period and the music of our own time, "the goal of hearing 'foreign' music with understanding and appreciation is not inherently unachievable" (S. Davies 2001, 235). Second, in response to Kivy's paradox of historical musicology, Davies grants that the phenomenology of the modern listener and that of the period listener will almost certainly differ, but maintains that the case for authentic performance is not compromised by such a concession. For authentic performance can achieve its goal – making the period piece accessible to the modern listener for her appreciation – even if such phenomenological differences exist.

Authenticity defined in terms of performance practice

Davies's case rests upon a conception of the goal of historically authentic performance that contrasts markedly with Kivy's claim, cited earlier, that we should assess a performance of a performable work in terms of its "aesthetic payoff," where this is measured in terms of qualities of the listener's experience. But Kivy's further claim, that historical listening bears upon the appreciation of a musical work by helping us to understand what a composer has attempted and achieved, suggests a new way of presenting the case for authentic performance – a way compatible with the general thrust of Davies's argument. Why shouldn't we think of sonically authentic performances as a source of *understanding* of the musical works performed, understanding that can then enter into our historically informed listening to other performances of the piece, or, indeed, to that very performance? This would yield an "aesthetic payoff" by contributing to musical appreciation in the kinds of ways that Kivy identifies in his account of historical listening. This kind of defense of authentic performance is best set out in terms of our third notion of authenticity. This defines authenticity not purely in terms of the sound of a performance, but in terms of the performance means and performance practices that the composer expected to be operative in performances of the work. As we shall see, there are a number of ways in which our understanding of a work may be augmented by listening to performances that are authentic in this sense.

If authentic performance is to be justified by its (indirect) contribution to the understanding and appreciation of a musical work, this presupposes a conception of what the musical work is, an issue that we examined in Chapter 2. Interestingly, Kivy defends his assumption that any case for historically authentic performance must rest upon its "aesthetic" payoff by suggesting that the alternative would require an analysis of the musical work which took composer's intentions to be partly constitutive of the work (1995, 150–151). While Kivy declines to provide an analysis of the nature of the musical work, our present reflections suggest that some such analysis will be necessary if we are to determine what *counts* as an "aesthetic payoff." Indeed, as we shall see, it is in terms of the instrumentalist and contextualist conceptions of the musical work considered in Chapter 2 that the most compelling defenses of authentic performance can be given.

Edidin draws a useful distinction between two kinds of evaluations that we can make of a particular performance of a performable work (1991, 396). On the one hand, we can treat the performance as to some extent an autonomous event, to be evaluated in terms of its own musical qualities and the skills of the performer, even if we acknowledge that these qualities are realized and these skills exercised within the performative envelope of a particular performable work. On the other hand, we can assess the performance *as* a performance of a particular performable work. Here we may compare it to other performances of the work and relate at least some of the qualities found in the performance to the work itself in the way discussed in the first section of Chapter 3. The claim that performances, whether historically authentic or not, should be held accountable to their "aesthetic payoff" is most obviously read as a claim about how we should assess them as autonomous events. What we must now explore is how performances that are authentic in the third sense might be held to be valuable *as performances of a work* in virtue of what they contribute to our understanding of that work.

In Chapter 1, we saw that our appreciative interest in an artwork is always interrogative. We seek not merely to engage with a sensible manifold but also to understand why the manifold is ordered in the way that it is. We thereby refer the manifold to the generative activity of the creator of the work. This applies no less to performable works than to their performances. As we have seen, a performable work prescribes certain things for its correct performances. But, we may ask, why does the work prescribe the particular things that it does? If we are contextualists, we will think that at least some of these prescribed features are to be explained in terms of the historically situated judgments of the composer. Indeed, Kivy himself offers such an explanation in relating Beethoven's strategy in the opening measures of his Symphony No. 1 to what had been done by Haydn and Mozart. But, while the explanation of prescribed features of a performable work may cite the musicohistorical context in which a composer was working, it may also appeal to aspects of period performance practice. Edidin speaks here of composers "writing idiomatically for their performers" (1991, 405), composing in light of how the anticipated performers, in conforming to period conventions of performative practice, would execute various passages in the score. In such cases, he argues, we can expect that composers "respond consciously or unconsciously to their awareness of prevailing practice in various ways." Only where prevailing period practice is employed in the performance of the piece can we determine certain of its intended aesthetic values – values not only intended by the composer but also realized when the piece is played as he expected. This extends to the use of period instruments, where, again, we can think of composers as "writing idiomatically for those instruments" (Edidin 1991, 407), taking account of the strengths and limitations of the means through which they expect their works to be realized. More generally, we may expect composers to work creatively within the constraints that their musico-historical contexts present, thereby "making virtues of necessity" (398). The contextualist, therefore, can expect that a proper interrogative understanding of a given musical work will be advanced through performances that are authentic in their employment of period instruments and their respect for period performance practice.

This may also apply to the locations in which composers expect their works to be performed. Both Kivy and Stephen Davies (1987, 41) cite works of the Venetian composer Giovanni Gabrieli that were composed for performance in San Marco, which has very distinctive acoustics. Kivy comments that such works "must lose some palpable musical qualities, expressive ones to a large degree, when deprived of this very special setting" (1995, 97). To fully grasp the expressive properties of such works, then, it seems that we must hear them performed in the architectural environment for which they were composed, or in an environment that simulates it – the latter is presumably impossible in practice in the case of San Marco. We need to take account, in appreciating such works, of how the composer exploited the situational possibilities, working creatively within external constraints.

Levinson, whose contextualism incorporates the instrumentalist's requirement that prescribed instruments be used in correct performances of a work, argues that, if we are to grasp those qualities of a work that bear upon its appreciation, it is not enough that an authentic performance *sound* (objectively) the way that an (ideal) performance would sound if played on period instruments according to period performance practice. In Davies's original defense of historically authentic performance, as we saw, the primary motivation for using period instruments was that only their use allows faithful reproduction of the relevant sound qualities. Levinson, however, insists that actual period instruments must be used if we are to realize certain representational and expressive properties of the work (see Levinson 1990a). He reiterates his more general instrumentalist claim, familiar from Chapter 2, that "part of the expressive character of a piece of music *as heard* derives from our sense of how it is *being made* in performance" (Levinson

1990a, 395). He further relates this to the idea that "expressive content in music ... is centrally predicated on the construability of musical gestures as akin to, or as relatable to, human behavorial expressions of emotion" (398).[12] He offers a number of examples of this phenomenon. A rapid upward glissando in keyboard music often conveys a sense of momentary abandon, and this is grounded in our awareness of the kind of physical interaction with the keyboard required to produce such a sound. And it is in virtue of the sorts of movements that a cellist will make in rendering certain passages that we hear those passages as having a caressing quality. Where period instruments are used in performance, our awareness of the ways in which these instruments differ from their modern counterparts in physical construction and mode of operation and, as a result, differ in their *sonic capacity*, may affect their gestural potential, and thus their expressive meaning, even if, in some cases, they produce identical sounds to the modern equivalents.

If Young and Kivy are right about the gap between sonic and sensible authenticity, then some of the expressive properties to which Levinson alludes may not be directly available to us. But authentic performance may still increase our understanding of the expressive qualities those works must have had for a contemporary audience, if, as Davies suggests, such understanding does not require that we simulate period experience in all respects. In the same way, *pace* Kivy, our failure to experience surprise or shock in hearing the opening measures of Beethoven's Symphony No. 1 does not negate the importance of hearing those measures played as Beethoven prescribed, for we can thereby better understand how those measures would have struck his contemporaries. More generally, it seems that, if we are swayed by arguments for contextualist or instrumentalist conceptions of the musical work, we can accord a role to authentic performance, understood in terms of conformity to period performance practice, in the appreciative understanding of musical works.

This is not to argue that *only* performances of musical works that are authentic in this sense are of value, or that a performer is under an obligation to perform works in this way. But it is to suggest that, the further our conception of musical works departs from pure sonicism, the more value historically authentic performances can have for our appreciative understanding of performable works as the particular works that they are. But this raises a consideration to which we alluded earlier. Will there not be a tension between the demands placed on a performer by the task of performing a work authentically in the above sense and the performer's desire for personal authenticity in her playing? Kivy raises this concern (1995, 271–286). He argues that the more we insist upon the historical authenticity of performance, the more we restrict the personal authenticity of the performer. Indeed, he claims, a primary motivation for the historical performance movement is a desire to eliminate the gap between the "text," representing what the composer prescribes, and the performance of the prescribed work (Kivy 1995, 276). As we saw earlier, one thing that distinguishes the performed arts from other multiple arts is the role of interpretation in the generation of work-instances. This helps us to understand Kivy's observation that what is really at issue in debates over the desirability of historically authentic performance is "whether you want the art music of the Western historical tradition to remain a *performing* art or to cease to be one" (271). What is also at issue, if Kivy is right, is whether, as he wishes to maintain, at least some performances of performable works are works of art in their own right. For only if we can credit features of a performance to the exercise of creative freedom on the part of the performer can we take the kind of interest in the performance qua performance that we have seen to be distinctive of our interest in an artwork qua artwork.

Fortunately for the limited defense of historically authentic performance mounted in the preceding paragraphs, we need not, in accepting this defense, commit ourselves to the scenario that Kivy describes. We have based the case for historical authenticity on the requirements for understanding, and thereby properly appreciating, performable works construed as essentially contextualized entities. But, in so doing, we have not foreclosed on other more traditionally "aesthetic" values that might be sought in the performance of performable works, even if such performances fail to be work-instances, in the technical sense. A performer seeking to increase the Kivian "aesthetic payoff" of her performance might ignore considerations of authenticity and even depart in certain respects from the score while still succeeding in producing a performance of a given work. We might value such a performance, which is of the work, as an autonomous event while not valuing it *as* a performance of the work performed, taking it to provide very little appreciative insight into, or understanding of, the latter.

But more crucially, why think that there cannot be an exercise of personal authenticity in historically authentic performances of period performable works, if, as Kivy rightly holds, those works were generally intended by their composers as proper subjects for interpretation by performers? For surely performers contemporary with the composer of a period piece were able to exercise their own creative freedom in performing those works. Many different interpretations fall within the performative envelope furnished by the explicit prescriptions and implicit understandings of the composer. A modern performer or ensemble seeking to provide an authentic performance of such a work has, in principle, exactly the same range of interpretive possibilities as period players. The difference lies in the accessibility of possibilities within that range. Only through dedication to exploring the potentialities of period instruments and period performative practice will modern performers come to realize the interpretive possibilities of the work taken as the historical individual that it is. But, when modern players dedicate themselves in this way, their performances can exhibit freedom, creativity, and other performative values. Thus there is no obstacle to our treating historically authentic performances by such accomplished performers as works of art, if we are inclined to view performances as works of art in the first place. Nor is there a problem in reconciling personal authenticity with historical authenticity. Artists of all stripes can manifest personal authenticity within the constraints of a chosen artistic discipline or practice. We don't think that the sonneteer denies herself the chance of personal authenticity in her work by opting to work in this form rather than in free verse, for example.

In conclusion, we may note one consequence of the contextualist or instrumentalist defense of authentic performance that we have presented. If we do insist on the importance of historically authentic performance for the appreciation of at least some performable works, can we reasonably claim to be in a position to appreciate those musical works of which we have heard performances? The vast majority of such performances, after all, are surely not authentic, or even, strictly speaking, correct. One option might be to defend the artistic relevance of authenticity without insisting on the need for authenticity in *actual* performances. For, it might be said, the requirements of authentic (and, indeed, correct) performance serve as a standard for judging whether qualities of an actual performance can be referred to a performable work. What matters is whether a given quality in a particular performance of a work *would*, or *could*, be a quality of a hypothetical authentic performance of that work.[13]

But whether authentic performance can generally serve as such a standard is questionable. How, for example, am I to know whether qualities experienced in listening to a non-authentic performance – in St. Paul's Cathedral, for example – of a work composed for performance in San Marco would be present in an authentic performance unless I have heard the work authentically performed in San Marco? The defender of a contextualist or instrumentalist conception of the performable work must, I think, bite the bullet here and grant the imperfections in our appreciative understanding of musical works from which we are historically distanced. The contextualist will lament this fact, but will not be moved to revise her theory. For it is simply a consequence of the contextualized nature of what we are trying to appreciate, given the context in which we ourselves are operating.

Notes

1.   See S. Davies 2001, 110–111, on the two kinds of interpretation required for the performance of a scored performable work.
2.   For a more extended discussion of these matters, see S. Davies 2001, 103–107.

3. See Edidin 1991, 404.
4. The most extended philosophical examination of the issues is in Kivy 1995. An earlier book on the subject is Leppard 1988. Kenyon 1988 is a specialized collection of papers by philosophers and musicologists. A lively exchange on the subject can be found in S. Davies 1987, 1988, and Young 1988. Other papers include: Baugh 1988; Goehr 1989; Edidin 1991; and Rubidge 1996. A critical review of the literature can be found in S. Davies 2001, ch. 5, where Davies also further develops the position defended in his earlier papers.
5. See Kivy 1995, chs. 5 and 9; Edidin 1991, 415.
6. See Kivy 1995, ch. 1, for these distinctions. See also Young 1988 and Edidin 1991.
7. For discussion of the relevance of Dipert's paper for issues concerning authentic performance, see Edidin 1991, 413–415; Kivy 1995, 43–45; S. Davies 2001, 231–234.
8. See S. Davies 2001, 234–237, for a defense of this claim, See also the discussion of "sensible authenticity" below.
9. We shall return below to Kivy's contention that the "aesthetic payoff" of a performance of a performable work is the proper criterion for evaluating that performance.
10. For a more detailed defense and response to criticisms, see S. Davies 2001, ch. 5.
11. See Baugh 1988, 482: "The original world of the work vanishes with the first public."
12. Stephen Davies has made similar claims in more recent papers, where he describes musical performance as the bodying forth of human action. See, for example, his 2008, 369–371.
13. See D. Davies 2004, 218, for a tentative endorsement of this proposal.

5

Challenges to the Classical Paradigm in Music

1 Introduction: The Classical Paradigm in the Performing Arts

In the last three chapters, we have examined the classical paradigm. The latter provides us with an account of what it is to be, and to be appreciated as, an artistic performance. According to the classical paradigm, performances are *of* performable works and play a necessary part in their appreciation. Performable works prescribe certain things to performers, and are appreciated for the qualities realizable in performances that satisfy these prescriptions. Theorists differ, as we have seen, as to the kinds of things that are prescribed and the nature of the things that do the prescribing. Performers are also in a sense collaborators with composers, for they are expected to exercise their creative freedom in interpreting what is prescribed. Only where this kind of interpretation is called for in generating work-instances of a multiple artwork do we think of it as a performable work. This, we will recall, grounds Kivy's concern that the demand for historically authentic performance threatens the status of musical works as performable works because it denies the performer a sufficient degree of interpretive freedom.

The need for interpretation in artistic performances is clear if we compare music to film. Many individuals play a part in enabling a film to be screened – those who generate a copy of the master encoding of the film, for example, and those who project the film by means of this copy in a cinema. But we do not take such individuals to be "performing" the film. They merely realize for the viewer, in the screening, already determined appreciable qualities of the film. They do not themselves determine some of these qualities

Philosophy of the Performing Arts, First Edition. David Davies.
© 2011 David Davies. Published 2011 by Blackwell Publishing Ltd.

through the exercise of their creative freedom. It is because the performance of a performable work requires interpretation that we have a use for a notion of authenticity that differs from the one that applies to artworks outside the performed arts. Authenticity here involves being true to the work in one's interpretation.

In examining the classical paradigm we have restricted our attention almost entirely to performances of musical works. Indeed, our focus has been even narrower, since our examples have been nineteenth- and twentieth-century classical compositions in the Western tradition such as Sibelius's Second Symphony. In the case of performances like the one with which we began Chapter 2, it is difficult to deny the explanatory force of the classical paradigm as an account of what transpires. The performance is clearly advertised as *a* performance *of* Sibelius's Second Symphony, where the symphony must, it seems, be something distinct from the particular performance. It is attended by persons such as Berthold who bring to their experience of the performance a critical and appreciative ear schooled both in a knowledge of what is being performed and a history of attending other performances labeled as being "of" the same thing. The musicians and the conductor conceive their performance as an interpretation of this thing, and are guided, in rehearsal and in concert performance, by a score that they correctly take to record certain prescriptions laid down by Sibelius in 1902.

To say that a performance is rightly subsumed under the classical paradigm is not to deny that our appreciative interest may focus more on the creative brilliance (or otherwise!) of the interpretation than on the work interpreted. More significantly, in bringing a given performance under the paradigm we do not foreclose on the possibility that the performance may be, and may be appreciable as, a work of art in its own right. This was part of our answer to Kivy's worries about historically authentic performance at the end of Chapter 4. But it is also the right way to respond to those who suggest, conversely, that, if we are to uphold the artistic status of what performers do, we must deny that the performances are of independent works (see, for example, Jacobs 1990).

Assuming, then, that what Berthold attended was indeed a performance of a performable work, understood in the manner of the classical paradigm, we can ask to what extent this is also the case for other performances in the performing arts. In assessing the *scope* of the classical paradigm, we must consider whether it applies more generally to musical performances, and whether it also applies to performances in theater and dance. In line with the methodological considerations that have guided us thus far, we shall focus on the practices of performers, critics, and audience members. Our task is to determine whether those practices are best explained in terms of the paradigm, or in terms of some alternative model of artistic performance.

To see how the classical paradigm might be extended to the performing arts more generally, we may consider Paul Thom's account of the latter. Thom defines a performable work as "the directed content of a performance directive" issued by the artist (1993, 44). Such a directive prescribes what must be done to execute the work. In line with Wolterstorff and Stephen Davies, Thom holds that a directive must be understood against a background of assumptions concerning performance practice that the artist shares with those he or she expects to perform the work. His account allows performable works to differ from one another in a number of ways (Thom 1993, 51–55). First, we may, but need not, have an explicit specification of the content of the directive. What matters is that this content be somehow transmissible so that, as with a musical score, we have a point of reference in determining when we have different performances of the same work, and when we have performances of two different works. But nothing in the model excludes performable works that are orally transmitted and that undergo a measure of change through such transmission over time. We might expect musical performances in medieval times and in non-Western cultures to be of performable works that fit this description. Second, the directive may be more or less determinate in its prescriptions. Thom cites, as an example of a "minimalist" directive, La Monte Young's *Composition 1960 #7* which prescribes only that a B and an F sharp be "held for a long time" (Thom 1993, 54). Goodman cites a kind of "deviant scoring" for musical works used by John Cage in his 1960 work *Concert for Piano and Orchestra, Solo for Piano*:

> Dots for single notes are placed within a rectangle; across the rectangle, at varying angles and perhaps intersecting, run five straight lines for (severally) frequency, duration, timbre, amplitude, and succession. The significant factors determining the sounds indicated by a dot are the perpendicular distances from the dot to these lines. (Goodman 1976, 187–188)

Goodman is concerned that this method of "scoring" fails to meet the requirements for a notation. But, as we saw in Chapter 3, as long as we let the circumstances of performance play a part in determining what work a performance is of, there are no obstacles to the use of such heterodox means of specifying performable works.

Thom's account generalizes from musical performances to the other performing arts through another dimension in which artists' directives can vary: the medium in which the content of the directive is to be executed. In the case of music, what is prescribed is the production of a particular sequence of sounds; in the case of dance, it is the production of a sequence of bodily motions, and in the case of theater it is the production of a sequence of verbal (usually) and non-verbal actions. Thom doesn't think that all artistic performances fit this model. There can be performances that are not of works – the most obvious examples being improvisations – in any of the performance media just noted. But, he maintains, a performance of a performable work is generally aesthetically richer and more satisfying than an improvised performance (Thom 1993, 69–72). First, an improvisation is unlikely to have the same degree of structural complexity as a performance of a performable work, given the manner in which it is created. Furthermore, we will not be able to enjoy the performance both for its own sake and for the way in which it interprets a performable work. Thus, while Thom questions what he terms the "valorization" of the work over performance, he takes the classical paradigm to have wide scope in the performing arts, and also takes this to be generally a good thing.

A number of writers, however, have offered more or less radical challenges to these assumptions. In assessing these challenges, we shall, in the remainder of this chapter, begin with performances of Western classical music, and then examine other musical genres. In the following chapter, we shall look at theater and dance, and also consider the suggestion that, far from having narrower scope than many think, the classical paradigm actually has wider scope, encompassing at least some works of literature.

2   The Scope of the Paradigm in Classical Music

Some have suggested that, while a particular model of artistic performance may fit a performance of Sibelius's Second Symphony very well, the same model cannot usefully be applied to other performances in the classical tradition, for example those of early music. There is disagreement, however, as to where precisely to draw the line, and how radical a departure from the classical paradigm is required to accommodate such cases. For some, this is merely a family squabble within the broader camp of the paradigm, to be resolved by adopting different versions of the latter for different musical periods. Levinson, for example, prefaces his arguments for an instrumentalist and contextualist conception of the musical work by explicitly confining the scope of his inquiry to "that paradigm of a musical work, the fully notated 'classical' composition of Western culture, for example, Beethoven's Quintet for piano and winds in E-flat, op. 16" (1980, 64–65). In response to criticisms from Kivy, he grants that instrumentalism will not hold for "most music before 1750" (Levinson 1990b, 232). Thus he seems to subscribe to two different conceptions of what a musical work prescribes for its performances: instrumentalism for works created after 1750, and non-instrumentalism for most works created prior to 1750. Stephen Davies espouses a related kind of pluralism for classical musical works while also remaining within the classical paradigm. Classical works for performance, he argues, can be more or less "thick" or "thin" in their constitutive properties (S. Davies 2001, 20). An eighteenth-century work such as Mozart's Divertimento in D, K. 136, is thin in that its prescriptions leave considerable freedom to the performer in determining the acoustic properties of a performance. Thinness is often a consequence of the fact that instrumentation is left open. A work such as Bach's *Goldberg Variations*, for example, can be played on different keyboard instruments, so specific timbral properties are not prescribed. In the case of a comparatively thick work like Stravinsky's *The Rite of Spring*, on the other hand, "a great many of the properties heard in a performance are crucial to its identity, and must be reproduced in a fully faithful rendition of the work" (S. Davies 2001, 20).

Neither Levinson nor Davies calls into question the applicability of the classical paradigm itself to the Western musical tradition as a whole. A more radical challenge, however, is posed by Lydia Goehr's (2007) analysis of eighteenth-century practices of musical performance. Goehr argues that what she terms "the work-concept" – the concept of what we have termed the performable musical work –developed only at the end of the eighteenth century. Prior to that date, it played no part in regulating musical practice, even though we treat eighteenth-century compositions as performable works. She identifies various aspects of eighteenth-century musical practice that were grounded in a key difference in the function of musical performance at that time (Goehr 2007, ch. 7). Since the early nineteenth century, performances of classical music have usually taken place in a "concert" environment whose primary purpose is to present the music performed. Eighteenth-century performances, however, usually served an extra-musical function, most obviously by accompanying religious services. As a result, the character and duration of a performance was determined largely by the needs of the extra-musical event which it supplemented. Performances were frequently interrupted by other elements in the religious services that they accompanied, for example. The primary concern of performers, therefore, was to make the music fit the extra-musical events. Because of the variable nature of these events, those responsible for the performance did not think of themselves as composing or performing something that might be repeated as a whole in other contexts. Rather, in adapting to the needs of a particular performance situation, musicians made liberal use of passages from other performances, either their own earlier performances or those of other performers. It was such elements or themes, capable of being incorporated into distinct performances as needed, rather than the contents of performances as a whole, that were thought of as repeatable.

This explains both the enormous number of different "works" that we ascribe to composers such as Vivaldi and Scarlatti and the overlap in musical material between these "works." Furthermore, because of the need to adapt a performance to the needs of the particular extra-musical function that it served, there was little occasion for rehearsal prior to performance. Only the most general prescriptions were provided for the performers, necessitating much embellishment on their part. Indeed, it was often not known in advance which instrumentation and musicians would be available for a performance. Performers therefore had to adapt to meet the contingencies that presented themselves. A further consideration helped to entrench this state of affairs. Until the end of the eighteenth century, no notation existed that would permit a full enough specification of a composer's prescriptions to allow a performance in accordance with these prescriptions to take place in the absence of the composer himself. Where scores were published corresponding to eighteenth-century performances, they were identified with the particular performance occasion rather than with an independent performable work, or they were treated as exercises for musicians to enable them to better develop their performative skills.

Goehr draws the following conclusions from these features of eighteenth-century musical performance practice:

> The idea of a work of music existing as a fixed creation independently of its many possible performances had no regulative force in a practice that demanded adaptable and functional music, and which allowed an open interchange of musical material. Musicians did not see works as much as they saw individual performances themselves to be the direct outcome of their compositional activity. (Goehr 2007, 185–186)

To say that the concept of the performable work had no "regulative force" in eighteenth-century musical practice is to say that it did not regulate what musicians did or, presumably, how what they did was viewed by those attending the events where music was performed. If this is correct, then locating eighteenth-century musical performances within the classical paradigm cannot be expected to help us understand why they had the features that they did. Given our assumption that subsuming performances under the paradigm is justified just in case it *does* have some kind of explanatory payoff, Goehr's analysis suggests that, even in Western classical music, the scope of the classical paradigm is more limited than we might have thought. While nothing prevents us from treating the eighteenth-century scores that are available to us as the basis for multiple performances, it seems wrong to think of the original performances from which these scores are derived as themselves performances of performable works in the sense required by the classical paradigm, or to think of these scores as themselves representing eighteenth-century performable works.

This conclusion might be disputed, however. Kivy, discussing Goehr's work, describes as "intolerable" the thought that Western art music was not a performed art until the nineteenth century (Kivy 1995, 262–263). He argues that, even if we grant that there was not, in eighteenth-century musical practice, anything meeting our strict conception of the performable musical work, we can nonetheless preserve a performance/work distinction that applies to such practice. For the eighteenth-century musical community placed a high value on improvisation of a sort "that required for its enjoyment the concept of a pre-planned, preformed, and enduring kind of music as the standard against which it could be measured" (Kivy 1995, 263). The value ascribed to improvisation, Kivy maintains, requires as a foil the idea of performance from a notation, or from memory of a notated, previously existing, work.

We cannot fully assess the force of this response until we look more closely – in Chapter 8 – at improvisation in general, as a feature of musical practice, and at its bearing upon the applicability of the classical paradigm to that practice. However, it isn't clear, given Goehr's account of eighteenth-century musical practice, that the foil against which improvisation would have to be measured must be the performance of a previously existing performable work. For, as we saw, she claims that performance practice drew very freely not on pre-existing works but on pre-existing elements that could be enlisted in adapting a performance to the needs of a given extra-musical event. Improvisation, then, could be valued as a way of developing or embellishing upon such elements, or as a way in which such elements are synthesized into a single performance, without the need for the pre-existing repeatable *works* that the classical paradigm demands.

In a more extended critical response to Goehr, Stephen Davies argues that her conclusions rest upon two assumptions (S. Davies 2001, 86–92). First, in surveying the musical tradition, she focuses on striking *dis*continuities between musical performances before and after 1800. Second, the discontinuities upon which she focuses depend upon her selection of the works of Beethoven as paradigmatic of the work-concept. These works are, in Davies's terminology, relatively thick, and their scores are taken to be strictly binding on performers. Given this choice of paradigm, it is not surprising that Goehr is impressed by discontinuities in performance practice. But, Davies maintains, she fails to pay proper respect to important continuities between nineteenth-century musical practice and that of earlier periods. There is, he claims, ample evidence of an interest in the authorial role of composers going back to at least the twelfth and thirteenth centuries. Also, the absence of a notation prior to 1800 capable of freeing the performance of a work from the supervisory presence of the composer does not show that there were no works before that time, but only that such works were necessarily somewhat thinner in what they required of performers. According to Davies, Goehr downplays historical continuities in her claim about the work-concept because, given her paradigms, she sees this concept as emerging only when certain notions admittedly found in earlier musical practice come to function together in a unified way – the notions of "composition, performance, autonomy, repeatability, permanence and perfect compliance." Davies, on the other hand, maintains that performance practice prior to 1800 was indeed regulated by the work-concept, as long as we do not conflate the latter with its thick interpretation in nineteenth-century Romanticism.

Davies is surely right in thinking that Goehr cannot take the thick Romantic construal of the work-concept as a given in arguing for the constructed nature of the notion of a musical work. But it isn't clear that her argument depends crucially upon such a construal. Like Kivy, Davies pays little attention to Goehr's claims about the distinctive function of musical performance prior to 1800. It is the purported discontinuity in function that supposedly explains why the work-concept comes to play a regulative role only after that date. Because musical performance pre-1800 is subject to the demands of an extra-musical event, there is no place, according to Goehr, for repeatable works, even if there is a place for repeatable elements that can be combined in individual performances. This allows her to account for the importance accorded pre-1800 to the authorial role of composers, as cited by Davies. Such importance may attach to the composition of those elements that can enter into such performative wholes. If it be replied that such elements are thin works, then it must be granted that they are not the works we standardly identify in this period. It is the change in the function of musical performance that, for Goehr, explains how the different elements cited by Davies, such as repeatability and composition, come together only after 1800 in a work-concept that regulates practice and individuates works in the way we customarily do.

3   Jazz, Rock, and the Classical Paradigm

Jazz

Talk of improvisation leads us very naturally to the topic of jazz. One obvious feature of jazz performance is the value placed upon the improvisational skills of the performers. Improvisation is clearly not sufficient for a performance to count as jazz, however, given its place in eighteenth-century classical music. What is also crucial is the way in which performers relate what they are doing to a particular tradition – the "jazz" tradition. But it is the central role accorded to improvisation that calls into question whether jazz performance can usefully be brought under the classical paradigm. Many jazz performances takes as their starting point a performable work written for performance by "straight," rather than predominantly improvisatory, ensembles. However, given the ways in which a jazz performance is allowed to depart from the prescriptions for such a work, and given the value placed on these departures, it might be asked whether the performance stands to the performable work in the right relationship to count as a performance *of* that work. Stephen Davies, for example, argues that renditions of jazz "standards" – such as the performance of "My Funny Valentine" by the Miles Davis Quintet on December 2, 1964 – should not be subsumed under the classical paradigm:

> There is no reason to assume that a playing event beginning with a particular tune is best viewed as a performance of a work thinly specified via that tune. The improvisation is inspired by the tune and is "after" it, but the whole that is created can be regarded as new and unique. (S. Davies 2001, 10)

As we shall see in Chapter 8, this is a complex issue, and to clarify it we shall have to consider carefully both the nature of improvisation and the different ways in which it can enter into performance practice. To do justice to the phenomena, we may need to adopt a pluralist approach to jazz, paralleling the kind of approach canvassed above for classical performance. But I shall defer further discussion of this until Chapter 8.

Rock

Questions arise about the applicability of the classical paradigm to jazz because there are aspects of what goes on in live jazz performance that fit uneasily with the idea of performance as regulated by the goal of interpretively realizing a pre-existing set of prescriptions. The work, it might be said, cannot do justice to the performance – in Andrew Kania's witty characterization, jazz might seem to be all play and no work.[1] In the case of rock music, on the other hand, questions arise because of the significance, for the identity of the rock work, of what goes on in the recording studio and the consequent failure of live performance to do justice to our conception of the work.

In both classical music and jazz, it is natural to assume that the primary goal of a recording is to reproduce as accurately as possible the sound of a performance. This performance may be occurring on a stage or in a club, where what is recorded is an audible event intended to serve other purposes.

Or it may be taking place in a studio for the sole and express purpose of making the recording. In listening to the recording of Brahms's *Hungarian Dances* by Jascha Heifetz and Brooks Smith, for example, we assume that we are hearing a recording of what we might have heard had we been present in the studio on April 14, 1956 when Heifetz and Smith performed the piece. This impression is even stronger if we listen to the recording of the John Coltrane Quartet's live performance of "My Favorite Things" at the Newport Jazz Festival on July 7, 1963. In such cases, we do not expect the recording to reproduce all of the relevant sonic qualities of the performance. In this sense, a recording has a tertiary status for our appreciation of a classical work – the work itself is realized in the performance of which we are listening to the recording. And perhaps it has a secondary status in our appreciation of the work in the jazz example, if, as Stephen Davies suggests, we take the work in this case to be the performance itself.

A little reflection on classical and jazz recording practice suggests that this intuitive view of such recordings stands in need of some qualification. For example, while the "take" of the *Hungarian Dances* occurred on a single day, the take of Brahms's Sextet in G major, Op. 36, contained on the same CD took place on two consecutive days, the different movements being recorded separately.[2] More generally, it is standard practice in classical recording to splice together different takes in the interests of obtaining the best overall rendering of the piece. The recording of an individual live performance may not allow for the splicing of takes, but it does allow for various strategies that serve a similar interest. As Theodore Gracyk brings out very clearly in a critique of the idea of sound recording as capturing "what one would have heard" (1996, 87–90) the recording of the performance by the Coltrane Quartet involved various techniques for miking and mixing to produce a sound that could not have been heard by any individual listener at the Newport Jazz Festival. The recording of a live performance is importantly aperspectival whereas our hearing of that performance is always perspectival. Also, the recording may provide a better balance of the individual contributions than would have been available during the live performance, either because of dynamic differences between the instruments or because of failings in the system of amplification used on stage.

However, even when we modify our view of recordings of classical and jazz performances in light of these kinds of considerations, performances retain a certain primacy, for the purposes of appreciation, over recordings. The recording aims to present what was performed in a way that does best service to the achievements of the performers, even if this departs significantly in the ways just described from "what would have been heard" when those performances took place. Theodore Gracyk (1996) has argued, however, that the same does not apply to the central works of rock music by artists such as Elvis Presley, the Beatles, the Rolling Stones, Bruce Springsteen, and Led Zeppelin. Here, the sound we associate with the work depends essentially upon the use of various kinds of technological resources in the recording process. In such cases, there is no actual or even possible live performance that sounds like what we hear when we listen to the recording. Generally, the sound that we associate with a rock work is the result of skillful construction in a studio. This involves various elements recorded at different times and in different places and technologically modified in various ways so that the resulting sounds as they feature in the recording may differ dramatically from the sounds originally recorded. For example, individual rock musicians and singers regularly overdub their initial performances, harmonizing with their own voices or soloing over their own initial solos. Members of a band often record their contributions individually rather than in a group performance, and guest musicians may add their contributions in different cities where they are given access to copies of the bed tracks. Furthermore, many elements in rock recordings owe nothing to the recording of live performances, being generated purely electronically. Producers such as George Martin for the Beatles perform many wonders in the studio by dropping things into and lifting them out of recordings, reversing tapes, and integrating sound material from a variety of sources in a collage fashion, as in the coda to "All You Need is Love." Gracyk provides a rich range of examples of such practices in familiar rock works.[3]

Does this present a problem for the application of the classical paradigm to rock music? Gracyk argues that it does, and that the rock work is the recording, rather than the song recorded – the electronically encoded result of what gets done in the studio that is then played back by the listener rather than performed by musicians. There is no performance of which the work is a recording, nor does the work receive performances at live concerts. Stephen Davies, on the other hand, believes that in general the classical paradigm still applies, save in a few cases that parallel purely electronic works in the classical tradition. We shall begin by looking at Davies's attempt to extend his pluralistic account of musical works to accommodate rock music. Then we shall compare this to Gracyk's account, and to an attempt by Andrew Kania to mediate between these views.

We noted earlier that Davies distinguishes between thin and thick performable works in terms of the constraints they impose on their right performances. But Davies also endorses a broader pluralism concerning musical works (2001, ch. 1). He distinguishes, first, between works that are, and works that are not, for performance. He then divides works for performance – our performable works – into works for live performance and works for studio performance. Taking the first of these points, Davies recognizes that some musical works are created not for performance of any kind but for *playback*. Such pieces, which he terms "purely electronic," are constituted in a studio using various kinds of technological resources. They exist in virtue of being encoded in some way, and are to be played back by means of a mechanical device capable of retrieving what is stored. As in the case of films whose instances are screenings, the instances of such works are *soundings* generated from accurately cloned copies of the master encoding, and not performances of any kind. Davies cites, as examples, works of *musique concrète* by composers such as Pierre Schaeffer and the electronic music of Herbert Eimert.

Works for performance, on the other hand, require for their realization that some role be played by a performer. In the familiar case of works for *live* performance, we have a prescription, issued by the composer, as to what must be done by musicians in order to perform the piece. In the case of a work for *studio* performance, on the other hand, what is prescribed is that the musicians' skills be exercised in a studio where the sounds produced can be "taped, superimposed, mixed, and modified, until a composite is produced" (S. Davies 2001, 31). Such works

> require the electronic manipulation of the materials finding their way into the performance. Normally they are not created in real time. Parts are laid down one after the other, and accumulate by addition and juxtaposition. Usually the result would be impossible to perform in real time ... The composite mix is carefully constructed in a complex editing process. The performance is completed when the master tape is finalized. (S. Davies 2001, 34–35)

Davies claims that rock works are generally works for studio performance, although he grants that some works – such as the Beatles' "A Day in the Life" – are better viewed as purely electronic. To view such works as purely electronic is to treat all of the electronic manipulations of and additions to the original recordings in the studio as constitutive of the work, rather than as representing merely one way in which the work can be performed in the studio through electronic manipulation of recordings.

Gracyk, on the other hand, equates rock works in general with purely electronic works in Davies's sense. While he points to the same phenomena that Davies describes in the preceding passage, he argues that the focus of critical and appreciative interest and attention in rock music is the distinctive *sound* of the recording available to receivers in playback, rather than the sound of a performance made available through the recording. He seeks to counter not only the idea that recordings are recordings of performances in the standard sense – *live* performances – but also the idea that live performances are performances *of* the rock work, now construed as the recording. While performers frequently try to replicate distinctive aspects of the sound of the recording, this, insofar as it is governed by an interest in mirroring rather than *interpreting* the recording, would not count as a *performance* of the recording, as we have defined this notion. And recordings, because they are so thick in terms of their constitutive properties, are not the kinds of things that allow of interpretive performance in the first place. Gracyk does, however, leave a place for performed works in rock music:

> Recordings are the primary link between the rock artist and the audience, and the primary object of critical attention. These musical works are *played* on appropriate machines, not performed … The relevant work (the recording) frequently manifests another work, usually a song, without being a performance of that song. (Gracyk 1996, 18)

As Davies points out in responding to Gracyk, it is not immediately clear how we should mediate between these two views, each of which points to the same general features of the production of rock recordings. Both Davies and Gracyk hold their accounts answerable to the same criteria, namely, our musical and critical practice (see S. Davies 2001, 9–10). Furthermore, on both accounts works require the electronic manipulation of raw sonic materials for their realization, and are issued as discs for playback – although, for Davies, the work is not to be identified with an individual recording resulting from such manipulations but with a work for studio performance that allows of different studio realizations. Davies nonetheless marshals a number of considerations in support of his view (2001, 31–34). First, he questions the notion of "manifestation" to which Gracyk appeals. How is it possible, he asks, for a recording to "manifest" a song without thereby being a performance of that song?[4] Second, he points to two features of our musical practice that he thinks fit better with his account than with Gracyk's. First, one of the things that is valued in rock works is the musicians' skill in playing their instruments, the same skill that is central to the appreciation of live performances. This suggests that recordings are viewed as continuous with live performances in their values and traditions, something captured in the idea that rock works are still works for performance, but for performance augmented by the resources of the studio. Second, rerecordings and "covers" are treated as performances or interpretations of the original work. For example, Joe Cocker's recording of Lennon and McCartney's "With a Little Help from My Friends" is regarded as a new interpretation of the Beatles' work. But if rock works were purely electronic, then we should treat the Cocker recording as an autonomous and independent, if derivative, work. Davies stresses that the work for studio performance is not to be identified with what is specified in the sheet music, for the latter is typically far too thin to accurately represent the work. Rather, it is understood, in the case of such works, that the performance is to be "thickened and stiffened by electronic interventions and editing" (S. Davies 2001, 35), even though it is left open precisely how this should be done. Davies concedes, however, that the case for viewing rock works as purely electronic is strengthened if, as Gracyk and others have suggested, we take the rock work to be the album – for example, Springsteen's *Born to Run* – rather than the individual track (S. Davies 2001, 34).

Andrew Kania (2006) has defended Gracyk's general approach by suggesting how it might accommodate the features of our practice to which Davies appeals. Rock works, he maintains, are indeed thick recordings – he terms these "rock *tracks*" – that also manifest thin rock *songs*. Manifestation is a relation that may, but need not, involve being an instance of what is manifested. But, even if the recording is an instance of a song, in some sense, it is not a performance of the song. In live performances, however, what is performed *is* the song which the track manifests, rather than the recorded track. While a live performance may in many ways seek to reproduce aspects of the sound of the track, it also introduces other elements that are specific to the context of live performance – for example, an extended introduction and coda, or alternative lyrics – and may radically depart from the sound of the track. The idea that live performances are performances of *songs*, then, is preferable to Davies's view of such performances as attempts at live replication of works for studio performance.

Kania argues that the value placed upon the instrumental skills manifested in recordings does not pose a problem for this view, since the manner in which the sounds in a track were produced may bear upon the aesthetic properties we ascribe to the rock work. Nor is there a problem accounting for our treatment of cover versions. While Davies wants to explain this in terms of there being different (studio) performances of the same work for studio performance, Kania talks instead of different tracks that are intended to manifest the same song. He points, here, to an analogy with remakes in cinema: "Just as we compare film remakes with their originals, yet do not think of films as performances of the narrative they have in common, so we compare cover versions without thinking of them as performances of the songs they manifest" (Kania 2006, 409). In both cases, we treat the two entities as works in their own right. While it is certainly possible to see the entities as distinct performances of a shared work, such an approach is uninteresting given the thinness of what they share.

This final observation by Kania seems to be crucial when we try to decide between the idea that rock works are purely electronic recordings and the idea that they are works for studio performance. For, as we have seen, our notion of a performable work is tied to the idea of interpretation in performance, and to the idea of performances as more or less true to the work. Davies resists the idea that works for studio performance are individuated in terms of the thin requirements of their sheet music. But, if all we add, in characterizing such works, is the understanding that the live studio perform-ance is to be augmented by the use of (unspecified) studio resources, this leaves little room for the idea that we can compare two studio recordings in terms of their being true to the work for studio performance, over and above their being studio recordings that comply with the sheet music. Thus it isn't clear that the notion of a "work for studio performance," understood to be distinct from a work for live performance, meets the conditions we have established for something to count as a performable work. If so, then Gracyk and Kania make a powerful case for locating the rock work outside of the classical paradigm, even though rock performances remain within the paradigm insofar as we view them as performances of (thin) songs.

4   Non-Western Music and the Classical Paradigm

The musical genres considered thus far belong to the broadly Western musical tradition. An obvious question, therefore, is whether the classical paradigm can accommodate music produced and appreciated outside that tradition. A couple of disanalogies might suggest that it cannot. First, as compara-tive anthropologists and ethnomusicologists have stressed, music in other cultures is generally closely tied to some non-artistic function – religious, ritual, or social – rather than being designed for the kind of contempla-tive appreciation central to Western music since at least the early nineteenth century. We might ask then whether performances of such music qualify as *artistic*. Second, most music-making in other cultures proceeds without the use of musical notation. This raises the question whether, lacking such a notation, there are sufficient resources to create and preserve performable works of the sort required by the classical paradigm.

The first concern is easily answered if we define the kind of regard proper to artistic manifolds in the way that we did in Chapter 1. We there distanced "artistic regard" from the modernist idea that artistic manifolds call for a kind of disinterested contemplation. Artistic regard, we maintained, is the kind of regard that must be accorded to a manifold whose content has been articulated in the way that artworks articulate their contents. The question, then, is not whether music in another culture is intended for disinterested contemplation, which it may well not be, given the ritual, religious, or social function that it has in that culture. Rather, the question is whether the lis-tener must attend to the music "artistically" in order to grasp the articulated content that bears upon its capacity to serve that cultural function.[5]

The second concern is addressed by Stephen Davies in his reflections upon the music of the gamelan in Bali and Indonesia (2001, especially ch. 6;

2007).[6] Although notation is now sometimes used in the teaching of gamelan musicians, Davies stresses that the notated pieces were until recently transmitted orally. In such cases, a musician is taught a given part in a composition by personal instruction either from the composer or from another musician who has acquired the ability to play the part by these means (S. Davies 2001, 21, 289). Given that both composers and performers in this tradition have a clear sense of what a given composition requires and of the interpretive freedom available to musicians (285–286, 22), and that performances are treated as being *of* something composed (88), the requirements of the classical paradigm are clearly met. Balinese gamelan, Davies argues, "shows how works can be introduced and preserved over extended periods within an oral tradition, which, nevertheless, is never static or backward looking" (22). In the same way, the classical paradigm can accommodate orally preserved works in more conservative early Western traditions, such as Greek and Coptic chant.

Notes

1. See Kania, forthcoming.
2. See the notes for RCA Victor GD87965, issued 1988.
3. An interesting documentation of the process whereby a rock track is recorded can be found in Jean-Luc Godard's film *One Plus One* (sometimes titled *Sympathy for the Devil*). While Godard intends the film to function as a radical Marxist commentary on capitalism and imperialism, he takes as a central metaphor the process whereby the Rolling Stones transform the initial inchoate ideas for the song "Sympathy for the Devil" into the finished track released on the album *Beggars Banquet*. The film contains extensive live recordings of this process as it unfolded in the studio.
4. One model for the notion of "manifestation" might be the "ingredients" model of theatrical performance to be examined in Chapter 6.
5. Indeed, we need to think of artistic regard in this way if we are to accommodate, as art, many Renaissance paintings produced to serve a primarily religious devotional function.
6. See also Alperson et al. 2007.

6

The Scope of the Classical Paradigm: Theater, Dance, and Literature

1 Introduction: Berthold and Magda Go to the Theater

We re-encounter Berthold and Magda at the local theater in a provincial town they are visiting. The billboard outside the theater advertises a performance of *King Lear*, and it is this that has lured them inside. When the curtain rises in the otherwise empty auditorium, they immediately doubt the wisdom of their decision. The stage is adorned with scenery reminiscent of the illustrations in a Grimm's fairy tale, and it quickly becomes apparent that there are only a small number of people in the cast. One of them, dressed in a manner resembling Gandalf in the film version of *The Lord of the Rings*, is presumably supposed to be Lear. The solitary actress in the cast, who is attired like a hobbit, is identifiable as Cordelia by her relationship to the Gandalf-figure, who banishes her from his presence after she refuses to satisfy his desire that she profess her affection for him. It is conveyed by report that his strange behavior is the result of the fact that he has given away his possessions to his other daughters (not explicitly represented in the performance) who, having agreed to profess their love for him, have since tormented him terribly. The Gandalf-like figure is also tormented, but for his own instruction, by another hobbit-like figure clearly intended to be Lear's Fool. Much is made of a scene that seems to take place in a thunderstorm, in which the Gandalf-like figure loudly intones barely recognizable lines from Shakespeare's play – although this is arguably an improvement over the mumbled manner in which the actors generally deliver their lines.

Philosophy of the Performing Arts, First Edition. David Davies.
© 2011 David Davies. Published 2011 by Blackwell Publishing Ltd.

The sheer awfulness of the performance only fascinates Berthold and Magda for a little while, and they would have left but for the evident occurrence of a real thunderstorm outside. While sitting out the storm, they entertain themselves by looking at the architecture of the theater, which, unlike what is taking place on stage, is certainly worth looking at. The actors, however, continue undaunted by the obvious lack of interest of their audience. Thankfully for Berthold and Magda, many details of the narrative of *King Lear* not essential for the overall plot of the play, as well as all but the central characters, have been omitted, and after only an hour it is obvious that the denouement is approaching. However, as the female hobbit-figure is being led off stage to be executed, the Gandalf-figure springs to life, knocking down those guarding her, and they leave the stage arm in arm to the haunting strains of "Over the Rainbow." To a tumultuous silence, the curtain descends. Berthold and Magda, finally distracted from their distraction, are still in their seats as the curtain rises again (by accident it would seem) to reveal two stage hands beginning to dismantle the set. Seeing that they have an audience, the stage hands ham it up. "Finally," says Berthold, "something worth watching!"

The point of this cautionary tale is not merely to discourage the reader from venturing into provincial theaters. Nor, as might be the case were it to be told in Chapter 9, is the point to raise questions about the role of the audience in theatrical performance. As we shall see, some writers maintain that the presence of an attentive audience is a necessary condition for a theatrical performance to take place. Rather, the point in the present context is to raise the following question: assuming that what transpired before Berthold and Magda was indeed a theatrical performance, was it a performance of *King Lear*? Our interest in this question is of course an interest in the more general question: when is a theatrical performance a performance of a particular play? But our explorations in the previous chapter should alert us to a measure of ambiguity here. For we could be asking two things: (1) When is a theatrical performance a performance of a *particular* play – for example, a performance of *King Lear*? (2) When is a theatrical performance a performance *of* a particular play? Here we are asking whether the performance stands in the "performance of" relation to a performable work.

The first question presupposes that we *are* dealing with something that purports to be a performance of a performable work, and asks how we determine whether it is indeed a performance of a particular work. This is a matter internal to the classical paradigm as applied to theater. It is analogous to the issues examined in Chapter 2 concerning the kinds of thing that musical works prescribe for their correct performances. Our concern here is with the kinds of features prescribed by *theatrical* works for their right performances. The second question, however, asks about the applicability of the classical paradigm itself to theater. In the few references made in earlier chapters to theatrical rather than musical examples, we tacitly assumed that the classical paradigm does apply, at least to canonical theatrical performances advertised under such labels as *King Lear*. If this assumption is correct, then our concern, in asking the second question might be about the scope of the classical paradigm as applied to theater. Are some theatrical performances perhaps not helpfully viewed in this way? But we might also ask whether the classical paradigm fails to apply to theatrical performances *in general*. We shall address this more radical suggestion in section 3 below.

2   Theatrical Performances and Performable Works

Let us assume, for the moment, that it is right to think of canonical theatrical performances of the sort just described as performances *of* performable works such as *King Lear*. In terms of Thom's account sketched in Chapter 5, we are assuming that such performances stand in some suitable historical-intentional relation to the content of performance directives issued by creators of the works performed. A number of other prominent theorists have conceived theatrical performances in a similar fashion. Richard Wollheim, who, as we have seen, identifies musical works with types that have musical performances as their tokens, offers a parallel account of theatrical works (1980, 82–83) According to Wollheim, a theatrical performance is an interpretation of the prescriptions established by the author of the work performed. And Noël Carroll describes a performable theatrical work as a "recipe" which is "filled out" through the interpretations of those who perform the work (1998, 212–213).

   If canonical theatrical performances are indeed properly subsumed under the classical paradigm, then the questions that we addressed in Chapters 2 and 3 concerning performable works of music will also arise for performable works of theater. One question – the ontological one, as to the nature of the performable work – will presumably admit of a similar range of answers to those canvassed in the musical case. Performable works of theater might be viewed as pure types of some kind, or as indicated types, or as continuants, or as generative actions, or as fictional entities. More germane in the present context, we must ask which kinds of features performable works of theater prescribe for their correct performances, and in what respects such works require interpretation on the part of performers. Relatedly, when does something count as a performance of a particular theatrical work, whether correct or flawed? And finally, what will count as an authentic performance of a theatrical work, and do such performances have an artistic value that should lead us to seek them out?

Let me elaborate on these questions. First, if *King Lear*, for example, is a performable work, what kinds of features does it prescribe for its right performances? If we adopt the same general approach here as in the case of classical music, two things will bear upon how we answer this question: (1) explicit prescriptions by playwrights, presumably contained in playscripts – the latter will play a parallel role to scores in the case of scored classical works, and (2) understandings, in the performative communities to whom playscripts are addressed, as to what these prescriptions actually prescribe. There is an apparent tension, however, between this answer to our first question and a natural answer to our second question: when should we count something as a performance – correct or not – of a particular performable theatrical work? We saw that a necessary condition for an event to count as a performance of a particular scored musical work is that the performers aim to satisfy the explicit and implicit prescriptions embodied in the work's score. In classifying theatrical performances, however, it seems that we are quite willing to accommodate intentional departures from the explicit prescriptions in a playscript. Indeed, we seem willing to accommodate a wide range of such departures in different performances that we identify as being of the same play. This is most obvious in the case of "classic" dramas such as *King Lear* and *Hamlet*. These are almost always presented in an abridged or amended form of some kind, and in a manner that departs radically from the performative practice of Shakespeare's time.[1] Indeed, the director Peter Brook not only holds that Shakespeare's plays retain their identity through many different interpretations (Brook 1988, 78),[2] but also takes this to be consistent with making striking changes to the explicit prescriptions of the plays. We can see this in his own directorial practice. His 1962 production of *King Lear*, for example, not only excised substantial portions of the original text but also, in the interests of a broadly existential interpretation of the play, reallocated some speeches between characters.[3] Even where we have greater compliance with the text of a period play, it is very common to reset a performance bearing the name of that play in a different cultural or historical context. For example, directors see nothing wrong in setting a performance bearing the label *Measure for Measure* in Prohibition era Chicago. Something similar applies even to contemporary dramas, which frequently undergo considerable modification by the director in rehearsal, generally with the blessing of the playwright.

Can we reconcile these features of our theatrical practice with the requirements of the classical paradigm? One option would be to say that such features merely testify to a freer conception of what is permissible in a *performance* of a work, and are consistent with a conception of what is required in a *correct performance* of the work closely resembling the one that obtains in classical music. But why don't such willful departures from the requirements for correct performance of a work, as construed above, discredit the performers' claim to be performing that work? One way to answer this challenge would be to sever the connection – central in the musical case, as we have seen – between aiming to perform a given work, on the one hand, and aiming to produce a performance that conforms to the explicit and implicit instructions communicated by the author of that work, on the other. A performer of a given theatrical work, it might be claimed, must aim to be true to something somehow embodied in, but not identical to, the explicit and implicit instructions in the playscript. We shall turn shortly to some ways in which this might be understood.

A third question that arises with respect to musical performances falling under the classical paradigm concerns the nature and value of authentic performances. We saw, in Chapter 4, that historical authenticity is generally glossed in terms of being true to the work in some sense. But, while many performances seem to aim at being true to the text of a play, we find relatively little artistic or scholarly interest in the idea of staging historically authentic theatrical performances that, by analogy with historically authentic musical performances, attempt to replicate an ideal period performance of a theatrical work as defined by its contextualized playscript. There are indeed some who try to define theatrical authenticity in such terms. For example, Robert K. Sarlòs argues for the importance of reconstructing an ideal performance of a dramatic work that not only meets the explicit prescriptions of the text but also respects period performance practice in its style (see Sarlòs 1989). But, where such performances are presented, their interest seems more antiquarian than artistic. Consider, for example, the interests that seem to motivate the staging of Shakespearean plays at the reconstructed Globe Theatre.

This is, in fact, what we might expect if the defense of historically authentic performance of musical works mounted at the end of Chapter 4 is on the right track. The suggestion there, we may recall, was that performances of musical works that use period instruments and conform to period performative practice can serve our interest in understanding the performable works by providing us with insight into their constitutive prescriptions. To the extent that composers expect that their works will be performed in a certain way, these expectations may affect what a composer prescribes, given the kind of sound sequence he or she seeks to realize in performance. An authentic performance can provide some insight into such decisions on the composer's part, and this can supplement other knowledge we may have of the musico-historical context in which the composer was working.

In the theatrical case, on the other hand, where parallel contextual factors may bear upon the construction of a play, we can usually understand why the playwright constructed a play in a particular way in light of such factors merely by locating the text of the play in its historical setting. It is not obvious that we need to attend a historically authentic performance of, say, *King Lear*, to understand how certain features of period practice explain features of the play. Similarly, we do not need to attend a performance of a Shakespearean comedy with an all-male cast in order to understand various references to cross-dressing in the dialogue. It is sufficient that we understand that period performances used only male actors. Indeed, what seems to bear equally on our interrogative interest in Shakespearean drama is knowledge of the dramatist's expectations as to the conduct of the *audience*. For example, spectators tended to leave when a favored character died, which might explain why the deaths of major characters are grouped at the end of the play![4] But, again, to serve our interrogative interest in the play, we do not need to attend a performance in which the rest of the audience behaves in the way that period audiences did.

I asked a few paragraphs ago whether our willingness to accept, under the labels of particular dramatic works, performances that depart substantially from both playscript and period performance practice can be reconciled with the requirements of the classical paradigm. I suggested that this might be possible if being true to the work – that at which a performer of the work should aim – were less closely linked than in the musical case to being faithful to the artist's explicit or implicit instructions for the work. A looser construal of what it is to be true to the work might, I suggested, furnish us with guidelines enabling us to consider in a principled way whether a performance should count as being *of* a given play. It is only where we have such guidelines that the classical paradigm's notion of a performance being *of* a performable work can get any purchase. And such guidelines will also illuminate what it is to *succeed* in being true to a theatrical work if this is not to be understood in terms of the kind of authenticity sought in some performances of classical music. We might consider two proposals as to how truth to a theatrical work might be conceived, if not in terms of conformity to what is explicit or implicit in the playscript. First, it can be claimed that a performance of a performable theatrical work must aim to be true to *the story* or to *the fictional world* of the play, in some way. Second, following up on one suggested account of musical authenticity, authentic performance of a dramatic work might be held accountable to the *spirit* of the play, in some sense. Let us look at each of these suggestions in turn.

Woodruff furnishes us with a good example of the first approach. In line with his claim that theater in general is "the art that makes human action worth watching for a measured time," he proposes that we take the essence of a play "as a *piece of theater*" to be that which, in non-contested performances of the play, makes the action most worth watching (Woodruff 2008, 50). This, he suggests, is the principal characters and the plot, which are the reasons why we watch the play (58):

> To find the essence of a piece of mimetic theater, identify the main character (or characters) and the principal conflict (or conflicts) that are resolved in the plot. By "plot" I mean the structured action that keeps our attention and measures the time for a theatrical performance. By "character" I mean someone who attracts our close attention. (Woodruff 2008, 55)

In the case of *Hamlet*, for example, the barest essence of the play is that its main character is Hamlet and that it is about resolving certain conflicts generated by Hamlet's felt need to seek revenge for the killing of his father. It is not necessary, for a performance to be *of* Hamlet, that the dialogue specified in the text of the play be retained, or even that the outcome of the plot be identical. Woodruff allows that one could play *Hamlet* with a happy ending as long as one stuck closely enough to the structure of the play in other ways (2008, 61). If so, it might seem that what Berthold and Magda saw was indeed a performance of *King Lear*, as were the 1681 performances directed by Nahum Tate in which the Cordelia character was also spared, albeit in a less flamboyant fashion.

Woodruff mentions but accords relatively little significance to something that might be thought to be at least a necessary constraint on a performance's being of a particular play – namely, that it stand in an appropriate historical-intentional relation to the authoring of the play. In Chapter 4, we endorsed an analogous constraint upon something's being a performance (but not a work-instance) of a given musical work. Woodruff only comments that standing in a *Hamlet* "tradition" is not what makes a performance a performance of *Hamlet* (2008, 60). This is certainly true but it doesn't indicate what significance standing in such a tradition does have. However, it would not be difficult to supplement Woodruff's account with a historical-intentional condition on a performance's being of a given work.

A more serious concern is that, if we identify the essence of a play with its "characters and plot" in such a way that we allow at least some Nahum Tate-like performances to count as genuine performances of *Hamlet* or *Lear*, then it is not clear what justifies claiming that the characters in these performances *are* Hamlet or Lear. In a sense, we have exchanged one problem – what is essential for something to be a performance of a given play? – for another problem – what is essential for a character to be a particular character from a particular play? – without any obvious gain in tractability. What is it, for example, for the main character of a play to be Hamlet? Not, surely, just that he is a prince who is concerned to avenge the supposed murder of his father by his uncle possibly acting with the tacit collusion of his mother. Woodruff suggests that the more we supplement this thin description with other characteristics, such as being disturbed, brilliant, passionate, reflective, book-loving, yet capable of violence (2008, 50), the more willing we will be to identify a character with Hamlet. But what makes *these* traits the important ones? More generally, why are we willing to countenance a performance of *Hamlet* in which some things are changed, but much less willing to countenance a performance in which other things are changed, in the characters and plot?

In deciding which departures from a playscript of a play are consistent with a given character's presence in a performance, we might be attracted by an alternative strategy that would reverse Woodruff's approach. This character is Hamlet, or Lear, it might be said, because the play in which this character plays a particular role is *Hamlet* or *King Lear*,[5] where this is not itself to be decided merely by reference to characters or plot. If it is asked what *more* than plot and characters is involved in being a performance of *Hamlet* or *King Lear*, an answer might appeal to the "spirit" of each of these plays. This is the second strategy canvassed above that might reconcile a version of the classical paradigm as applied to theatrical performances with the way we label such performances in our theatrical practice. David Thacker, for example, claims that in staging a play like *Hamlet* or *King Lear*, "the aim is to find what the play is about and how to make that meaning clear." The director must "attempt to understand what the drift of the play was for Shakespeare and then search for some close contemporary equivalent that will make the play precise, clear, and immediate for the audience" (Thacker 1992, 23–24, cited in Rubidge 1996, 229). The idea, I take it, is that what is at least partly constitutive of a play is its *point*, what we take to be a playwright's reason for prescribing a particular sequence of actions involving particular characters embroiled in a particular plot. It is because we are doubtful whether Nahum Tate-like performances that transform a play like *King Lear* from an unbearable tragedy into something approaching a melodrama preserve the point of the play, in this sense, that we question whether they are performances of the play, however faithful they may be in other respects to its characters and plot.

Talk here of the point of a play calls for two comments. First, we may recall that the same term was used in Chapter 1 in discussing the nature of our artistic interest in a performance of Yvonne Rainer's *Room Service*. If our interest in something as an artistic manifold is always in part an interrogative interest in the ordering of that manifold, the hierarchical nature of any explanation of the ordering of a manifold refers us to an overriding aim or point that various subordinate aims subserve. This provides a reason for giving the point of a performable work priority in determining when we have a genuine performance of that work. In the theatrical case, things are slightly more complicated. When we take an artistic interest in a sequence of actions presented on a stage, or in a set of prescriptions for such a sequence of actions, what might be termed our "external" interrogative interest in the ordering of this sequence usually complements our "internal" interrogative interest in why the characters act as they do – our interest in what motivates them – and in what actually occurs in the plot. When an artistic manifold presents a narrative, both an internal and an external interrogative interest in that manifold are elements in a proper engagement with it *as* an artistic manifold.

But, second, it is crucial that we do justice to the manner in which the point of a standard dramatic work is embedded in the particularity of the narrative of that work. A related issue arose in the previous chapter when we considered Randall Dipert's observation that an artist's intentions are hierarchically ordered, with high level intentions that pertain to certain effects to be elicited in the audience. Aron Edidin, we may recall, notes that a composer's high level intention is not merely to produce a certain kind of effect in the listener, but to produce such an effect by particular musical means. In the same way, we might insist that the point of a play is not something that can be expressed in abstraction from the kinds of artistic material with which the artist is working. The point of *King Lear*, for example, is not merely to bring out for the viewer the supreme importance of certain human virtues in the face of the unbearable tragedies that beset us in our flawed attempts at happiness, but to do this through the viewer's reflection on the particular character and situation of Lear, as defined by the broad features of the plot. Thus, in stressing the importance of being true to the spirit – the point – of *King Lear* in performances of the play, we are not denying the relevance of character and plot. Rather, we are insisting that the import of departing from specific aspects of the scripted characters and plot can be gauged only when we weigh those aspects in the balance of the point that the play is making by means of those characters and that plot. This kind of complex measure of being true to a play might allow us to argue in a principled way that the relocation of modified versions of the characters and plot of *Measure for Measure* in Prohibition era Chicago is a genuine and interesting performance of Shakespeare's play while also arguing that what was presented before Berthold and Magda was not a performance of *King Lear*.

The kind of complex measure of truth to a play just sketched would, I think, provide us with the resources needed to defend the application of the classical paradigm to the kinds of contemporary dramatic performances we have been considering. It allows us to allocate such performances to particular performable works in a principled way, by requiring of a performance of a given work *W* that the performers stand in the right kind of historical-intentional relation to the authoring of *W* and intend that their performance be true to *W* in the sense defined. This construal of what it is for a theatrical performance to be *of* a performable dramatic work parallels in structure the account given earlier of musical performances that fall under the classical paradigm: the difference lies in the construal of what it is to be true to a work. And it also allows us to give a clear sense to the idea of correct performance in terms of *success* in being true to the work in this sense. The principles also have some bite in their critical bearing on our standard ways of classifying things. For example, it is far from clear that the emplotted point of Shakespeare's history plays is preserved in performances that drastically relocate them in such a way that we lose a purchase on those aspects of the original historical context of the drama upon which some of the emplotted point depends.[6]

3   Challenges to the Classical Paradigm in Theater

We have considered three ways in which one might characterize, by appeal to the notion of truth to a performable theatrical work, the conditions under which we have a performance of that work: (1) in terms of aiming to reproduce the letter of, and perhaps also the period style of, the work; (2) in terms of aiming to be true to the characters and plot of the work; and (3) in terms of aiming to be true to the emplotted point of the work. The first option, I have suggested, is rarely instanced in its strong form in theatrical performance, seems to be widely adhered to in a weaker form that aims merely at conformity to the playscript of a theatrical work. The third option, I have argued, is preferable to the second if we wish to subsume under the classical paradigm contemporary theatrical productions that are uninterested in being true to a theatrical work in the first sense. We might then see the first and third senses of truth to a theatrical work as defining two traditions of work-performance in theater – the more traditional text-based conception, and the more contemporary point-based conception. To count as performing a theatrical work at all, we might say, performers must at least intend to be true to the work in one of these senses. This intention may function only as a constraint on interpretation rather than as the primary motivation for the performance. When this intention *is* the primary motivation for a performance, however, it is natural to talk of a concern with authenticity and with truth to the work construed on the stricter reading of our first sense.

These two notions of truth to a theatrical work might seem analogous to the different roles ascribed to instrumentation in defining performable musical works, as noted in Chapter 5. But the latter is a historical change in the ways in which composers and performers thought about musical works, and thus, arguably, a change in the nature of the works themselves. In the theatrical case, on the other hand, our two conceptions of truth to a performable work are often applied to the *same* theatrical works. It is *King Lear*, for example, that supposedly admits of both text-based and point-based performances. But, if a performance is to be true to a work, should we not require that it conforms to the *artist*'s conception – or the artist's culture's conception – of what truth to a work involves, that is, of what a work prescribes for its correct performance? If so, then, unless Shakespeare endorsed both text-based and point-based construals of what his plays prescribe, at most one of our two conceptions of truth to a performed work will itself be true to Shakespeare's works – true, that is, to the playwright's sense – or the playwright's culture's sense – of what his or her works prescribe for their correct performance. I say "at most one" for reasons that will become clearer in Chapter 8, where we shall return to these questions.

What concerns us here, however, is that many productions that sail under the flags of well-known performable works seem to have no interest in being true to these works however construed. In his "existentialist" interpretation of *King Lear*, for example, Peter Brook had no qualms either about changing aspects of the characters and plot of the play as standardly understood, or about the possibility that his production was not true to the spirit of the play. He had no such qualms because he had no desire that his production should be true to Shakespeare's play in any of the senses just discussed. Rather, he saw himself as doing something quite different. But what is this "something quite different" that calls itself *King Lear* yet is not constrained by the require- ment of being true to Shakespeare's play in any of our senses?

Brook's conception of what he was doing owed much to the ideas of Jerzy Grotowski, one of the most influential theorists of theater in the second half of the twentieth century. James Hamilton has written about the influence of Grotowski and other twentieth-century theorists such as Bertolt Brecht and Antonin Artaud on developments in theatrical performance (2007, ch. 1). Artaud's "theater of cruelty" calls for a theater that employs distinc- tively theatrical means to achieve its ends. Such a call arises out of reflection on the nature of theater as an art form, and from the application to theater of the modernist idea that art forms should pursue artistic ends through the use of their distinctive media. Theater, Artaud maintained, should not be viewed as the handmaid of literature, and theatrical performances should not be thought of as accountable to independent literary works. Rather, the essential elements of theatrical performance are the performative capaci- ties of the actors as they bear upon an audience, and a performance should aim at the articulation of a particular artistic content through the manipula- tion and deployment of these elements. In Grotowski, this finds its expres- sion in the idea of a "poor theater" that takes as its resources only what the performer brings to the stage, eschewing the use of props and drawing the audience into a "therapeutic" engagement with the actors (see Grotowski 1988, 211–218). Where a performance takes place under the label of a per- formable work, as with Grotowski's 1964 production of *The Tragical History of Doctor Faustus*, Marlowe's play functions as a resource in the pursuit of these essentially theatrical goals, but there is no obligation to be true to the play in any of the ways just discussed.

If, in such cases, there is no imperative to be true to a performable work but a literary text is still drawn upon in certain ways, how should we conceive the relationship between the theatrical performance and the text? Hamilton proposes that we make sense of such theatrical practices in terms of what he labels the "ingredients model":

> [T]he texts used in theatrical performances [are] just so many *ingredients*, sources of works and other ideas for theatrical performances, alongside other ingredients that are available from a variety of other sources. Works of dramatic literature, in particular, are not regarded as especially or intrinsically fitting ingredients for performances. As ingredients they are but one kind among many possible resources of words for a theatrical performance. (J. Hamilton 2007, 31)

Hamilton cites the program for Grotowski's production of *The Constant Prince* which relates the production to the eponymous text by Calderón de la Barca in the following way: "The producer does not mean to play *The Constant Prince* as it is ... He aims at giving his own vision of the play, and the relation of his scenario to the original text is that of a musical variation to the original musical theme" (J. Hamilton 2007, 8).

These reflections on twentieth-century theatrical productions might suggest a pluralist view of theatrical performance. On such a view, while many – perhaps most – performances fall in one way or another under the classical paradigm, other productions and performances fit better with the ingredients model. Indeed, pluralism is necessary to account for theatrical performances that make no pretension to be *of* anything – for example, the largely improvisational *commedia delle'arte* tradition in Europe in the sixteenth and seventeenth centuries, and the flourishing contemporary tradition of improvisational performance. But, it might seem, the developments in theater that Hamilton describes must be understood as reactions against a theatrical tradition whose self-understanding is given by the classical paradigm. And this tradition is one that obtains not only in our own theatrical practice but also in other cultures where theater has a place.

But Hamilton does not advocate such a pluralism. He makes the much bolder claim that the ingredients model provides the best account of theatrical performance as a whole. And, as we shall see, he is not alone in questioning whether the classical paradigm has any part to play in a philosophical understanding of theater. He endorses and defends the following thesis: "A [theatrical] performance is ... never a performance *of* some other work nor is it ever a performance *of* a text or *of* anything initiated in a text; so no faithfulness standard – of any kind – is required for determining what work a performance is of." He also defends the thesis that "theatrical performances are artworks in their own rights" (J. Hamilton 2007, 32). But, as we have already noted in discussing musical performance, one can grant that artistic performances are artworks in their own right without thereby denying that they are performances of performable works. Indeed, Carroll's "recipe" view of theatrical works and theatrical performances freely admits the artistic standing of the performances. Thus we need to separate any arguments that Hamilton offers for his second thesis from arguments for his first thesis. Given this caveat, what reasons can be given for thinking that *no* theatrical performances fall under the classical paradigm, where the latter allows of interpretations in terms of truth to a performable work in either of our senses.

In a recent defense of his view, Hamilton claims that the direct argument for the general applicability of the ingredients model to theatrical performance is just the history of theater since the mid nineteenth century (see J. Hamilton 2009a, 5).[7] This, as it stands, is an odd claim to make. For Hamilton's attack on what he terms the "text-based" model of theatrical performance is predicated on the assumption that, prior to the contemporary developments initiated by figures like Artaud and Grotowski, theatrical companies conceived of what they were doing in terms of the classical paradigm. Theatrical performances were taken to be interpretations of theatrical works, as Wollheim and Carroll claim them to be. If the history of theater is to provide us with an argument for the general applicability of the ingredients model, then it seems we must take the self-understanding of those engaged in traditional theater to be mistaken. The claim must be that, properly understood, traditional theater, no less than contemporary avant-garde theater, accords to literary texts or performable works no more than an ingredient role in the generation of theatrical performances.

Hamilton does not provide the kind of extensive historical survey of actual theatrical practice that might seem necessary to support such a comprehensive "error theory" of traditional theatrical self-understanding. Thus, it seems, the burden must fall upon his more general claims about the ways in which theatrical companies, traditional and modern, prepare for a performance. These claims deserve serious consideration because, as we have seen, it is in terms of its ability to reflectively explain our critical and performative practice that a given model of artistic performance is to be assessed. We must ask whether, when pre-existing theatrical "works" play a part in the process generative of traditional theatrical performances, this is better explained by some version of the classical paradigm or by the ingredients model.

Hamilton relies upon a range of hypothetical theatrical productions, reflecting the range of things one might have encountered in a theater in the latter part of the twentieth century. In each case, we begin with a company of performers who have a copy of the text of *Hedda Gabler*, and the resulting performance issues out of a process of group rehearsal. In the first few cases, there is also a director who has a particular vision of the kind of performance to be produced. The resulting productions are very different, however, as we can see if we consider three examples.

The first two productions begin with a meeting of the company where scripts are distributed to the performers cast to play the different characters in Ibsen's play. In the most traditional production, *Hedda-to-Hedda*, the director precedes rehearsals by informing the company that their interpretation will, as far as possible, follow Ibsen's text and his stage directions. A second production, *Gabler at a Distance*, differs only in that the director's interpretation requires that the company incorporates a number of "Brechtian" devices:

> [A]t times an actor may say another character's lines, prefacing them with either "And he said ..." or "And she said ..." As the company rehearses, additional line reading techniques are introduced. Occasionally a performer will be called upon to preface her or his own character's lines with "And I said ..." The performers may be asked to state the stage directions Ibsen wrote in the script and others of the director's invention, so that each character sometimes describes what she or he does as she or he is doing it. During the rehearsal process, the company comes to employ other techniques that are consistent with whatever effects are achieved by the techniques already mentioned. (J. Hamilton 2007, 44–45)

One of the least traditional productions is *Something to Tell You*:

> A company takes every line in Ibsen's script and rewrites it as a sentence that some member of the company could say truthfully in front of and to an audience. The company makes most of those sentences simple declarative sentences. They write as conditionals sentences forming a certain number of key passages. The company thinks of places in which the same sentence could be repeated for interesting acoustic effect. The company decides who says what sentences, bearing in mind that each sentence could be said by more than one of them. The company now works on rhythmic and dynamic patterns, listening together to a lot of rock and roll and jazz, paying attention to rhythmic patterns and opportunities for musical irony in their script. The company organizes the resulting text for the performances using an explicitly musical form – for example, the result could be a set of themes and variations. The company rehearses and performs with the aim of creating the kind of sonic experience one gets from music. (J. Hamilton 2007, 47)

On either of our models of what it is to aim at a performance that is true to an independent theatrical work, *Hedda-to-Hedda* will qualify as a performance of *Hedda Gabler* and *Something to Tell You* will not. *Gabler at a Distance* obviously does not aim to be true to *Hedda Gabler* in our first sense, nor is it clear that it aims for truth to the work in our third sense, since the focus on Brechtian devices might not preserve the point of Ibsen's play. Hamilton, however, thinks that, rather than focusing on these kinds of considerations, we should be more impressed by continuities in the way in which the three productions were put together. His descriptions stress the elements of deliberation, extemporization, experimentation, and discovery that enter into the preparatory process, the choices open to the director and performers, and the fact that the text is always *used* by the performers to realize the general performative goals of the company – it is always a means to an independent performance, rather than something that, in itself, imposes any constraints on performance. As Hamilton characterizes this general feature of theatrical productions, "a company arrive at the first rehearsal and are given a script. There is no logically predetermined way for them to use the script. There is not even a requirement, of logic or of art, that they actually do use it. This is a situation in which a number of things can be decided" (J. Hamilton 2007, 203). This supports the further claim that where, as in *Hedda-to-Hedda*, we have the appearance of a theatrical performance falling under the classical paradigm, the performers are merely exercising one among a number of possible options as to how to use the script as an ingredient in a production.

Do these kinds of considerations support the claim that the history of theater establishes the general applicability of the ingredients model to theatrical performance? We should note two things. First, the argument as I have presented it assumes that, whatever their other differences, theatrical productions conform to a particular model of how public performances issue from the improvisatory and exploratory activity of an ensemble in rehearsal. In the tradition of preparing for theatrical performances with which we are familiar, the final form of a theatrical performance usually reflects changes made as a result of innovations introduced in rehearsal. This applies even to performances that seem to conform to the classical paradigm in striving, among other things, to facilitate the appreciation of a performable work. Furthermore, in theatrical practice, improvisations by performers in rehearsal may result in new constraints on subsequent performances.[8] We may term this the "ensemble revision" model of the genesis of theatrical performance. This model is widely acknowledged by contemporary playwrights and actors alike. Tom Stoppard, for example, thanks the director of *Jumpers* for "insights and inventiveness … throughout rehearsals," and Peggy Ashcroft characterizes rehearsal as "the giving birth" of performance. Preparation for the initial performance of a modern production, whether the germinating text is contemporary or historical, typically involves between 120 and 160 hours of rehearsals, the vast majority of these either partial rehearsals, attended by those actors involved in a given segment of the performance, or, more usually, group rehearsals involving the entire company.[9]

However, and this brings us to the second point, it is not clear that, even if we grant all of this, it is sufficient to establish that all theatrical performances make better sense under the ingredients model than under the classical paradigm. First, as we shall see in Chapter 8, the ensemble revision model of theatrical production is not universally applicable even within the Western theatrical tradition. Where there are, within this tradition, norms of theatrical production that don't involve ensemble revision of the sort found in Hamilton's range of scenarios, the foregoing argument for the ingredients model of theatrical performance cannot apply.

Second, even where we do have productions that involve ensemble revision, it isn't clear why this establishes that the ingredients model accounts for such productions better than the classical paradigm. Take *Hedda-for-Hedda*, for example. While performances of this production indeed reflect decisions and modifications made in rehearsal, those decisions and modifications seem to be governed by the company's overarching aim of being true to Ibsen's play in the first of our senses. Hamilton claims that, even if the company belongs to a tradition that always uses a text in this way, their treating it as the script of a performable work is still an unforced choice on their part, as the ingredients model requires. He supports this claim by appealing to an ideal companion company belonging to the same tradition who *would* see alternative ways of engaging with the text. So, where companies seek to faithfully realize an independent work, we have "performances that adopt constraints that are not binding in the tradition, but are taken as though they were" (J. Hamilton 2007, 210).

But this is rather mystifying. For suppose that we have a tradition where both performers and audience assume that the right, or the only, way to engage with the text of a dramatic work is to seek to mount a production that is faithful to the text of that work. In what sense does the observation that "objectively" there are other options open to both performers and audience show that performances intended by the performers and understood by the audience to be *of* a work are not really *of* the work at all? By analogy, it is "objectively" possible for musicians performing in a classical orchestra to treat the score as merely one "ingredient" in a group improvisation. But this surely does not demonstrate that their actual performance, which is intended by the performers and understood by the audience to conform to the classical paradigm, is not really *of* a musical work at all. Hamilton has responded to this kind of argument by rejecting the musical analogy on the grounds that the historical traditions of music and theater are quite different (J. Hamilton 2009b, 83). But this seems to beg the question, given that what is at issue is precisely how the theatrical tradition is rightly understood.

More generally, if we hold models of artistic performance accountable to their ability to reflectively explain critical and performative practice, the classical paradigm surely makes better sense of what is going on in *Hedda-to-Hedda* than the ingredients model, and avoids having to view the tradition of literary theater as massively self-deceived. This suggests that our initial response to Hamilton's presentation of the ingredients model as an explanation of performances like Grotowski's *The Constant Prince* was the right one. There is no single model – not even a single model of the classical paradigm, as we have seen – that can be usefully applied to theatrical performance as a whole. Theater, like music, requires a pluralistic approach which limits, but does not eliminate, the scope of the classical paradigm.

Hamilton is not the only person to argue for the general inapplicability of the classical paradigm to theater, however. David Osipovich (2006) has argued for a similar conclusion. Osipovich takes as his starting point a more restricted critique of the classical paradigm. David Saltz (2001) has argued that individual theatrical performances are properly seen as being *of productions*, not of theatrical works. Salz maintains that productions that bear the names of theatrical works are not rightly understood as guided by an overriding intention to be faithful to such works. Rather, the decisions that shape productions are often purely practical, depending upon such things as the nature of the performance space and the human resources available. Also, where decisions *are* made on artistic or aesthetic grounds, these often reflect the artistic or aesthetic goals of the company itself, rather than those of the playwright. Thus an independent theatrical work is, in Hamilton's terms, merely an ingredient upon which a company can draw in a production.

Osipovich argues for a more radical conclusion. Just as there are extra-work considerations that shape productions, so, he argues, there are extra-production considerations that shape performances. The "liveness model," as he terms it, takes a defining condition of theatrical performance to be the co-occurrence at a given time of an act of showing and an act of watching what is shown. Because the performers – those who are doing the showing – must always be sensitive to, and willing to respond to, the responses of those who are watching, all theatrical performances are "unscriptable" – that is to say, it is impossible in principle to specify in advance what the performers should do in order for the performance to succeed.

> [E]very time one [performs live] one has to decide, based on the audience's responses, whether *this* time a particular set of tactics will work. But the fact that this decision has to be made during the course of every performance … means that every performance has a unique set of circumstances. Because this set of aesthetically significant circumstances is based on the interaction of a particular audience with a particular cast on a given night, it is *unscriptable*, either beforehand or afterward, since every night the actors will have to decide if the way they have been "doing" it will work for this *particular house*. (Osipovich 2006, 464)

If all theatrical performances are by their very nature unscriptable than, it is claimed, there is no script against which they can be measured to gauge their fidelity or success, and thus they are never *of* something independent of themselves. This argument, if it applies to the idea that performances are of independent performable works, will apply equally to the idea that performances are of independent productions.

We shall examine in Chapter 9 the idea that artistic performance requires the presence of an audience. But we may wonder how the liveness model really calls into question the idea that at least some theatrical performances are *of* independent works or productions. For, as we saw in the previous section, the intention to be true to such a work or production can be understood in a number of ways: in terms of fidelity to a script of some kind, certainly, but also in terms of being true to the emplotted point of that work or production. If a troupe of performers indeed intends to be true to a work or production in this latter way, then, while the requirements of liveness may indeed lead to various departures from a script, they will lead to departures from truth to the work in the sense specified only if the performers betray the very aim of the performance. Indeed, a tacit recognition of this point seems built into the very argument for unscriptability. To ask whether a particular set of tactics will "work" for a particular house presupposes some goal that one is trying to achieve. It is only by reference to such a goal, as end, that one can question the efficacy of certain tactics, as means. That liveness calls for certain departures from a given script or way of presenting such a script only makes sense in terms of an end pursued. It is the idea of being true to the emplotted point of a work that arguably provides us with the end pursued in many contemporary theatrical performances, such as those staged by David Thacker, as we saw. Scriptability, then, only seems to be an issue if one thinks of truth to the work in terms of conformity to an explicit script. And, if a company's goal *is* to stage a performance that is true to a work in this first sense, it is *this* that will define the end pursued relative to which the demands of liveness must be answered. So in this case, it seems, the performance *is* scriptable.

4   Dance and the Classical Paradigm

In Chapter 1 we considered a dance performance attended by Noël Carroll and Sally Banes. In following their lead in describing it as a performance of Yvonne Rainer's *Room Service*, we treated the performance as one falling under the classical paradigm, and *Room Service* itself as a performable work. This seemed a natural way to talk at the time, before we started to think more carefully about the status of artistic performances. It is certainly the way in which we often talk about classical dance. We say that we saw a performance of Tchaikovsky's *The Nutcracker*, for example. But we might also say that we saw a performance of Balanchine's *The Nutcracker*, meaning that we saw a performance of the version of Tchaikovsky's work choreographed by George Balanchine for the New York City Ballet in 1954. Indeed, given the place that Balanchine's production has assumed in American cultural life, an American balletomane might be more likely to speak in the second way than in the first. This might seem analogous to saying that one saw a performance of Peter Brook's *King Lear*. As we saw in the previous section, we can distinguish, in theater, between works, productions, and performances, although theorists differ as to the kinds of dependence relations holding between these entities. However, as we shall see, the relationships between dance works, dance productions, and dance performances prove to be even more tangled. [10] Additionally, some writers have raised more fundamental questions about the applicability of the classical paradigm to dance performances. Interestingly, as we shall see, the reasons for this skepticism differ from those that have led us to prefer alternative models for at least some musical and theatrical performances.

If dance performances are to be rightly subsumed under the classical paradigm in its standard form, then our best explanation of what is going on in these performances must construe them as attempts to provide interpretive realizations of the prescriptions of particular performable works. These prescriptions must exist independently of particular performances and must allow of multiple realizations. We shall also need a viable notion of what it is for a dance performance to be a correct rendering of the work performed, and a serviceable means for determining at least in principle which performance events are performances of which works. While a performable work's defining prescriptions can be orally transmitted, they are conveyed, in the musical and theatrical cases with which we are most familiar, by a score or a script respectively. The simplest way to extend the classical paradigm to dance, then, would involve an analogous means of making explicit what a given performable work of dance prescribes.

Theorists who apply the classical paradigm to musical and theatrical performances generally take a similar approach to dance. Wollheim and Carroll, for example, take dance works to be types and dance performances to be their tokens. A performer produces a token of a dance work, qua type, by interpreting the "recipe" provided by the creator of the work. Graham McFee has provided the most detailed defense of such a view. "With dance, as with music," he maintains, "there are at least two 'objects of appreciation': the work itself and tonight's performance of it" (McFee 2000, 546). Dance performances are tokens of an abstract type, although, in addition to the work, we must acknowledge, as an intermediate type, a performer's interpretation of a role or dance. In performing a given dance work, the dancer(s)'s movements follow a recipe for the dance.

McFee proposes that we apply to dance the following (defeasible) "thesis of notationality" more generally applicable in the performed arts:[11] "Performance A and performance B are performances of the same work of art ... just in case both satisfy or instantiate some particular 'text' in a notation agreed by the knowledgeable in the art form to be an adequate notation for that art form" (McFee 2007).[12] According to McFee, our sense of the identity of a particular dance work, and of what is required for its correct performance, is tied to the idea of a characterization, in such a notation, of the sequence of movements to be executed by performers. Such a characterization distinguishes, in the actual sequence of movements executed by one who performs the dance, those features taken to be constitutive of the piece danced from other features that represent either interpretations or errors on the part of the performer. It is, then, in terms of the performer's or performers' intention to manifest the features captured in the notation that we can make sense of the idea that performances are of particular dances. As a matter of fact, as McFee admits, most contemporary dances are never notated. But what matters, he claims, is the notatability in principle of a performance of a dance. For the latter implies at least a tacit understanding of what is constitutive of the dance performed.

As critics have pointed out,[13] and as McFee (2007) has acknowledged, the thesis of notationality, whatever its virtues when applied to classical music, faces some serious problems if applied to dance. First, two notational systems for representing movement have been used in relation to dance performance. One of these, Labanotation, is applicable to movement in general while the other, Benesh notation, is usually viewed as more suitable for recording movements in classical ballet. There is not, as in the musical case, agreement amongst "the knowledgeable" as to whether either system can capture the relevant features of a given dance performance. This lack of consensus reflects aspects of the very nature of dance performance. As Francis Sparshott (2004) has argued, the idea that we can identify a dance work with a notatable prescription to perform a certain sequence of movements assumes that we have a notation capable of capturing those features of the movements that are constitutive of the work. The principal medium of dance, Sparshott maintains, is the unspeaking human body in motion and at rest. But the latter admits of many different levels of description. We can describe it in terms of the quasi-mechanical operation of systems of motor programs, for example, or of such systems as elements in the organic activity of a living being, or of the execution thereby of meaningful human gestures, or of these gestures as executed by a gendered human being of a particular age, or of the meanings of these gestures given the social status or context of the agent. Of course, we might say the same thing about any medium used in the arts. In painting, for example, as we saw in Chapter 1, it is standard to draw a distinction between the *physical* medium of pigment distributed on canvas and the *artistic* medium of brushstrokes, impasto, and composition (see D. Davies 2003). But the problem for dance, Sparshott suggests, is that the available notational systems represent movement and rest of the human body at a more basic level of description than seems appropriate if we are concerned with these as elements in an artistic medium. These notational systems break movements down into teachable steps, whereas the identity of the dance seems to require a more abstract level of description in terms of meaningful gestures.

Even if these difficulties can be overcome, there is a more fundamental problem. McFee assumes that what is constitutive of a dance work is a particular sequence of movements – the sequence that the notation is supposed to capture. But, if we look at how we characterize performances in dance practice, we find a much more complex phenomenon. Take as a simple example *The Nutcracker*. This work was commissioned as a ballet, with music and associated narrative by Tchaikovsky and choreography by either Marius Petipa or Lev Ivanov, and the first performance took place in St. Petersburg in December 1892. McFee's "notatability" conception of what the dance work prescribes for its performances would suggest that the constitutive features of the work are the movements specified in the choreography, presumably taken in concert with a score for the music that the movements are designed to accompany. However, this doesn't seem to fit the subsequent history of the work. While productions labeled as being of *The Nutcracker* over the first 30 or so years generally aimed to follow the original choreography, subsequent productions so labeled have freely departed from it. Indeed, this applies to some of the most famous productions generally taken to be of this work, such as Balanchine's 1954 production mentioned earlier and Baryshnikov's 1976 production. Both of these involved for the most part completely original choreography. If we ask what is common to all of the productions generally accepted as being of *The Nutcracker*, the least plausible answer is their choreography. But equally implausible, if we are not to radically overrule the classifications made in our practice, is the suggestion that they share a plot or a set of characters with the original production. Some accepted productions completely revise both plot and characters, and there is wide variation in apparently essential features of the narrative, such as the ending, the presence of a central romantic theme, and the status of much of what transpires as reality or fantasy. What is relatively constant is the use of Tchaikovsky's score, although even here there are variations in the ordering of the constituent pieces and sometimes supplementation with other material.

A notational theorist might, of course, simply deny that those purported performances of *The Nutcracker* that make no attempt to comply with the original choreography are rightly classified under that label. But *The Nutcracker* is simply an extreme example of a more general phenomenon in classical ballet, where performances taken to be of a given dance work are allowed to vary considerably in choreography. If the classical paradigm is to apply to such performances, we cannot identify the performable work with a specific set of prescriptions for movement.

But with what, then, should we identify it? Where a work originates in the composition of music specifically intended to accompany the presentation in dance of a particular narrative, we might hope to identify the work with this combination of music and narrative. While this may work for many classical ballets such as *Swan Lake*, we have seen that it can only strictly apply to *The Nutcracker* if we are willing to disqualify many purported performances of the work. Nor is it clear when we should say that a performance preserves the narrative of a work. In the face of productions such as Matthew Bourne's 2006 *Swan Lake*, with male swans, one can understand Selma Jean Cohen's earlier complaint that, "if plot and characters can be so radically altered, if dances can be shifted from one place to another, added or omitted, how can we identify *Swan Lake*?" (1982, ii). Our strategy for dealing with theatrical works that dramatically depart from what is prescribed in the playscript was to ask whether the production aims to preserve the emplotted point of the performable work. But the notion of the point of a classical ballet is less sharply drawn, and it is not obvious that a parallel strategy will be helpful here.

On the other hand, we cannot identify a dance work with the mere combination of a piece of music and the intention that this be used as a framework for dance of some unspecified kind. For one thing, there are contemporary and traditional dances that lack a musical accompaniment. For another, where a dance work avails itself of a previously existing piece of music, we do not want to say that all dances performed to that piece of music are performances of the same dance work. For example, the repertoire of a Montreal modern dance company in the early 1990s included an expressive routine performed to the accompaniment of Harold Budd's piece "Gypsy Violins." But, if another dance company's repertoire independently incorporates a very differently choreographed dance to be performed to that same piece of music, we surely have two separate works of dance.

What conclusions should we draw from these reflections? Perhaps only that, if we wish to apply the classical paradigm to dance, we must be prepared to countenance works that differ considerably in the kinds of things that are constitutive of them. Music, narrative, and choreography may all play constitutive roles for particular works, and our best guide in determining what is required for the performance of a particular work may be the classifications manifest in dance practice. Philosophers can perhaps do no more, here, than propose the classical paradigm as a general model and note certain general constraints on the individuation of works as I have just done. This is perhaps what we should expect, given the history of dance performance.[14] Dance has occupied an ambiguous position in the performing arts. On the one hand, most eighteenth-century thinking took the distinguishing feature of dance as an art to be its ability to represent actions. So conceived, dance is naturally allied to theater, and dance works may be thought to be individuated in a manner analogous to plays, albeit that in the latter case the "actions" are predominantly linguistic in nature – "speech acts," as these are often called. Classical ballets in this tradition seem to owe at least part of their identity to the narrative thread around which the individual dances are organized. Such works can therefore admit of alternative choreographies. As a result, the lack of an agreed notation for capturing finer details of the movements of dancers will not pose a serious obstacle to the idea of dance performances as performances of such works.

On the other hand, many modern dance productions eschew the representational possibilities of dance, and focus on formal or expressive properties, thereby allying dance more closely with music. In productions by choreographers such as Merce Cunningham, for example, the precise movements prescribed for the dancers seem to be crucial to the identity of the dance work – as crucial as is the precise sequence of prescribed sounds to the identity of a classical musical work.[15] Here, the lack of agreement on how to characterize the relevant movements – disagreement both on the notational system to be used and its adequacy – present more serious problems for the applicability of the classical paradigm if we accept the thesis of notationality for such productions.

There are further difficulties if we ascribe to notational representations of movements the role suggested by McFee. First, as noted earlier, there are no scores for most dance performances This, as Renee Conroy (2006) has noted, is partly because of the cost of scoring and the difficulty of getting competent notators. Furthermore, unlike in the musical case, there is no general expectation that either dancers or choreographers will be able to make or read scores for the dance performances in which they are involved. Second, and relatedly, where we do have notational representations of dance productions, they are usually made by professional notators who record what the dancers are doing in rehearsal under the direction of the choreographer. As we saw in looking at the Goodman argument in Chapter 3, however, the project of retrieving notational characterizations from performances is highly problematic, especially if this is to play a central part in the definition of performable works. It is in attempting to counter these difficulties that Goodman imposes very strict requirements on musical scores, excluding from the scored work any features of performance that might be scored in different ways, such as verbally indicated tempo and mood. In the case of dance, it is obviously a serious obstacle to the application of McFee's thesis of notationality to dance if, as we have already noted, there is no consensus as to how the fluid movements of the dancers are to be notated. For example, an arm movement can be represented either in terms of the position of the elbow or in terms of the position of elbow, wrist, and hand. While the notator, in recording what the dancers are doing, tries to distinguish between the movements prescribed by the dance and the interpretation of the dance by the dancer, this is a matter on which accomplished notators may differ. This supplements Sparshott's worries voiced earlier.

In fact, for most contemporary dances, we are in an even worse position if we want to refer a dance performance to the defining conditions of a particular dance work, perhaps as a precondition for restaging the *same* work. For what we usually possess is not a notational prescription for, or description of, a performance, but a video recording of the performance itself. Whereas the notator's decisions as to which features of the dancers' movements are constitutive of the dance and which are interpretive can at least be informed by the choreographer's instructions to the dancers, no such resources are available in a film of the finished performance. As Sarah Rubidge notes,

> video records, unlike scores and scripts, are over-determined. They inevitably document particular realizations of works by particular performers. They also record unselectively, and are ever in danger of rendering indeterminate or contingent features of a performance, such as particular performers' interpretations of a role, mistakes in execution of the work during the performance, differences in numbers of dancers as a result of injury, set, costume, and so on, determinate features of the work. (Rubidge 1996, 223)[16]

Since, as we have seen, the distinction between prescription and interpretation is central to the concept of the performable work, this represents a serious problem for dance as a performed art if specific choreography is taken to be constitutive of the dance work. It suggests that, in such cases, it is the particular performance, or production, supervised by the choreographer that functions as the work. With a piece like *Room Service*, for example, it seems that what groups performances as performances *of* that work is the presence of Rainer, as choreographer. Where we lack sufficient notational resources to identify a piece independently of the choreographer's presence, Martha Graham's remark, of her works, that "when I go, they go"[17] may strike us as a poignant acknowledgment of the situation.

It might be objected, however,[18] that this is too pessimistic a picture, one whose pessimism about the idea of dance as a performed art is grounded in a misguided acceptance of the role that McFee assigns to notatability in defining the performable work. We are, after all, familiar with performance traditions in folk and non-Western contexts that seem quite capable of preserving the identity of a performable work from performance to performance over many generations in the absence of any notational representation of the piece. For example, as noted in Chapter 5, Gregorian and Coptic chant traditions successfully preserved works of plainsong prior to the development of any means of notationally transcribing these works. More generally, oral cultures demonstrate remarkable abilities to preserve the integrity of linguistic cultural artifacts in the absence of written records. Furthermore, the problem with preserving work identity based on video recordings of performances might also seem to be overstated. For, as long as we can avail ourselves of persons schooled in the relevant performance traditions, we can rely on their judgments in determining which features of a recorded performance are constitutive of the dance performed. A similar solution might answer the problem voiced by Graham. While the choreographer of a work of modern dance may be a particularly sensitive interpreter of her own works, the works themselves are surely open to performative interpretation by others familiar with the choreographer's *oeuvre*.

These objections are well taken, but, in identifying the conditions under which a tradition of performable works can be sustained in the absence of notational representations of those works, they also alert us to the possibility of cases that are genuinely problematic because these conditions are not met. It is instructive here to reflect upon current debates about the practice of "dance reconstruction." For those such as Kenneth Archer and Millicent Hodgson (2000) who champion such a practice, the task is to "salvage what we can of … masterworks" in the history of dance. The aim is to present authentic performances of the works of great choreographers such as Nijinsky and Massine. I have argued that the general artistic relevance of authentic performance lies in its bearing on our interrogative understanding of performable works. But, whereas the use of period instruments in a performance may provide insight into why a composer prescribed a certain sound sequence, we face two difficulties if we try to extend this argument to dance. First, as we have seen, we often lack any clear notational representation of the works we are trying to "reconstruct," and are limited to various kinds of archival resources. If we *don't* have contemporaries who are themselves experienced in the relevant performative traditions, these resources themselves stand in need of interpretation. This also holds for video records. But where, as with many works of dance performed prior to the inception of video recording, we lack a visual record of performances, there is a different problem. Many of the aesthetic qualities of past dance performances that might help to explain why they were choreographed in a particular way depend not upon anything susceptible to notational or other written record, but upon the embodied skills of the dancers with whom the choreographer was working. Rubidge notes, here, that

> the possibility of "authentic" (in the sense of historically accurate) dance per-formances, even from earlier in [the twentieth] century, is severely reduced. A significant element of the work itself is literally embodied in the dancer's movement. Personal style in dance is affected by the individual dancer's pref-erence for particular ways of moving, by dance training, and, perhaps more significantly, by the cultural environment in which the dancers operate. (Rubidge 1996, 225)

Conroy similarly notes that, even in the case of historical dance perform-ances whose performers are still active, "critical movement elements fall from kinesthetic memory as the body takes on new information" (2007). While there is a parallel problem in historically authentic musical perform-ances concerning the ways in which period musicians *played* period instru-ments, the problem in an art form where bodily movement itself seems to be the medium is especially acute.[19] We do not have to share the general postmodernist hostility to enduring performable works expressed by Mark Franko (1989), one of the most trenchant critics of dance reconstruction, to understand his skepticism as to the ability of the latter to contribute to our understanding of past dance performance.

We have seen that serious questions can be raised about the utility of apply-ing the classical paradigm to at least some works of dance. In earlier sections of this chapter, we identified the conditions that need to be met if the paradigm is to make best sense of our practice in particular areas of the performing arts. It remains an open question to what extent these conditions are met in spe-cific dance traditions. There is certainly the appearance of an active tradition of dance works upon which choreographers are able to draw. But the ephem-eral nature of much dance performance calls into question whether it always makes sense, here, to think of enduring and reperformable works that inform the creative activity of successive generations. Where we lack a firm sense of what a given historical "work" of dance prescribes, it may be better to see later productions as using elements from earlier productions as ingredients in some-what the way that Hamilton urges us to see theatrical productions.

5   The Novel as Performable Work?

Thus far, in this and the previous chapter, we have been exploring the applicability of the classical paradigm to artistic performances in what are usually viewed as the performing arts – music, theater, and dance. Peter Kivy (2006), however, has recently defended the surprising thesis that literature in general – not just drama or even poetry – should be viewed as a performed art, analogous to music. The novel, he maintains, is properly viewed as a performable work whose performances are readings – datable events – enacted by readers. Reading itself, then, is a performing art. The literary text, like the musical score, is a notational prescription for generating instances of the work. Furthermore, silent readings of novels are analogous to performances of musical works "in the head" by score readers: "We hear stories in the head, the way Beethoven, when he read the scores of Handel, heard musical performances in the head" (Kivy 2006, 63). Performances of literary works in the head can be seen as expressive "soundings" which, as in the case of soundings of musical works by score readers, embody an interpretation of the overall sense of the work. The silent reader, Kivy maintains, expressively impersonates the storyteller, while at the same time critically commenting and reflecting on the content of the narrative. Such reflection takes place in the "gaps" that punctuate, and the "afterlife" that follows, the reading performance in the narrow sense. The case for viewing silent reading as a performance of the literary work, he claims, depends upon the sense it makes of our reading experience.

There are, however, reasons to question Kivy's claim. The "storyteller" we supposedly impersonate is the person held responsible for constructing the story. Where novels have impersonal third-person narrators – as, for example, in Graham Greene's *The Heart of the Matter* – the silent reader impersonates whoever is taken to be telling the story – Greene himself on some accounts, or, more plausibly, a fictional author of some kind. What, however, of a novel with a first-person narrator, such as *David Copperfield*? It seems that the reader impersonates the storyteller who is himself impersonating David Copperfield, since that is what the model takes a storyteller to do in telling a first-person fictional narrative. In the case of direct quotation in such a fiction, the reader must presumably impersonate the storyteller impersonating the narrator impersonating one of the characters. But this seems to be a somewhat baroque description of the phenomenology of reading. If silent readers do indeed expressively sound direct quotations in a fictional narrative in distinctive ways, it seems more intuitive to say that they impersonate the character herself, rather than enact the complex set of nested impersonations just sketched.

Even if Kivy were correct about the phenomenology of reading, however, it is questionable whether this could establish that the reading of literary fictions is a performing art. One concern is whether the sounding of the literary text in the head of the reader qualifies as a performance, given our elucidation of this notion in Chapter 1. A performer, as we saw, is guided in her actions by the anticipated eye or ear of an intended audience of those actions. Is it plausible, however, to think that the reader serves as her own intended audience in her sounding of the work? But perhaps Kivy can argue that the reader's critical assessment of her own performance in such cases is no more problematic that the sight-reader's critical assessment of her sounding of a musical work in her head. More crucially, however, even if we allow that the reader can "perform" the literary text, this doesn't show that literature is a performed art. For what makes music and drama performed arts is not merely that aficionados attend performances of plays and musical works, but that it is only through engagement with such performances that theatrical and musical works can be properly appreciated and evaluated. It is the role that performances by practitioners of the performing arts play in the appreciation and evaluation of works that make theater and music performed arts. But if this is true, then descriptive facts about the phenomenology of our reading experiences, however insightful, cannot serve as the principal argument for viewing the reading of fictional literature as a performing art analogous to musical performance. What needs to be shown is how such phenomenological facts bear upon the appreciation and evaluation of literary works. Only if the sort of "performance" that Kivy describes bears upon the appreciation of a work of literary fiction in a manner analogous to the way in which a performance (public or in the head) of a musical work bears upon *its* appreciation can our ability to "perform" a literary work in the head support the conclusion that literature is properly viewed as a performed art and reading as the related performing art.

In certain respects, this challenge might be met. There may indeed be a role, in the proper appreciation of at least some literary fictions, for the reader's expressive sounding in the head of the utterances of characters in the novel, for this may bear upon what is true in the story concerning these characters. But, to be accorded such a role, the sounding must contribute to understanding and appreciation of the fiction over and above the contribution made thereto by the *interpretation* of the characters upon which the expressive sounding is itself based. It must be in virtue of how the utterances sound when voiced in the head that some appreciation-relevant fact about the literary work is made manifest to the receiver. Clearly there are cases where this is so. For example, the humorous dimensions of certain comic characters depend in this way on how their utterances would sound.[20] But in general it is unclear that this condition on artistic relevance will be satisfied. And, if we turn to the narrative elements in storytelling, it is much more difficult to see how expressive sounding plays a part in the appreciation of the work, save where the sound of the words itself contributes to the work's appreciable properties – where literature performs certain more standardly poetic functions in virtue of the sounds of the text.

What seems crucial to appreciating a novel is grasping a structure of meanings embodied in a linguistic medium. This includes both what is going on in the narrative and the more general thematic significance that it has. In order to grasp the work as a structure of meanings, the reader has to extract the relevant structure from the text before her, and this may require a complex range of activities, at least some of which – relating to direct quotation, for example – may be thought of as soundings of elements in the work. Related activities might include those exercises of the imagination necessary in order to grasp certain psychological truths in the story. So it may be important to think of silent readers as playing a role in realizing the work through their activity, which suggests that silent reading is in this respect more like score reading than like looking at a painting. Kivy's presentation of the case for a performative element in literature may serve to awaken us to the significance of such aspects of literary experience. But, for the reasons stated, I don't think this should persuade us that literature is usefully thought of as a performed art.

Notes

1. For some indication as to *how* drastically Shakespearean performative practice, and indeed Shakespearean receptive practice, differs from our own, see the discussion of Stern 2000 in Chapter 8.
2. I owe this and some of the other references in the following paragraphs to Rubidge 1996.
3. For an indication of the ways in which Brook's production departed from Shakespeare's prescriptions, see his 1971 film *King Lear* which preserved the central ideas of his theatrical production.
4. For this and other details about the reception of dramatic performances in Shakespearean and Restoration theater, see Stern 2000 and the discussion of her work in Chapter 8.
5. Or stands in some appropriate historical-intentional relation to *Hamlet* or *King Lear*. We presumably wish to allow characters from one play to appear in another play, as in Tom Stoppard's 1966 play *Rosenkrantz and Guildenstern are Dead*. Thus the condition specified in the text for being Hamlet, Lear, etc. is a sufficient but not a necessary one.
6. I owe this observation to Andrew Kania.
7. In his 2009b in the same volume, Hamilton defends his account against its critics.
8. We shall consider in Chapter 8 whether this qualifies as a form of what I term "improvisational composition."
9. I draw in this paragraph on Stern 2000, 5–8.
10. Important extended philosophical treatments of dance can be found in Sparshott 1988; 1995; and McFee 1992. A number of helpful critical surveys of the issues in the philosophy of dance have appeared in the last few

years. See, for example, McFee 2000, Carroll 2003, Sparshott 2004, and Van Camp 2009.

11. McFee 1992, 88–111. McFee defended his view in his 2007.

12. Original formulation in McFee 1992, 97–98.

13. For concerns about whether a notated "score" can play this kind of role in dance, see Rubidge 1996 and Conroy 2006. I draw upon both of these sources in the following discussion.

14. For an overview of the historical development of thinking about dance, see Carroll 2003.

15. For a formalist conception of what a performed work of dance prescribes for performances, see Anderson 1975.

16. Rubidge 1996, 223. These concerns are part of a more general worry about the ability of recordings to capture and convey to viewers elements that are crucial to the understanding and appreciation of theatrical and dance performance.

17. Cited in Conroy 2007. I draw on references in Conroy's paper in the discussion of dance reconstruction in the following paragraphs.

18. Stephen Davies raised these points in private communication.

19. Stephen Davies (private communication) has pointed out a parallel difficulty in music relating to the use of the voice. We lack evidence that would allow us to determine how medieval singers sang, given the possibility of voicing sounds in different places in the throat.

20. Here, however, we might question whether the sounding is a matter of interpretation rather than mere execution. Recall the essentially interpretive dimension of performance in the performing arts.

Part Two
Performance as Art

7

Performances as Artworks

1   Introduction: Spontaneous Performance in the Arts

On January 24, 1975, Keith Jarrett walked onto the stage of the Opera House in Köln, West Germany, seated himself at the piano, played four single notes that mimicked the house intermission bell, and then performed uninterrupted for just over 26 minutes. After a pause, he again performed uninterrupted for over 33 minutes, and then, at the urging of the audience, performed for a further seven minutes. He did this without a score, and without any prior planning or rehearsal relating to the form that this specific performance would take. The performance, which drew on a number of different musical traditions such as classical piano, jazz, and blues, was, almost as an afterthought, recorded by the sound engineers. The recording was later heard by Manfred Eicher of ECM records with whom Jarrett had done some earlier recordings. *The Köln Concert* was released on a double LP later that year, and on a CD in 1980. Having sold more than 3.5 million copies, it is the best-selling solo jazz recording of all time. Some years later, Jarrett was persuaded to release an authorized transcription of the performance, but he stressed that it was intended to document the event, not to establish a set of prescriptions for a performable work. Unfortunately, as a brief visit to YouTube indicates, some have been unable to resist the temptation to "perform" the piece, in more or less listenable ways.

I have chosen Jarrett's performance to begin the second part of this book because it has both an iconic and an ambiguous status that fits well with some of the questions we are going to examine. In the first place, Jarrett's

Philosophy of the Performing Arts, First Edition. David Davies.
© 2011 David Davies. Published 2011 by Blackwell Publishing Ltd.

performance obviously involves improvisation. Indeed, it is striking in that it was not preceded by any prior decisions as to what would be played (save, perhaps, for the opening four notes!), whereas improvised performances with which we are more familiar take a pre-existing "frame" as the structure for improvisation. This frame may be a melody or song composed for "straight" performance – such as "My Favorite Things," to which John Coltrane returned again and again as a basis for the improvisational explorations of his ensembles. Or it may be something composed with the specific intention that it be used as a frame for improvisation, as with Miles Davis's "Blue in Green." As Jarrett makes clear in discussions of his solo performances, however, he sees his explorations as open-ended: "When I think of improvising, I think of going from zero to zero – or wherever it goes. I'm not connecting one thing to another."[1] We shall examine the different roles that improvisation can play in artistic performance in the next chapter.

Second, the iconic status of Jarrett's performance provides us with perhaps the most intuitively persuasive example of an artistic performance in the first of the senses that we distinguished in Chapter 1 – a performance that is artistic in virtue of itself being a work of art.[2] We shall have to ask, however, whether these intuitions are to be trusted. For some have seen a tension between the ephemeral nature of a performance – even a recorded performance – and the "enduring" nature of works of art.

Third, Jarrett's performance differs in at least one notable respect from the artistic performances falling outside the classical paradigm discussed in the previous chapter. In giving an account of at least some theatrical and dance performances, it is tempting to adopt a version of the ingredients model. But even the ingredients model generally holds that individual performances are of *something* – namely, they are performances of *productions*, which are staged on different occasions to different audiences. We noted in the previous chapter that, in performances in the performed arts, we can distinguish three elements, of which at least two are nearly always present: first, a performable work; second, a production, often of a performable work; and third, a performance-event. Performative interpretation of a performable work generally occurs in the preparations for staging a production of the work, although performers may still interpret their roles in different ways for different individual performances. The same tripartite model can be applied to many jazz performances, where an individual rendition of a standard might be described as a performance of something repeatable, namely, the ensemble's interpretation of the standard. The latter, like a production of a play, provides the narrower frame within which the ensemble improvises on different occasions of performance.[3] With performances fitting the ingredients model, on the other hand, we have a production that is not *of* a performable work, but that takes such a work as one of its ingredients. The individual performance then, *pace* Osipovich, is *of* that production. Jarrett's actions, however, exemplify the possibility of a performance that is neither of a performable work nor of a production. If we are to view it as an artistic performance, therefore, it seems that our only option is to view it as a focus of artistic appreciation in its own right, and this might seem to commit us to viewing it as an artwork.

In this chapter, we shall look at two questions, and also lay the basis for more detailed examination, in the following two chapters, of related issues. The first question is whether an individual performance-event such as Jarrett's actions on January 24, 1975 can indeed be an artwork, and thus be what we termed in Chapter 1 a "performance-work." To answer this question, we must reflect upon what is involved in the appreciation of Jarrett's performance and how this relates to the kind of appreciation proper to artworks. This will allow us to assess the charge that individual performances fail to meet at least some conditions for being a work of art. If we answer the first question positively, it is natural to pose a second question concerning those performance-events that are performances of performable works – "work-performances," as we termed them in Chapter 1 – or performances of productions understood in the manner of the ingredients model – "production-performances" as we may now term them. Can work-performances or production-performances also be artworks? In other words, are at least some work-performances or production-performances also performance-works? In previous chapters we alluded to this possibility in resisting the suggestion that, if we are to do justice to the virtues of individual performances or productions, we must deny that they are *of* works. Obviously, if there are good reasons to think that some work-performances can be performance-works, we undermine one of the reasons offered for limiting the scope of the classical paradigm in the performing arts.

In addressing these two questions, we shall also reflect upon what it is to appreciate "for its own sake" a performance-event presented in the context of the performing arts. We might expect the qualities central to appreciating such an event to differ in crucial ways from those bearing on the appreciation of artworks outside the performing arts, and from those bearing on the appreciation of performable works through their performances. For example, it might seem crucial for the appreciation of Jarrett's performance that it is entirely spontaneous in the sense that it involves no prior planning as to its structure.[4] As such, it is the manifestation in real time of the creative imagination and physical skills of the performer. In order to clarify whether such an artistic performance can be a work of art, we shall draw upon our discussion in Chapter 1 of the features that distinguish artistic from non-artistic performances. This will also provide the background for our detailed examination, in the following two chapters, of improvisation, rehearsal, the role of the audience in live performance, and the embodied nature of the performer.

2   The Artistic Status of Performances Outside the Classical Paradigm

Jarrett's performance at the Opera House in Köln is not, as we have seen, an artistic performance in the second of the two senses distinguished in Chapter 1. It is not a performance that instantiates something else that is a work of art, nor is it a performance that instantiates a production that has an artwork as one of its ingredients. Is it, nonetheless, an artistic performance in the first sense, something that is itself a work of art? Our general methodological principle counsels us to look to our artistic practice for guidance, while holding this practice accountable to rational reflection. But practice, here, is not on the face of it very helpful. Jarrett's musical performance is certainly presented in the same kind of location, to the same kind of audience, paying the same general kind of attention, as performances of performable works such as Chopin's nocturnes. But, as yet, we have seen no reason to conclude that performances of performable works are *themselves* works of art. Indeed, it would sound a little strange to say, on emerging from a Chopin piano recital, that one had just heard two works of art. If it would in fact be correct to say such a thing, we cannot rest this conclusion merely on an appeal to our ordinary ways of talking about performances.

Paul Thom appeals to our linguistic intuitions in arguing *against* according the status of work of art to a performance like Jarrett's. He maintains, first, that there is a unified conception of "work of art" that applies across the arts: "A work of art can be defined as an enduring thing, created in some medium (such as oil on canvas) by an author (such as a painter) in order to be beheld in a particular kind of way (namely, to be viewed aesthetically)" (Thom 1993, 28). Performable works, Thom argues, satisfy this description if we view them, as he does, as directives for performance which are appreciable in virtue of their performances. For, even though the performances themselves are ephemeral, the performance directives endure. In the case of a purely improvised performance like Jarrett's, however, there is merely the production of a sound sequence on a particular occasion. Thom rejects the idea that a performance like Jarrett's itself brings into existence an enduring performance directive binding on future performances. We shall examine the idea of what can be termed "improvisational composition" in more detail in Chapter 8. He concludes that such a performance itself neither endures nor instantiates something else that endures. What was offered for the appreciation of the audience in Köln, therefore, was not a work of art, but only an "aesthetic object," an arrangement of aesthetic qualities.

In a response to Thom, Peter Kivy trades linguistic intuitions with his opponent (Kivy 1995, 124–128). He disputes both the claim that it is part of our concept of a work of art that the latter must be an enduring entity, and the claim that performances do not endure. A performance endures, Kivy argues, insofar as it is repeatable. And performances are repeatable because numerically distinct performances by an orchestra can manifest the same interpretation of the work performed. This latter point seems questionable however, in that it conflates questions about performances and questions about productions and interpretations. A production of a play, like a conductor's interpretation of a symphony, certainly endures in the sense that there can be different performances of that production or interpretation at different times. In this sense, a production or interpretation, no less than a play or a symphony, can be characterized in terms of an enduring performance directive. But individual performances do not endure, nor are they repeatable. And the question of concern to Thom, and indeed to us, is whether individual performances – not productions – can be works of art.

Kivy's first claim – that a work of art need not endure – is more difficult to assess if we are appealing to linguistic intuitions. It might be thought to weigh in favor of Thom's intuitions that, if we allow that Jarrett's ephemeral performance on January 24, 1975, preserved through recording, is a work of art, we must presumably say the same for all of the other wholly improvised solo performances given by Jarrett over the past 40-odd years. It would be odd, after all, to say that the contingent fact that Jarrett's performance was recorded is part of what makes it an artwork. Surely, if it had not been recorded, this would not have affected any of the qualities that make it artistically interesting – the qualities that presumably make it an artwork if indeed it is one. It would have deprived us only of the ability to appreciate an artwork, assuming it to be one. But then we must maintain that many ephemeral events only appreciable by a small number of people present at a given place and time – Jarrett's unrecorded concerts, for example – can be artworks. This kind of consideration is not decisive, however, since it isn't clear why one who shares Kivy's rather than Thom's intuitions shouldn't happily embrace this consequence.

We will perhaps make more headway if we consider different aspects of our practice regarding performances in the performing arts. Philip Alperson (1984) argues that jazz improvisations, as individual events, should be treated as artistic performances in our first sense, and thus as artworks. He argues this on the grounds that the criteria that we bring to bear in our appreciative assessment of improvised performances are in many cases the same as those that we bring to bear in our appreciative assessment of performable musical works. Alperson notes, first, that improvisers share with composers the task of constructing sequences of sounds that are intended to articulate an artistic content. Thus, in each case, we can appreciate the qualities that the resulting sound sequences possess as musical constructions – qualities such as "intelligible development, internal unity, coherence, originality, ingenuity, etc., the artful employment of prevailing idioms, and the emergence of an individual style" (Alperson 1984, 22).

Alperson notes, however, that, if these are taken to be the sole criteria for evaluating improvisations, it is likely that, in general, they will compare unfavorably with performable works. For it is difficult to achieve, on the fly so to speak, the kind of structural complexity that composers can confer on their compositions. Composers are able to reflect and revise, to have at their creative disposal at a time both earlier and later elements in the same composition, and to correct, on further thought, false steps that seem initially promising. Improvisers lack such resources, however.[5] Alperson counters by insisting that the proper appreciation of improvisations requires that we view them not merely in terms of the musical constructions that are their products but also in terms of the actions that generate these products. These actions, no less than their products, can be the objects of aesthetic contemplation. In the first place, we can appreciate, in the actions of improvisers, the same qualities that are manifest in performances of performable works – "sensitivity, lyricism, and general virtuosity," for example. However, what distinguishes the actions of the improviser are the risks that she takes, precisely because she is creating a musical structure without the resources for revision available to the composer. What is a liability if we consider the improvisation purely as a musical construction thus becomes an asset when we consider it as an action.

Our aesthetic interest in an improvised performance such as Jarrett's, then, is an interest in both the musical construction and the action of constructing it. In a recent piece on the Köln concert, Corinna da Fonseca-Wollheim (2008) makes a similar point. Commenting on the attempts of amateurs to "perform" the Köln Concert on the basis of the transcriptions, she remarks that

> without the live, improvised element, the magic is lost. Unlike a piece of classical music, "The Köln Concert" is a masterpiece only in its recorded format. And it requires an audience that participates in the unfolding act of creation each time anew. Thus the listener becomes involved in the search for a theme's development, shares in the elation when Mr. Jarrett finds a beautiful new tune, experiences the joy of hearing him play with it. When he pauses on a chord, unsure of where to go next, it seems as if much more than the immediate future of this music hangs in the balance. When he shifts to a new key, it feels as if a door has been pushed open, inviting the listener to explore new rooms and hallways.

Furthermore, in listening to an improvised performance in this way, we disregard things that might concern us in listening to a performance of a performable work. Alperson quotes Francis Sparshott to this effect:

> When the musician improvises, we make allowances for fluffs, interruptions, squawks, and all sorts of distracting concomitants that we assume to be no part of the performance. But we also allow for his forgetting what he was doing, trying to do two things at once, changing his mind about where he is going, starting more hares than he can chase at once, picking up where he thought he had left off but resuming what was not quite there in the first place, discovering and pursuing tendencies in what he has done that would have taken a rather different form if he had thought of them at the time, and so on. (Sparshott 1982, 255)

Do these kinds of considerations show that an improvised performance like Jarrett's can be a work of art? Thom thinks not. Responding to Alperson, he maintains that the qualities we appreciate in good improvisations – "spontaneity, excitement, and the display of an ability to solve problems and be inventive without preparation" (Thom 1993, 63), for example – are qualities they possess as objects of aesthetic beholding, not as artworks. For, he again insists, artworks must be enduring entities. It seems, then, as if we are back at the same impasse of conflicting intuitions that led us to look at Alperson's account in the first place. Indeed, it might be thought that, if we are trying to establish that improvised performances in the performing arts can be artworks, the strategy of pointing to the kinds of criteria to which we appeal in evaluating such performances is an unpromising one. For none of the kinds of criteria that Alperson cites is exclusive to the evaluation of *artworks*. The criteria cited for assessing musical constructions are applicable to constructions in general, including philosophy papers. And the criteria of "sensitivity, lyricism, and general virtuosity" applicable to an improviser's playing of her instrument would also be appropriate for judging the performance of a lecturer, as long as we operate with a suitably broad conception of "lyricism." And any lecturer who works without a "script" takes the same kind of risk as the improvising musician. Thus we cannot demonstrate that improvisational performances in the performing arts are artworks by pointing to the fact that these criteria are applied to such performances. For they are also applied to many things that are clearly *not* works of art.

At this point, I think the right strategy is to question the distinction upon which Thom is relying in his argument – the distinction between artworks, as enduring entities, and artistic performances, as transient objects of aesthetic beholding. Rather than focus on the criteria used in assessing improvised performances in the arts, we should ask about the kinds of things being assessed. Here, I think, we should remind ourselves of our discussion, in Chapter 1, of the features that distinguish artworks in general from objects of reflective attention outside the arts. The suggestion, it will be recalled, is that artworks call for a distinctive kind of regard, and that they do so in virtue of the ways in which they articulate their contents. To determine the artistic contents of an artwork requires *close attention* to the details of its artistic vehicle which often *exemplifies* properties ascribable to the work. Artworks tends to articulate their contents by means of many *different properties* of their vehicles, and to do so in a "*hierarchical*" manner, where higher level content is articulated through lower level content. Artworks therefore call for a distinctive kind of regard if we are to ascertain not only what their vehicles represent, express, or exemplify at the most immediate level, but also, at the more thematic level, the point of the vehicles having the manifest features that they do. This inflects the interrogative interest that we take in the manifold in trying to make sense of it in terms of reasons for its being ordered in the way that it is.[6]

If an improvisatory performance like Jarrett's *Köln Concert* is to be viewed as an artwork, Jarrett's actions on stage on January 24, 1975 must be the work's artistic vehicle, and these actions must have been executed with the intention of articulating an artistic content accessible only to receivers who accord that vehicle the distinctive kind of regard for which artworks call. Alperson's general characterization of our interest in improvisatory performance, together with da Fonseca-Wollheim's description of the kind of attention for which Jarrett's performance calls, certainly suggest that these requirements are met. The performance, as artistic vehicle, articulates its content through the timbral richness of the sequence of sounds produced. The expressive qualities of the latter, and the ways in which they draw upon the different musical traditions to which Jarrett refers in his playing, also serve to communicate higher order content. Furthermore, those features of musical constructions to which Alperson refers reinforce our interrogative interest in the manner in which the musical manifold is ordered, even if that ordering is the result of irreversible decisions made in real time rather than of an extended process of reflective construction.

What space remains, then, for Thom's distinction between artworks and objects of aesthetic contemplation? Our interest in Jarrett's performance is an interest in something intentionally done, just as our interest in an enduring artistic artifact is an interest in something intentionally made. In both cases, however, there is a process–product ambiguity in talk of something done or made. There is the intentional act of doing or making something, and there is the product or result of that doing or making. In Jarrett's case, the result is the performed musical composition that articulates a particular artistic content. The *Köln Concert*, as the result of Jarrett's activity, is in this broad sense an artifact. On the other hand, to take an interest in something as an "object of aesthetic contemplation" generally prescinds from its status as an artifact. Our most obvious models of "objects of aesthetic contempla-tion" are natural phenomena such as landscapes, mountains, and perhaps fogs at sea. Once we think of an object of contemplation as something made or done, our interest becomes interrogative. We seek *reasons* rather than natural causes for its being ordered in the way that it is. If we are right in our account of what is distinctive of our interest in artworks – namely a particular kind of interrogative interest in the manifold that results from a (usually) completed action – then it is difficult to see why the non-enduring nature of individual performances should be relevant to their status as artworks. Indeed, our *encounters* with artworks, whereby we are able to engage with them in the distinctive manner that I have described, are always ephemeral, however last-ing their effects on us may be. That something that we encounter in this way may itself be ephemeral, available only on a particular occasion of reception, may be regrettable, but doesn't seem to have any real bearing on the artistic status of that thing. Thus, by a more circuitous but I hope more satisfying route, we return to Kivy's original objection to Thom: it isn't clear why we should share the intuition that only enduring things can be artworks. While we *could* stipulatively restrict the term "artwork" to things that endure, this stipulation doesn't seem to be grounded in anything bearing essentially on the ways in which artworks work.

3   The Artistic Status of Performances Within the Classical Paradigm

We reflected a few pages ago on the oddness of saying, as one emerges from hearing a piano recital of Chopin's nocturnes, that one has just heard two works of art. Should our willingness to allow that performances falling outside the classical paradigm, like Jarrett's *Köln Concert*, can be artworks lead us to a similar view of performances of performable works? Can I really get two works for the price of one when I attend a performance of a perform-able work? (And, if so, should we conceal this fact from promoters lest they raise their prices?)

Peter Kivy cites approvingly an argument by Thomas Carson Mark (1981) that, if accepted, would have the effect of artistically enfranchising per-formances of performable works. Mark argues that we should think of the performer of a performable work as like someone who puts a quoted pas-sage to use as a way of making an utterance of their own. For example, if Berthold, inviting Magda to accompany him on an evening foray along the South Bank, addresses her with the words "Let us go then, you and I, when the evening is spread out against the sky like a patient etherized upon a table," he is not merely quoting the opening lines of T. S. Eliot's "The Love Song of J. Alfred Prufrock." He is also using them to express his own desire that he and Magda set out on an excursion. In the same way, Mark maintains, the performer of a performable work doesn't merely "quote" in accordance with the musical directives of the composer, but also uses what is "quoted" to make an artistic statement of her own. In so doing, the performer confers upon the resulting performance aesthetically important qualities distinct from those of the quoted work. If then, as Kivy suggests, we identify a work of art with "an artifactual collection of aesthetically important properties" (1995, 118), the performance qua artistic statement by the performer is itself an artwork distinct from the work being performed. Since we are assuming that realizations of performable works require the interpretive contribution of performers, and thus that all performers confer upon their performances aesthetically significant properties distinct from those required by the work performed, we seem to have a general argument for viewing all work-performances as themselves artworks – performance-works as we have termed them. Mark summarizes his argument as follows:

> When we have a performance of a work of music we have … two assertions: there is the work of music itself, which is a statement or assertion by the composer, and there is the additional assertion which is the performance … The performance is not simply an interpretation (though it requires or involves one) or a presentation (though it requires that too since it involves producing an instance of the work): it is *another* work of art. (Mark 1981, 320; cited in Kivy 1995, 119)

There seems to be something right but also something wrong with this argument. On the one hand, we should surely agree that, when a performer does indeed use the prescriptions of a performable work to make a distinctive artistic statement of her own, this is properly regarded as a distinct work, if, as argued in the previous section, performances can be artworks. Indeed, the prevalence of this phenomenon in theatrical and dance performance is one of the considerations that lends credibility to the ingredients model. We are not surprised to discover, in attending a performance of a traditional play, that the director and company are to some extent making use of the play to comment on issues of interest to them. This is why we think of Brook's "existentialist" production of *King Lear*, for example, as a work to be assessed in its own right. When we turn to music, we also find striking examples of the same kind of phenomenon. Accomplished performers like Glenn Gould are celebrated for the independent vision that they bring to their performances of classical works. Their ways of interpreting and performing those works articulate an artistic content of their own.

On the other hand, the status of a work-performance as an independent work of art shouldn't be thought to follow simply from the fact that the performer uses the performance to make *a statement* of her own. Berthold uses Eliot's lines to express his own invitation, but there is only one artwork in the vicinity, even though there is a measure of interpretation in his use of the quoted passage. The personal statement that the performer makes in performing a performable work must be articulated *artistically*, in line with the analysis of this notion sketched in Chapter 1. Nor should the status of a work-performance as an independent work be thought to follow simply from the fact that the performance involves *interpretation*, for we need to ask what general purpose the performer's interpretation serves. Thom talks, for example, of the need for interpretation even in performances that aim for authenticity in the sense discussed in Chapter 4. Authenticity and interpretation go together, he argues: "To perform authentically is to do at least what the work directs; to interpret is to go beyond what the work directs in ways that illumine its directives" (Thom 1993, 95). But where the aim of interpretation is indeed to "illumine [the] directives" of a performable work, why should we think that the interpretive performance is itself a work distinct from the work being performed? The purpose of the performance in such a case is to do justice to the work performed, not to bring into existence a separate work that may compete for the audience's attention. The distinctive artistic values that are made apparent to receivers by such a performance are values that the performers take to be implicit in the performable work, although it may require great interpretive and performative virtuosity to discover this.

It is, of course, true that, to the extent that performance involves interpretation, it brings into being aesthetic qualities that are not *mandated* by the performable work, some of which may be intentionally added by the performer without any suggestion that they are somehow implicit in the work. Thus Kivy is right in thinking that we have an artifactual collection of aesthetic qualities for which the performer, not the composer, is responsible. But it is wrong to think, as Kivy suggests, that, if this is the case, then we must have an independent work of art. It may be, as in the case of the performer striving for authenticity, that the aesthetic qualities furnished by the performer are realizations of the aesthetic potentiality of the performable work – they are aesthetic qualities that the prescriptions of the composer *make possible*, without themselves being prescribed. The performance counts as an independent work, however, only if the aesthetic qualities not mandated by the prescriptions of the performable work serve the performer's purpose of articulating an artistic content of her own – one not referable to the performable work.

But this raises a more general worry about the idea of work-performances as performance-works. As we saw in Chapter 4, for a performance to count as the performance of a particular performable work W, the performer must be guided by the prescriptions constitutive of W so that the performance aims to comply with those prescriptions. We saw that the prescriptions themselves may need to be relativized to the context in which they were generated if we are to know what they in fact prescribe. We have also agreed that there is always further room for interpretation of those prescriptions on the part of the performer. But, as has just been argued, for a performance to count as a performance-work, it must aim to articulate an artistic content of its own. To what extent can a performer have *both* the aim required if her performance is to be a work-performance and the aim required if her performance is to be a performance-work? As we shall see in the next chapter, this problem is particularly pressing when we ask about the status of improvisations by jazz musicians on standards.

Another way to bring out this difficulty is to reflect on the kinds of properties of an improvised performance like Jarrett's that Alperson cites in arguing that such performances are artworks. We disagreed with Alperson's strategy of citing such properties for such a purpose, but it may be instructive to see how this strategy would fare when applied to work-performances. There were, we may recall, three kinds of properties: first, the properties of the performance viewed as a musical construction, analogous to the properties for which we admire performable works; second, the properties of the performance qua action, such as virtuosity and sensitivity; and third, the properties of the performance insofar as it involves the generation of a musical structure in real time.

Consider the first kind of property. A performance of a performable work seems to owe most of its properties as a musical construction to the work performed. For, in order to count as a performance of the work, the performer must intend to comply with the composer's prescriptions, and these prescriptions determine many of the structural compositional features to which Alperson refers: "intelligible development, internal unity, coherence, originality, ingenuity, etc., the artful employment of prevailing idioms, and the emergence of an individual style." Those such features that might be credited to the performer – coherence (in interpretation), originality, and individual style in particular – seem to be performative virtues rather than qualities that contribute towards the articulation of a distinct artistic statement by the performer. A performance of a performable work is also unlikely to have the third kind of property, unless it does so in virtue of the way in which the performer interprets the composer's prescriptions.

As for the second kind of property, this, in the case of a performance of a performable work, again seems to pertain to how the work is performed. It isn't obvious how it can substantively contribute to the making of an independent artistic statement by the performer or performers without violating the composer's prescriptions.

On the other hand, suppose that a performer working with the score of a performable work does satisfy Alperson's conditions, in virtue of being herself responsible for the structural qualities of the performance, or though giving an expressive interpretation of the work distinct from what the composer might have intended, or through generating such qualities on the fly. Then if, following Alperson, we take the presence of such properties to license viewing the performance as an artwork, it is unclear why it is better to view this as a performance *of* the performable work, rather than viewing it as a performance which uses the latter as an ingredient. For it is unclear how, in this case, the performer can have the requisite intentions to count as performing the work.

This is not to say that there cannot be performances that are both *of* performable works and performance-works in their own right. For there to be such performances, it is necessary that the performer can at the same time aim to satisfy the prescriptions of the performable work and articulate through her performance what we regard as an artistic content of her own. This may involve originality and coherence in interpretation in the interests of articulating a distinctive content that reflects the performer's own individual style. But it may also derive from a certain looseness in what the performable work prescribes, and a consequent greater freedom accorded to the performer to use the work as a medium for the articulation of contents of her own. As suggested in Chapter 6, there are reasons to think that such a looser conception of what a work prescribes is operative in theater and dance. This is why it is possible (although perhaps not correct) to think of a performance of what is often referred to as "Peter Brook's *King Lear*" as being both a performance of a work by Shakespeare and a performance of a production by Brook.

Our response to Mark's argument, therefore, should be that, while he identifies a genuine possibility – a work-performance that is also a performance-work – there is a tension between the requirements for being the former and the requirements for being the latter. As a result, it seems likely that events that meet both sets of requirements will not be the norm in those performed arts whose prescriptions are taken to be fairly strictly binding, such as classical music. While we may indeed appreciate a performance of a performable musical work for the aesthetic qualities attributable to the interpretation and virtuosity of the performer, this will only sometimes justify thinking of the performance as a distinct work, rather than, to use Thom's terminology, as a distinct object of aesthetic contemplation. But events meeting the requirements for being both a work-performance and a performance-work seem more readily available in a performed art like theater where there is a looser conception of what a performable work prescribes. If so, then we can freely acknowledge many theatrical performances as performance-works without denying their status as work-performances. This suggests that, in theater at least, the scope of the ingredients model is less extensive than Hamilton takes it to be. But it also suggests that the ingredients model may be more widely applicable in music, something we shall explore in the next chapter.

Notes

1. From Mike Dibbs's documentary *Keith Jarrett: The Art of Improvisation* (Euro Arts 2005), cited in da Fonseca-Wollheim 2008.
2. I shall, again for convenience, speak of the focus of our artistic appreciation as itself a work of art, and thus of a performance-work as a performance that, qua focus of appreciation, is itself an artwork. As noted in Chapter 1, I have argued elsewhere (2004) that artworks in general are not themselves the focuses of appreciation specified by artists, but the actions that artists perform in specifying those focuses. Since nothing here rests upon this distinction, I conform here to the standard understanding of such matters.
3. In some cases, the apparent "improvisation" is in a more literal sense a performance *of* a repeatable production, the performer repeating on different occasions a preconceived "improvisation" on a given number. For some examples of this, see A. Hamilton 2007, 201–204.
4. As we shall see in our more detailed examination of improvisation in the next chapter, that Jarrett's performance was entirely spontaneous in the sense specified is quite compatible with his having drawn, both structurally and in the selection of motifs, upon his prior performances and rehearsals, not to mention his understanding of generic and harmonic conventions.
5. Alperson credits Denis Dutton, in conversation, with this observation. For a similar point, see Thom 1993, 65–66.
6. In our attempts to appreciate artworks, we also take an interrogative interest in the individual elements of which the artistic vehicle is composed and through whose individual features the content of the work is articulated. These elements are not themselves artworks, of course, but our interrogative interest in them refers them to artworks – the artworks to whose articulated artistic content we assume they are designed to contribute.

8

Elements of Performance I: Improvisation and Rehearsal

1 Introduction

Artistic performances, we have seen, play one, and sometimes both, of two roles in the appreciation of artworks. Some performances are themselves artworks, and many performances contribute to our appreciation of the performable works *of which* they are performances. Indeed a performance may be at one and the same time both an artwork and a performance of a distinct performable work. In Part One we looked at the ways in which performances bear upon the appreciation of performable works. In this and the following chapter, I focus on certain distinctive features of performances themselves, features that distinguish the performing arts both from singular arts like painting and sculpture and from other multiple arts like film and literature.

We have already introduced improvisation, one of the topics of this chapter. We looked at the contribution that improvisation can make in determining the appreciable qualities of a performance, and at how a pure improvisation can itself be an artwork. In this chapter we shall ask a more fundamental question regarding the *nature* of improvisation, and examine different roles that improvisation can play in artistic performance. Improvisation might be thought to contrast with another feature of most performances in the performing arts – their being preceded by rehearsals involving the performers. We might think that it is a precondition for something to count as an improvisation that it *not* have been prefigured in rehearsal. But improvisation and rehearsal raise some similar issues bearing upon the understanding

Philosophy of the Performing Arts, First Edition. David Davies.

of artistic performances. First, both improvisation and rehearsal enter into the processes whereby particular performances come to have the manifest features that they do. Just as it may matter, for our appreciative understanding of certain artistic performances, that they involve improvisation on the part of the performers, so it may matter, for our appreciation of other artistic performances, that they issue from a particular kind of rehearsal process. Indeed, we saw in Chapter 6 how the role of ensemble revision in rehearsals for theatrical performances might be thought to bear upon whether these performances are rightly subsumed under the classical paradigm. Second, improvisation and rehearsal might both be viewed as modes of *composition* of performable works. We need to determine the conditions under which what we have termed "improvisational composition" might take place, whether in performance or in rehearsal.

A third distinguishing feature of artistic performances is that they are normally directed at an audience that shares a physical space at a given time with the performers. Film, on the other hand, is normally directed at an audience that occupies a distinct space at a later time. This opens up the possibility of integrating interactions with the audience into an artistic performance. We have already addressed, in Chapter 1, the kind of regard that artworks in general demand from their receivers. But we need to examine more closely two distinctive aspects of the relation between audience and work in the performing arts. First, we must determine to what extent it is definitive of an artistic performance that it is *for* an audience that is present at the time of performance. Second, we must inquire as to the kind of audience response that is sought or that is appropriate. This will be one of our concerns in Chapter 9. A second concern will be the ways in which, in theater and dance, the bodies of performers themselves figure in the artistic vehicles of performances.

2   The Nature of Improvisation

We noted in the previous chapter the "process–product" ambiguity of a term like "improvisation" as it applies to musical performance. The term may refer either to the product of a performer's activity or to the activity itself. If we are interested in the essential features that distinguish improvisations from other things, however, it seems more promising to focus on the performer's activity. For, even if, as we have seen, there are features that tend to distinguish the products of musical improvisation from the products of reflective composition, these features are not always present, and their presence is to be viewed as a consequence of the process that brings them into being.[1] In the previous chapter we followed most theorists in taking the distinguishing feature of improvisational activity to be its *spontaneity*, the lack of a preconception on the part of the performer as to how given elements in the performance should unfold. Alperson, for example, takes it to be a matter of general agreement that "improvising music is, in some sense, a spontaneous kind of music making" (1984, 17). Stephen Davies similarly characterizes improvisations, or "music making *simpliciter*," as "spontaneous and unregulated musical playings that are not of works" (2001, 11).

There are, however, some who dissent from this happy consensus. In a response to Alperson, Carol S. Gould and Kenneth Keaton (2000) argue that what they term "fluency" in departing from a score is what is crucial for improvisation. Spontaneity need not be present. They argue for this conclusion in the context of making two further points. First, they reject the idea that the distinction between jazz performance and classical performance is that the former involves improvisation and the latter involves interpretation. Second, and relatedly, they claim that performance in the performing arts always involves a measure of improvisation. When we describe a performance *itself* as an improvisation, we are merely registering a difference in the extent to which the performance as a whole requires that the performers depart from pre-existing compositional material. While we shall side with the standard view that spontaneity is the core of improvisation, we may better understand what that view entails if we consider Gould and Keaton's arguments for their alternative proposal.

Gould and Keaton advance a number of considerations that are intended to place jazz performance and classical performance on a comparable footing. They point first to the value placed upon improvisation in the classical tradition in the eighteenth and early nineteenth centuries, something we noted in Chapter 5 in discussing Goehr's challenge to the classical paradigm. They cite improvisational feats by J. S. Bach, Mozart, and Beethoven, and also the improvisational demands made by performable works of that period that employed such devices as the concerto cadenza and the basso continuo. Second, they argue that improvisation in jazz, like interpretation in classical music, presupposes a tradition that furnishes both norms that determine what is acceptable and existing patterns upon which performers are able to draw. A musical tradition, then, provides both the jazz musician and the performer of classical music with a necessary background for her performances. Improvisation, they maintain, "has a logic of its own … All improvisation in musical performance relies on the foundations of the particular musical tradition in which the work exists" (Gould and Keaton 2000, 146).

Third, they argue that there is an intimate connection between improvisation and interpretation. They maintain that, just as all performance requires interpretation, so all interpretation requires improvisation:

> Every performance requires the performer to improvise ... A player will respond to a variety of elements in performance. While melodies and harmonies may be specified in advance, the precise realization of dynamics, rhythmic subtleties, timbre, intonation, and articulation arises at the moment of the performance, and will vary (often considerably) from performance to performance, even when the piece is played by the same musician. (Gould and Keaton 2000, 145)

Finally, they offer an example intended to show that spontaneity is not a necessary condition for improvisation. They cite a performance of Haydn's Cello Concerto in D by the cellist Lynn Harrell in which Harrell added a series of decorative notes not prescribed in the score, apparently both for aesthetic reasons and as a vehicle for self-expression. Harrell's interpolation, they maintain "is undeniably a case of improvisation" even though Harrell "most likely worked out the sequence before the performance," so that the performance was not spontaneous (Gould and Keaton 2000, 146).

Do these arguments threaten the consensus view that spontaneity is the core of improvisation? The first thing to note is that proponents of the "spontaneity" view explicitly acknowledge both the place of improvisation in the classical musical tradition and the ways in which jazz improvisation is embedded in a tradition of playing. Alperson notes that "the history of Western music is replete with examples of musicians such as ... Bach, Handel, Mozart, and Beethoven, all of whom were well known for their ability to improvise complex musical pieces" (1984, 22), while Davies discusses a famous improvisational performance by J. S. Bach, of which more below, and also cites the following account, by a near-contemporary, of Mozart's prodigious improvisational talents:

> Even in the sixth year of his age ... one had only to give [Mozart] the first subject that came to mind for a fugue or an invention ... he would develop it ... as long as one wished ... he would improvise fugally on a subject for hours ... he would extemporize with inexhaustible inspiration. (S. Davies 2001, 13)

There is no suggestion here that improvisation can serve as the distinguishing mark of jazz as opposed to classical performance.

As for the ways in which improvisations are embedded in a tradition upon which the improvising musician draws, both Alperson and Davies dwell on this at some length. Alperson cautions against thinking that the spontaneity of an improvisation means that it is created out of nothing: "Even the freest improviser, far from creating *ex nihilo*, improvises against some sort of musical context" (1984, 22). Richard Cochrane recounts a cautionary anecdote by Ekkehard Jost that illustrates this fact: "A sceptical saxophonist was invited to join a free-jazz session. On being told to 'do his own thing,' he proceeded to play 'I Do Like to Be Beside the Seaside' throughout the session. '[His] associates were extremely angry about this and told him not to bother to come again'" (see Cochrane 2000, 142 n. 22). In a similar vein, Stephen Davies stresses that improvisations are subject to "the general social, stylistic, formal, syntactic, and other constraints governing the culture's music." In a passage that may recall our discussion in Chapter 5 of the ways in which eighteenth-century performers drew upon elements from other performances, he also remarks on the importance for the improviser of resources available in the tradition:

> The musician usually acquires a repertoire of phrases and figurations. Some of these will be of her own invention and others belong more widely to the performing community. When she improvises, she draws on this stock. The difference between formulaic improvisation and excitingly original improvisation often lies in how the units are combined, contrasted, and developed, not in their novelty. (S. Davies 2001, 12)

The claim that spontaneity is the essence of improvisation is, it would appear, quite compatible with an acknowledgment of the role of tradition in improvisation.

Second, Gould and Keaton's claim that all interpretation involves improvisation seems to operate with a much weaker notion of improvisation than the one that concerns Alperson and that is manifest in eighteenth-century classical music. Alperson, it will be recalled, stresses that there is an element of composition in improvisation. He cites the *New Grove Dictionary of Music*, which defines improvisation as "the creation of a musical work ... as it is being performed" (Alperson 1984, 20–21). It is because the product of an improvisation is a novel musical construction that we can appreciate in it some of the same kinds of qualities that we appreciate in a performable musical work. Similarly, what classical improvisers such as Mozart and J. S. Bach did was to generate a musical structure without being guided by pre-existing prescriptions. But Gould and Keaton, in the passage just cited, grant that the interpreting musician does not exercise creative freedom in respect of the musical structure of her performance. She improvises only in respect of the way in which this structure is realized in sound. Even if there is a sense in which the interpreter improvises, then, this does not bear upon one of the distinctive values of improvisation, both in the classical tradition and in jazz.

As a result, Gould and Keaton's case against the "spontaneity" view of improvisation must rest on Harrell's performance, which purports to be an example of non-spontaneous improvisation. But this "example" seems to beg the question at issue. For, if Harrell indeed worked out his embellishments of the Haydn work in advance, then why should we accept, as they claim, that the performance was "undeniably" an improvisation? If the performance was indeed preconceived, then we cannot properly take the kind of distinctive interest in it that we take in improvisational action, since there was no risk of the relevant sort. The only danger for Harrell, presumably, was of professional censure for departing from Haydn's score. Alperson and Davies can therefore simply reject Gould and Keaton's description of this situation as one of improvisation. Since the burden of proof in such cases lies on the one who seeks to overturn a consensus, Gould and Keaton do not seem to have given us good reason to reject the "spontaneity" view.

3 Improvisation and Performable Works: Three Models

In the previous chapter, we took, as an example of an improvised performance, Keith Jarrett's solo concert in Köln on January 24, 1975. One reason for choosing this example, as we noted, was that there is clearly no pre-existing performable work *of which* this was a performance. We were therefore able to consider without other distractions the artistic status of Jarrett's performance. But many improvised performances in jazz are commonly described as if they *are* performances of performable works. The musicians announce, for example, that they are going to play "Body and Soul," and afterwards we discuss their performance in those terms. However, as noted at the end of the previous chapter, there seems to be a tension between the demands that a performable work makes on its performers and the creative freedom we associate with improvisation. We must consider how best to describe these kinds of performances. We must also consider the converse possibility that at least some improvisations are *of* a performable work in virtue of the fact that the performance itself counts as the *composition* of that work. Such a possibility is implicit in the idea that improvisation is a kind of composition. If we are willing to say that Jarrett composed the particular musical construction he performed on January 24, 1975, why shouldn't we also say that, in so doing, Jarrett brought into being a set of prescriptions for future performances, and thus a performable work? Might it be that the YouTube pianists to whom I made disparaging reference in the previous chapter are more accurately viewed as performers of such a piece?

To clarify these issues, it will be helpful to distinguish three ways in which improvisation might enter into a performance in the performing arts.

Improvisation on a theme

In the most familiar scenario, a performer or a group of performers begins with an existing "theme" upon which they proceed to improvise. As we saw in the previous section, the improvisation develops subject to certain constraints that are operative in the relevant performative community and tradition. In many cases, the theme is based upon the prescriptions for a performable work of some kind. In jazz ensemble performances of this sort, musical ideas based upon a musical work's prescriptions frame the performance in a fairly literal sense. Such ideas provide the performance with both its starting point and its terminus – the "head" to which the musicians return – while also functioning as a reference point for the intervening improvisations. But it is rarely the prescriptions themselves that play this role. It would be unusual for a jazz improvisation on a standard theme to begin or end with a straight performance that complies in detail with what the work prescribes. Rather, performers feel free to embroider upon these prescriptions, altering the melody or chord structure, or modifying the tempo or time signature, in the interests of a particular improvisational project. As a result, different improvisational performances of a melodically complex standard such as "You Don't Know What Love Is" can differ dramatically not only in their freely improvisational passages but also in their framing thematic ideas. Indeed, as we shall see shortly, it is an open question whether such performances are indeed *of* performable works. This question clearly arises when improvisations taking their initial direction from a standard theme have a more open-ended structure. Indeed, some of Coltrane's later performances under the title of "My Favorite Things" abandoned even the convention that the performance begin with a recognizable execution of the theme. But the preceding examples must be distinguished from another kind of jazz improvisation on a theme, where the basis for the improvised performance is something designed expressly to function as a frame for improvisation. This applies to such pieces as Miles Davis's "Blue in Green" and Thelonius Monk's "Straight, No Chaser."

Improvisation on a theme is also a feature of some theatrical and dance performances. Consider, for example, James Hamilton's more radical *Hedda Gabler* variation *Something to Tell You*, described in Chapter 6. While this production, as Hamilton presents it, involves performances based on rehearsals, we can easily imagine an improvisational performance standing in the same kind of relation to Ibsen's text. Actors participate in such a performance by spontaneously adapting lines from Ibsen's play to make statements of their own, responding to the improvisations of their fellow performers. As in the case of musical improvisations upon a standard theme, the prescriptions for Ibsen's performable work constrain the improvisational activities of the company not by dictating what they should do but by providing a framework within which the acceptability of improvisational moves is determined. How such constraints operate in a given case is up to the company – our modified version of *Something to Tell You* is simply one example of how Ibsen's text might function as such a constraint. A theatrical analogue of the second type of musical improvisation on a theme, where the theme has been designed as a framework for improvisation, can be found in some fringe theatrical performances where the actors are provided, either by other actors or by the audience, with subjects upon which to improvise. This is a well-used device in comedy improvisation performances. As long as participants and audience have a shared understanding as to how the choice of a subject constrains the performers in their improvisations, this will count as improvisation on a theme as the term is being used here. Unclear cases arise when it is less clear that the performers' activities are subject to such constraints, as in the kinds of open-ended improvisations proposed by Jarrett. It would presumably be incorrect to describe the *Köln Concert*, or even its first "movement," as an improvisation on the theme of the Opera House intermission bell! We might talk in such a case of "improvisation *from* a theme" rather than improvisation *on* a theme.

Where the theme upon which performers improvise is provided by the score or text of a performable work, do we have a performance *of* that work? Certainly, we talk of such improvisations in this way, and this is how they are catalogued on recordings. But, as we saw in Chapter 6, it may be convenient to talk in this way when the performable work is merely an *ingredient* in a performance. In fact, philosophers have disagreed quite markedly over whether improvisations on a theme are, or can be, performances of performable works. Stephen Davies has, at different times, identified himself with both sides in this debate. In earlier papers,[2] he maintained that improvised renditions of standards like "My Funny Valentine" are performances of those works.[3] The performable works are to be viewed as comparatively thin – all that they prescribe for their playing is a melody and an associated chord sequence. But in this respect they are comparable to folk songs like "Wild Mountain Thyme" which admit of many acoustically different legitimate performances.

Davies's considered position,[4] however, is that, as suggested at the end of Chapter 6, work-performance and improvisation have competing aims. In improvising on a theme, it might be said, the performer uses it "as a springboard …, a foundation from which the performer pushes off." The performer of a performable work, then, "is always answerable to the piece," whereas "we expect a successful improvisation to explore hitherto untried ideas." Furthermore, as we have seen, improvisers pursue, and are appreciated for realizing, different kinds of values in their performances from those pursued in work-performances. Davies, however, is skeptical as to whether these are the key distinctions between improvisations and performances of thin works. For some improvisations are very tightly structured around their themes, while some performed works only loosely specify what they prescribe and allow for considerable freedom on the part of performers. The crucial difference, for Davies, lies in the practices with respect to which performers situate themselves and upon which they draw. The practices governing improvisation and work-performance differ in that "the former aims at the presentation of real-time music making constrained only by the grammatical conventions of a style, and the latter is dedicated to the delivery of a faithful instance of a previously composed work, even if it also has other purposes" (S. Davies 2001, 19).

In support of Davies's considered account, we might ask whether, when a performer improvises on a theme furnished by a performable work, the performance can serve arguably the central function of a work-performance, namely, enabling us to better appreciate the work performed. As we saw in Chapter 3, the aesthetic qualities realized in a work-performance can be referred analogically to the performable work whose prescriptions make these qualities of the performance possible. But it is unclear whether we can refer qualities of an improvised performance of, say, "My Funny Valentine" to the performable work in this way. For not only will there be violations of the prescriptions for correct performance of that work, but also (1) the performers are not *aiming* to fulfill those prescriptions, even in the initial statement of the theme, and (2) it is very unlikely that the valuable qualities to be found in the performance could be realized in a performance that *did* fulfill those prescriptions. This is not to say that we *couldn't* gain insight into a performable work from an improvisatory performance that took the prescriptions of that work as the basis for its theme, for such a performance might bring out values that could be sought in performances of the work. But even in this case, the performance will not itself be of the work, since it will not stand in the right kind of historical-intentional relation to the latter's prescriptions.

However, while Davies may be right about performances of standards, a different story seems appropriate for cases like "Blue in Green," which prescribe that performers use a given structure as a frame for improvisation. It seems better, here, to view the improvisational frame as a performable work that constrains performance in a looser way than traditional scores. An improvisation that takes the prescriptions for "Blue in Green" as its theme is guided by a frame designed for that purpose, and the performers intend to do what the work prescribes. In such cases, we can rightly refer qualities of the performance to the frame, taken as a performable work, admiring or criticizing the latter for the possibilities it offers to improvisers. The improvised performance thereby serves the central function of a work-performance in virtue of also serving as an improvisation. Thus, in this case at least, the goals of work-performance and of improvisation are in harmony rather than in conflict.

Improvisational composition

We noted above Alperson's claim that there is an element of composition in improvisation. He cites the *New Grove Dictionary of Music*, which defines improvisation as "the creation of a musical work ... as it is being performed." Alperson has in mind the improviser's responsibility for the musical structure of her performance on a given occasion, and his claim is that this performance-event can itself be viewed as an artwork. But it is tempting to think that the improviser may also compose a musical work in the more standard sense – a performable work that lends itself to other occasions of performance.[5] As I suggested earlier, we may term this "improvisational composition": we have a performance which is an improvisation but which also serves at the same time as an act of composition by prescribing a set of performance constraints for a performable work.

While improvisational composition represents a possibility in the performing arts, there is some disagreement as to whether this possibility is ever actualized, and, indeed, as to the conditions that would have to be satisfied if it were to be actualized. Obviously, the clearest proof that something is possible is an actual example, and Peter Kivy (1983) has defended the idea of improvisational composition in this way. He cites a famous occasion when J. S. Bach was challenged by Frederick the Great to improvise upon a given theme that the latter provided. Bach duly obliged and then later produced a score for his improvised performance, the result being the performable work known as *The Musical Offering*. Kivy insists that *The Musical Offering* was composed by Bach in the act of improvisation, and that what he did later was merely to transcribe the work he had already composed.

Critics less favorably disposed towards the idea of improvisational composition challenge Kivy's description of this episode in two different ways. First, they contest his account of the historical facts. There is some evidence that the work notated by Bach that we know as *The Musical Offering* departs in certain respects from the performance given for Frederick.[6] Such departures might have been due to failures by the performer to play what he intended, in which case we may still speak of the piece being composed in the process of improvisation while denying that it was correctly performed in that process. But they might also be due to the performer's further reflections on what had been improvised and his or her subsequent decision that the notated version would be better than the performed one. The second, more serious, challenge to Kivy's claim is conceptual. Thom puts this in terms of a distinction between *inventing music* and *constituting something as a musical work*. He argues that while Bach may have been doing the former during his improvisation, a separate kind of activity is required to do the latter (Thom 1993, 66). To constitute something as a musical work, as we have seen, is to prescribe that certain features must be present in correct performances of the work. But any given performance of a work will always be thicker in its appreciable audible qualities than the work of which it is a performance, because of the role of interpretation in performance. This, we may recall from Chapter 6, is one of the problems with the idea of performable works in dance: the notator attempts to record an actual dance performance rather than prescribing in advance what the dancers are to do. To constitute something as a musical work through a process of improvisation, therefore, requires something that renders determinate which features of the improvisation are to be constitutive of the work. This could be either a prior or simultaneous decision on the part of the performer, or, more likely, the existence of a set of public conventions that the performer can rely upon to determine what the constitutive features are. The act of composition in the Bach case must be seen as contemporaneous not with the act of improvisation but with the act of scoring. For it is only at this point that the relevant decisions are made in a binding form. Others have made similar points. Wolterstorff, for example, points out that to compose a musical work we must select "that particular set of requirements for correctness of occurrence to be found in the score," something the improviser is unlikely to do while in the very process of improvising (Wolterstorff 1980, 64). And Stephen Davies argues that, whether or not Bach wrote, in the score for *The Musical Offering*, what he actually performed for Frederick, he always had the option of prescribing, for that work, something other than what he performed (S. Davies 2001, 15).

Do these arguments show that improvisational composition is impossible? They certainly suggest that, if a performer is to be counted as composing a performable work at the very same time that she is improvising, this is because she is carrying out two distinct actions at that time – the act of improvising and the act of composing. Thus the act of improvising per se is not an act of composing, because the latter requires that some of the features of the performed sequence of sounds be selected as prescriptive for the performable work. However, we can imagine a situation in which what serves as the act of improvising also counts as the act of composing. This will be the case if the selection of certain features of the improvised sequence of sounds as prescriptive is made not by the performer as she is playing but by certain conventions in place at the time of performance. Such conventions might be generally acknowledged in the musical community to which the performer belongs, or they might result from a prior decision on her part. The conventions would have to take the following form: to improvise a sequence of sounds S is to prescribe features $F(S)$ for instances of a work W. Indeed, this is precisely what the Goodman argument that we examined in Chapter 3 assumes is possible for classical performable works – that we can unequivocally derive a score for a work from a correct performance. If such conventions are in place, then the improviser does not herself have to perform a distinct act of composition. Rather, in virtue of the conventions, her doing one thing – carrying out a given improvisation – counts as her doing something else – composing a particular performable work. Improvisational composition is possible, then, if (1) there is in place a set of conventions that determine what the performable work *is*, given the performance, and (2) the performer(s) draw(s) on these conventions in intending the performance to be an act of composition. It is highly questionable whether these two conditions are met in jazz improvisations. Indeed, Stephen Davies maintains that this would go against "the ethos of music like jazz" (2001, 14). But improvisational composition remains as a theoretical possibility here and in the other performing arts.

Pure improvisation

We have considered thus far the possibility of improvisations that issue from, and improvisations that issue in, performable works. The remaining possibility is of improvisations that stand in neither of these relationships to such works. We explored this possibility in the previous chapter, taking Jarrett's *Köln Concert* as our example. The performance itself is the artistic vehicle through which appreciable qualities are articulated. A similar analysis might apply to the kind of "free jazz" associated with Chicago ensembles in the 1960s and with European jazz in the following decade.[7] As in the case of Jarrett, the free jazz musicians often drew on various musical traditions as ingredients in their improvisations. But it seems implausible to think of their performances either as *of* pre-existing performable works or as *generating* such works.

4   Improvisation and Recording

If we accept Kivy's version of the story, Bach's feat illustrates how an improvisation-event that occurs at a particular place and time can be properly appreciated by those who were not present at that event. If the improvisation can be captured in a notation in a way that permits others to *perform* what was improvised, then, it might be thought, we are as well placed as Frederick the Great to appreciate the improvisational performance that we know as *The Musical Offering*, given a suitably gifted performer. But to draw this conclusion is to forget one of the points that Alperson and others have stressed about the appreciation of an improvisation. What we value in an improvised performance is not only, and perhaps not even primarily, the musical construction generated by the performer. It is also the improvisational action that produces that construction in the very process of generating the sounds that make up the performance. And with this difference in the values sought and found in improvisational performance goes a difference in the kind of listening that is required. Improvisational performance calls for a listening that attends to the manifest choices of the performer and screens out infelicities that might otherwise be taken to be serious flaws. When a contemporary performer gives a rendition of The Musical Offering, on the other hand, she is simply interpreting a performed work, and the element of choice and risk is no longer present in the performance in the way it was for Bach and for his audience.[8]

However, if we think about the possibility of appreciating an improvisational performance at which we are not present, what most naturally comes to mind is not an example like The Musical Offering. Rather, we think we can appreciate Jarrett's Köln Concert, or John Coltrane's performance of "My Favorite Things" at the Newport Jazz Festival on July 7, 1963, through recordings of those events. The recording is of the very event of the performer(s) improvising a sequence of sounds. Thus it might seem to provide a more solid basis than a transcription for appreciating an improvisation subsequent to its occurrence.

Matters are, as ever, more complex, however. Philosophers who have addressed this issue usually begin by noting a challenge posed by the composer and critic Roger Sessions to recorded music in general. Music, Sessions claimed,

> ceases to have interest for us ... the instant we become aware of the fact of literal repetition, of mechanical reproduction, when we know and can anticipate exactly how a given phrase is going to be modeled, exactly how long a given fermata is to be held, exactly what quality of accent or articulation, of acceleration or retard, will occur at a given moment. When the music ceases to be fresh for us in this sense, it ceases to be alive, and we can say in the most real sense that it ceases to be music. (Sessions 1950, 70–71)[9]

To defend musical recordings against the charge that they somehow destroy crucial features of musical performance, we need first to clarify the aspects of musical performance to which Sessions' argument might apply.[10] Since he stresses our ability to anticipate details of a recorded performance when we listen more than once to a recording of it, some commentators have taken the relevant aspects of a musical performance to be the structure of the sound sequence performed or the particular inflections given to the notes – color, timbre, dynamics, etc. These are indeed the qualities to which Sessions refers in his text. In that case, we might consider empirical work on the capacity of listeners to remember such details of a performance. Some critics of Sessions have appealed here to work by the philosopher of cogni-tive science Diana Raffman. Raffman (1993, chs. 4 and 5) argues that the mental schemata used by human memory to represent aspects of our expe-rience are not fine-grained enough to preserve the distinctive inflections of a musical performance. Gracyk, appealing to this work, suggests that this in part explains why we are still engaged by familiar rock works even after listening many times to their recordings (1996, 57ff., 236). The particular tone of the guitar solo on the Kingsmen's "Louie Louie," for example, can still deliver "the thrill of the unexpected" even when we feel we know every musical detail of the recording.

Other commentators have been less impressed by this line of argument, however.[11] For one thing, it admits of no obvious extension to *structural* fea-tures of a recorded musical performance, which we can presumably register in memory, and which will then, according to Sessions' argument, become increasingly familiar, and incapable of surprising us, with repeated auditions of the recording. Second, even in the case of those performative inflections that we cannot memorize in their full glory, we can surely anticipate *the thrill* of hearing a particular passage or solo, if not the "color" of the passage or solo itself. Thus we lose the *surprise* of being thrilled, even if we are still thrilled, by the distinctive tone of the guitar solo on "Louie Louie." And, third, it is not clear that what applies to our general powers of recall also applies to our experience in listening to a familiar recording of a musical work. Stephen Davies makes this point against Gracyk's use of Raffman's research. Even if we grant that people are incapable of "replaying" every detail of a recording in memory, "the issue … is whether they can anticipate what is coming next as they listen to a recording. My experience suggests to me that this is possible. If I know the disc very well, sometimes I have an eidetic aural 'picture' of what is about to happen a few milliseconds before it occurs" (S. Davies 2001, 305).

While Sessions intended his argument to apply to the artistic contents articulated in recordings of performable works, his argument can also be applied to recordings of *improvisations*, and here it takes a very different focus. Lee B. Brown, in a couple of papers (1996, 2000) has questioned whether recordings can do justice not to the content of an improvised per-formance but to the fact that it is improvised. Can a recording preserve "the spontaneous dimensions of musical performances" (Brown 2000, 117)? A recording of an improvisation differs from a later performance that rep-licates the sound structure of an improvisation – as in *The Musical Offering* example – in presenting a performance that itself involves real-time choices as to its own development. But it is questionable whether it can also make this aspect of the performance "live" to listeners, and thus whether listeners can thereby appreciate the improvised performance. Indeed, Brown argues, the same considerations apply to non-improvisational but highly inflected *interpretations* of performable works, since they also involve real-time, if not spontaneous, actions. Stephen Davies has responded that the listener's knowledge that she is hearing a recording of an improvised performance can inform her listening, thereby enabling her to appreciate those features of the performance that, as seen in Chapter 7, bear upon the proper appreciation of an improvisation qua activity of the performer. (2001, 305–306).

Brown, however, raises some additional concerns about the impact of recording technology on improvisational performance. First, he notes that it is only with the resources provided by recording technology that it becomes possible to analyze jazz performance. "Traditional jazz analysis" can proceed only if the analyst has the ability to listen repeatedly to the improvised performance. This might suggest that recording technology makes a positive contribution towards a better understanding and appreciation of improvised music. But Brown sympathizes with what he terms "postmodernist" critics of traditional jazz analysis who argue that, in their concern with structural features of improvised performances, analysts treat such performances as if they were pieces of pre-composed music, ignoring thereby the very spontaneity that makes them improvisations in the first place.

A second concern expressed by Brown is that the availability of recording technology has influenced jazz practice in ways that run counter to the ideal of improvisation. Whereas one might assume that, in jazz at least, the goal of recording is to capture the spontaneity of live performance, jazz musicians are increasingly using studio techniques such as overdubbing in their own recordings. This, in turn, is having an effect on the way that audiences listen to jazz, both live and recorded, making them more interested in the sonic possibilities of the recordings and less interested in the rawness and spontaneity of live performance.[12] Not only, then, are recordings an unsatisfactory medium for the appreciation of jazz performance, but the kinds of recordings being made by many jazz musicians are undermining the proper medium for such appreciation, the live concert in which musicians make real-time choices in their playing and audience members see these choices as essential to the appreciation of the performance.

However, it would be wrong to paint too negative a picture of the place of recordings in the jazz tradition.[13] First, as noted above, Brown grants that recordings have made possible the analysis and understanding of structural features of jazz improvisations. This understanding surely has a place in our appreciation of jazz performance, even if, with Brown, we insist on the importance of the spontaneity of such performances. To appreciate the spontaneity of a particular performance is to appreciate something specific that was done spontaneously, and this appreciation can only be sharpened by the kind of structural insights into that "doing" that analysis makes possible.

Second, while Brown may be right in questioning the use of studio techniques in manipulating the sound of traditional types of improvisatory jazz performances, such techniques are crucial to those recent developments in jazz broadly labeled as "jazz fusion." It is surely not difficult for the cultivated listener to adjust her expectations when listening to recordings of traditional jazz performance so that she seeks out different values in such performances from the ones she seeks out in fusion recordings.

5   The Place of Rehearsal in the Performing Arts

In examining the place of improvisation in the performing arts, I have focused for the most part upon musical performances. As the brief discussion of theatrical improvisation may have indicated, however, the conclusions that we have reached concerning improvisation in music admit of fairly easy generalization to theater and dance. Our focus on musical improvisation was partly motivated by the fact that it is philosophers of music who are largely responsible for the literature on improvisation in the performing arts. Indeed, it is to philosophers of music that we owe much of the philosophical literature on the performing arts in general. Perhaps this last fact also explains the relative neglect of rehearsal in that literature. For, to the extent that musical performances are subsumed under the classical paradigm, rehearsal seems to be of little philosophical interest. Given a performable musical work that an ensemble intends to perform, the primary purpose of rehearsal is to arrive at a shared understanding of how that work is to be interpreted in the resulting performance and to anticipate difficulties that might arise in harmonizing the contributions of individual members of the ensemble.

Rehearsal in theater and dance, however, is philosophically interesting precisely to the extent that it calls into question whether the classical paradigm can be extended to theatrical and dance performances. We may recall from Chapter 6 that the role of ensemble revision in theatrical rehearsals might seem to support the ingredients model over the classical paradigm as an account of at least some theatrical performances. Indeed, where rehearsals involve ensemble revision they raise some of the same issues as improvisation, since they have a compositional dimension. The final form of a theatrical or dance performance involving such rehearsals usually incorporates substantive changes made as a result of innovations introduced in rehearsal. Furthermore, it is a feature of dance and theatrical practice that improvisations by performers in rehearsal may result in new constraints on subsequent performances. Does this, then, give us a less problematic example of improvisational composition?

It seems not. The same considerations that led us to question Kivy's account of Bach's *Musical Offering* seem to be operative here. However brilliant or innovative a performer's improvisations in rehearsal may be, they acquire status as elements in a production or performance only as a result of a decision to accord them that status taken after the fact. Indeed, this decision is usually taken by another party or other parties, either a director or choreographer or the rest of the company. There are no conventions whereby innovations introduced in rehearsal are *ipso facto* accorded status as elements in the production or performance, so the conditions that we suggested for genuine improvisational composition are not met. This is not to denigrate in any way the role of rehearsal in the generation of theatrical and dance performances, however. As in our earlier discussion, the point here is a conceptual one.

Our interest in the present context, however, is precisely in the creative import of what transpires in rehearsal and its bearing upon some issues that we left undecided in Chapter 6 concerning the scope of the classical paradigm in theater.[14] Where, as in contemporary theater,[15] it is common for improvisations and discoveries by performers during group rehearsal to be incorporated into the finished performance, this clearly undermines any version of the classical paradigm that draws a sharp distinction between an act of composition by the author of a playscript and acts of interpretively realizing that playscript once it has been composed. The idea of theatrical works as scripts that only require realization through the performative norms of an interpreting community seems to make little sense here. As we noted in Chapter 6, this might motivate a non-text-based model of what a theatrical work prescribes for its correct performances, rather than a repudiation of the idea that theatrical performances are *of* works at all.

The "ensemble revision" model of theatrical preparation upon which Hamilton relies in sketching his hypothetical *Hedda Gabler* cases is so familiar to contemporary students of theater that it is natural to project it back earlier than 1850, when he begins his outline of the historical background to the exciting developments in twentieth-century theater reflected in such productions as *Something to Tell You*. In the absence of any illuminating evidence about rehearsal practice in, say, Shakespearean or Restoration drama, scholars have nonetheless assumed that the ensemble revision model obtained. Fredson Bowers (1955), for example, advised editors of Shakespeare that they must take account of the revisions to the plays in group rehearsals, while Gary Taylor's *Reinventing Shakespeare* (1989) rests on the assumption that Shakespeare's plays evolved through group rehearsal.[16] It is therefore very interesting to consider the insights into the process of theatrical preparation in English drama from the sixteenth to the eighteenth centuries presented by Tiffany Stern in the first serious scholarly studies of these matters

(2000, 2004). While I cannot hope to do justice to the richness of these studies and of the examples of theatrical practice discussed, a summary of the principal conclusions will, I think, allow us to consider their import for the alternative models of theatrical performance examined so far.

One constant in the hypothetical scenarios sketched by Hamilton is a company, possibly including a director, that uses a text in light of a shared conception of the goals of their intended performance. Another constant is a process of working towards the realization of those goals through group rehearsals and ensemble revision. Neither of these elements is present in the preparations for performances of sixteenth- to eighteenth-century English drama. One does find increasingly the presence of persons who played some of the roles of the modern director, however. These persons were the theater manager, most famously personified by Garrick at Drury Lane in the late eighteenth century, and the prompter, who possessed, and sometimes independently revised, the only complete set of specifications for the performance. But producers or directors in the modern sense appear only around the time that Hamilton's survey of the historical background begins, in the mid nineteenth century.[17]

Second, the idea of ensemble revision, central to our modern sense of how a play is prepared for presentation, has almost no application in sixteenth- to eighteenth-century English theater. This is primarily because there was little if any group rehearsal prior to performance, the latter seeming to be a necessary condition for ensemble revision to take place. Nor did the preparatory process begin with the sharing of a text to be used in some way. Preparation began and generally continued with the distribution of "parts" to individual actors, such parts containing only the actor's own speeches and a short one- to four-word cue (usually not specifically assigned to another character). Rehearsal was almost entirely one-on-one, sometimes including coaching from the author, the prompter, or the manager. Actors also found clues as to how their part was to be played internal to the text they received. Transitions from prose to verse, for example, indicated a change in emotion or demeanor.

The aim of individual rehearsal – known as "study" – was for the actor to learn how to speak and act his or her part. But study provided the actor with no insight into what else might be going on in the play. If there was a group rehearsal prior to the first performance, the individual actors came to it with their contributions already established. The principal purpose of such a rehearsal was to try to coordinate the contributions of the individual actors.[18] This depended, in actual performance, on the activities of the prompter who, being the only person with a record of the entire production, not only was charged with prompting words and actions on the part of the actors, but also directed blocking. The prompter therefore functioned very much like a musical conductor at an orchestral performance. Like a conductor, the prompter was part of the overall spectacle to which the audience attended.

One reason for proceeding in this way was the sheer number of plays put on by any given company, and thus the number of parts that any individual actor had to "study." But it meant that the spectacle confronting the audience was very different from the one with which we are familiar. Since actors prepared for the performance only by learning their own parts; they had no assigned roles when not actually speaking, and often fell out of character and conversed *in propria persona* with the audience. The "social" nature of theatrical perform-ance, stressed by Hamilton, was even more apparent here, audience members freely heckling and eliciting responses from actors. Audience members, too, viewed what was presented more as an assemblage of parts than as an ensem-ble production, and, as noted in Chapter 6, would often walk out when the parts that interested them no longer had a place in the presentation.

Performance practices at this time are clearly difficult to reconcile with a text-based construal of performable theatrical works. The contribution of the author was increasingly marginalized, especially when compared to modern practice where living playwrights are often involved in the rehearsal process. Playwrights, like contemporary screenwriters, furnished an initial text that, in the Restoration and even more in the eighteenth century, was usually radically transformed by the manager or prompter, whose task was to "theatricalize" the drama. Unless he was involved in individual rehearsals of one or more of the actors, further input by the author occurred only fol-lowing the first night, when the audience was canvassed for its views on the performance. The author was then expected to revise the play to meet their demands. Since the author was paid receipts only on the second or third night, and since there would be no audience unless the requested changes were made, authors generally complied with what was requested.

The first night, known as "the trial," was effectively an open rehearsal, not of *the acting of the play* but of *the play itself*, its writing and plot. Since it was expected that changes would be made, actors were not overly worried about learning all of their lines, so the acting on the first night was generally bad. Samuel Pepys apparently refused to attend first nights for this reason (Stern 2000, 188). The attraction of the first night, however – something for which the public was willing to pay twice the usual fee – was that one not only got to judge, but also to play a part in the revision of, the play. The general opin-ion was that it was only on the second night – assuming the play survived to a second night – that the play was presented in its finished form.

But, if sixteenth- to eighteenth-century English theatrical practice fits badly with the text-based model of theatrical performance, it fits equally badly with the ingredients model if the latter is taken to include ensemble revision. For, if we ask how performances in this period stand in relation to the *revision* of texts, we see that ensemble revision played almost no part, that much revision took place in "theatricalizing" the play even before the distribution of parts to the actors, and that the other principal source of revisions was the opinions of the audience on "first night." Furthermore, revisions after the distribution of parts were nearly always within speeches, or involved the deletion of exchanges between parts, so as to avoid affecting the "cues."[19]

But, it might be thought, the ingredients model doesn't *require* ensemble revision, even if this is a prominent feature of modern theatrical practice. The crucial question is whether we can identify something in sixteenth- to eighteenth-century practice that functions as a performable work. One final feature of sixteenth- to eighteenth-century English theatrical practice is relevant here. I noted earlier that rehearsal was almost entirely individual in nature, with actors being schooled by author, manager, or prompter, or even another actor, on how their part should be played. It was also assumed that, however the part was played by the first actor to whom it was assigned, this was how the part was to be played by other actors in any subsequent productions. The individual rehearsal of later actors was a training in mimicking the performance of earlier actors who had played the part. This meant that there was no real conception of an actor (or, indeed, anyone else, such as the prompter) *interpreting* a part, since it was assumed that there was only one way in which it could be played. Garrick's contribution, in the late eighteenth century, was to school actors – again in private study – to act parts from earlier plays in a new way. But Garrick was simply trying to replace one fixed way of playing the part with another equally fixed way. Prior to Garrick, it was assumed that a revival of a play would preserve the parts from earlier productions. Where changes *were* made in a revival of an earlier production, they were not artistically motivated, but reflected practical considerations, such as the lack of a relevant skill by the new actor playing a part, or the architectural features of the theater in which the performance was to take place.

The preparatory process as a whole, incorporating the first night and the subsequent revisions, seems to eventuate in something that subsequent performances and productions aim, and are expected to aim, to present to audiences. Thus we might view such subsequent performances as of works, so construed – collections of parts to be played in certain ways and an encompassing narrative into which those parts enter.[20] But, if we take sixteenth- to eighteenth-century English theatrical performances after the first night to be of works so conceived, responsibility for those works obviously cannot be assigned to any single individual, let alone to the hapless author. A comparison with cinematic works is tempting here. It has been argued that films are "multiply authored," by their screenwriters, actors, directors, and so on.[21] Similarly, in sixteenth- to eighteenth-century English theatrical practice, the playwright provides something like a screenplay; the manager, like a director, "theatricalizes" this to get something that works for the stage; the actors contribute to the resulting work to a large extent in ignorance of how what they are doing fits into the performance as a whole, and the audience, like a focus group, gets to have its say on things.

If sixteenth- to eighteenth-century English theatrical practice does indeed operate with the conception of a performable theatrical work as a collection of parts, this yields a further account of what is required if a performance is to be true to a work. Truth to a work so conceived is in some respects stricter than truth to a work defined in relation to a text, since the latter allows for different interpretations of characters. It also in some ways resembles truth to a work defined in relation to an emplotted point. For we might expect this point to be partly conveyed through the interpretation of the characters, and thus through the parts. But, as noted in Chapter 6, our intuitive notion of what it is for a performance to be true to a work seems to require that *the work itself* determine the sense in which a correct performance must be true to that work. In that case, if the Shakespearean conception of *King Lear* is of something constituted not just of a text (or perhaps a set of closely related texts) but also of a collection of parts which interpret that text in a specific way, then performances that aim merely to be faithful to the text, or to the emplotted point of the play, are in an important sense not performances *of* the play. For the kind of fidelity at which they aim fails to reflect the nature of the work itself. When, as in Chapter 6, we seek to reconcile contemporary performances purporting to be of Shakespearean plays with the classical paradigm by appealing to a notion of being true to the emplotted point of a play, we project our present sense of dramatic art onto a very different tradition. Our willingness to countenance a plurality of interpretations of Shakespearean and Restoration dramas whose legitimacy depends upon their intended fidelity to the emplotted point of the play would surely bemuse our period counterparts. Such interpretations are, however, best understood in terms of the classical paradigm that they strive, but fail, to emulate, rather than in terms of the ingredients model. For they aspire to be true to an independent work, even if they misconstrue what truth to that work requires.

Our brief examination of what may strike us as a largely alien form of theatrical practice should further caution us against trying to impose a single model on theatrical performance. The ingredients model fits very well the kinds of increasingly radical and experimental performances we encounter as we move further away from *Hedda-to-Hedda*. But it is difficult to see how it applies to sixteenth- to eighteenth-century English theatrical practice, or indeed to traditional theatrical performances that understand themselves in terms of the text-based model. Much theatrical practice is best modeled on the classical paradigm, since the goal of being true to an independent work explains much of what is going on in performances. But these performances often fail to conform to the classical paradigm as ordinarily conceived because the company operates with a conception of truth to a work that does not reflect the conception of the latter that is partly constitutive of the work they seek to perform. The classical paradigm is a model for thinking about what goes on in the performing arts in general. It is a limited model, and it is important to see this, but there is no reason to think that it is only in music that we have performances that accord with that paradigm.

Notes

1. For an interesting discussion of what he terms the "improvised feel," see A. Hamilton 2007, 198–207.
2. See, for example, S. Davies 1987.
3. This view is also defended in Young and Matheson 2000.
4. See S. Davies 2001, 16–19.
5. S. Davies (2001, 13) seems to misread Alperson as at least implying that improvisers can compose repeatable musical works. He identifies Alperson's view with that of Kivy, to be discussed below. But Alperson, while defending the idea of improvisations as works of art in their own right, explicitly rejects the idea of improvisational composition in our sense, and does so for the same kinds of reasons as Davies. See Alperson 1984, 26.
6. See S. Davies 2001, 13.
7. See Cochrane 2000 on how we should think about such pure improvisational works.
8. As Andrew Kania (private communication) has pointed out, a contemporary performance of *The Musical Offering* may help us to appreciate *Bach's* achievement. For, in attending to that performance, we can *imagine* that it is an improvisation, and thereby better appreciate what it would be to improvise such a piece.
9. This passage is cited in Gracyk 1996, 54; Brown 2000, 113; and S. Davies 2001, 305.
10. See Brown 2000.
11. See Brown 2000, 113–114; S. Davies 2001, 305.
12. S. Davies (2003, 307–313) makes a related point about the implications of recording for the interpretation and appreciation of works intended for live performance. The values sought in an interpretation of such a work when that work is performed for a live audience differ from the values sought in an interpretation when the work is performed in a studio for the purposes of issuing a recording.
13. I am grateful to Andrew Kania for raising these issues.
14. I focus here on theater rather than dance because, as we saw in Chapter 6, different issues bear upon the scope of the classical paradigm in the two performing arts.
15. See the examples cited from Stern 2000, 5–8 in Chapter 6.
16. See, again, Stern 2000, 3–4.

17. This is reflected in the fact that, as Stern notes, the *OED* identifies the first use of the term "director" in connection with theatrical performance as occurring in 1938, and the first use of "producer" to denote a person producing a dramatic performance as occurring in 1891 (2000, 8, 9 n. 29).
18. Note the parallel with the purpose of rehearsals for musical ensembles, as described above. Stephen Davies has pointed out, in private communication, that there is a further parallel. In orchestral rehearsal, musicians usually only get their individual parts, the conductor alone having the full score.
19. It is important to bear in mind here that the "second night" was the second *performance* of the play, which might not occur for some days after the "first night." As noted above, companies would put on a number of different plays at the same time. Thus even quite substantial revisions between the "first night" and the "second night" could be effected by the playwright and implemented by the players.
20. Note that these works, while they owe some of their features to what happens in performance, are not *composed* in performance. Composition is a matter of the decisions made at different stages in the process leading up to the second night, decisions that accommodate some revisions occurring in or suggested by performance but don't accommodate others. Thus we do not have here a plausible candidate for improvisational composition.
21. See Gaut 1997.

9

Elements of Performance II: Audience and Embodiment

1   Can There Be Artistic Performance Without an Audience?

When we last encountered Berthold and Magda, they were sitting in a provincial theater regretting their choice of evening entertainment. We also left hanging unresolved in that theater, however, a question about what had in fact taken place. Much of what happened on stage did so without being attended to by an audience. For, we will recall, the audience consisted solely of Berthold and Magda, who found other things to engage their attention as the actors toiled. But Paul Woodruff assigns an attentive audience a constitutive role in a theatrical performance. As we have seen, he defines theater as "the art by which human beings make or find human action worth watching, in a measured time and place," and maintains that we have a theatrical *event* only when both performer(s) and audience are exercising this art (2008, 18). If so then, while Berthold and Magda may have attended a performance by actors *in* a theater, they didn't attend a performance *of* theater.

Of course, there is nothing to prevent Woodruff from *stipulating* that he will use the term "theatrical event" in the foregoing sense. And it is tempting to read him in this way, given his concession that what transpires in the absence of a suitably attentive audience may be a *performance* even though it is not theater: "Take away the audience and the watching ends. If no one is watching, it's not theater, though it may truly be a performance" (Woodruff 2008, 42). But Paul Thom adopts what seems to be an even stricter line, holding that in the absence of an audience one doesn't even have a *performance*.

Philosophy of the Performing Arts, First Edition. David Davies.
© 2011 David Davies. Published 2011 by Blackwell Publishing Ltd.

We need to see what reasons support these intuitively surprising conclusions, and why one might take a different view of the issues. I shall focus on whether artistic performance in general requires an audience, while also looking in particular at theatrical performance, the kind of performance that concerns Woodruff. This will lead us to consider whether the audience stands in a relation to a theatrical performance different from the one in which it stands to performances in the other performing arts.

In Chapter 1, I suggested that someone counts as performing only if they are guided in their actions by the anticipated evaluative attentions of an intended audience who, it is assumed, will judge those actions according to certain criteria. I also argued that one can perform even if one's intended audience is not actually attending to what is done. Recall Basil twirling his umbrella on his way to the station. His actions are designed to produce a particular effect on his intended audience – his watching neighbors. But, I suggested, he is no less of a performer if, unbeknownst to him, no one is actually watching. If, as I supposed, the presence of an actual audience is unnecessary for Basil's actions to qualify as a performance, why should matters be any different when we turn to performances in the arts?

Nelson Goodman broadly concurs with this assessment of the situation (1984, 142–143). The intended function of performances in the arts, according to Goodman, is to affect how we organize and perceive a world, and this presupposes that the work is comprehended by an audience. But he allows that there can be genuine artistic performances in the absence of an audience, although such performances will of necessity fail to fulfill their intended function. Such events, Goodman holds, are genuine performances just as novels that never find a readership are genuine novels, and paintings that are never exhibited for the appreciation of others are genuine paintings. All that matters in each of these cases, we might say, is that we rightly explain certain features of the ordering of the artistic manifold – in the case of artistic performances, the actions executed by the performer – in terms of the artist's judgments as to how such an ordering *would* affect intended receivers. Even in the absence of the attending eyes and ears of Berthold and Magda, then, the event presented on stage in the provincial theater will count as a performance as long as the company's actions are shaped by the anticipated eyes and ears of an intended audience. Let me "fit audience find, though few," said Milton.[1] Or indeed, we might add, *if any*.

Thom, however, insists that there is no performance without an actual audience. A performance, he maintains, must always be "directed towards some kind of audience" (Thom 1993, 172). This is not the same as being presented before an audience, since sporting events, while they are usually presented before spectators, are not performances in the relevant sense (179). For actions to be "directed towards" an audience, there must be some kind of *address* by the agents to the audience. This, in part, is what is lacking in sporting events, where the energies and attentions of a player are focused on other players or other elements of the game, even if there are in fact spectators present. In a performance, this address relates to what the performers are manifestly doing. To perform is to display something to the audience – a series of actions or sounds, say – and, in so doing, to address the audience in the following terms: "attend to this!" (173). Artistic performances differ from other kinds of displays – for example, a merchant's display of his wares – in the kind of attention that they solicit from spectators. A performance in the performing arts demands that the spectator engage in what Thom terms a "playful beholding" which *interprets* what is presented. This "playful beholding" is a feature of the audience's attention and can take a number of forms. Audience attention can play "between the performer's present actions and recollected past actions or anticipated future ones," or "between one performer and another," or "between content and vehicle," or "between a particular performance as a whole and another performance of the same work," or "between aspects of the performance and aspects of their own lives," or "between what occurs inside the performance space and what has occurred or may occur outside it" (205). The attention solicited is therefore not merely passive but demands activity on the part of the spectator.

Performing, Thom maintains, takes place in the context of performance institutions. The latter involve both a performance setting – a space set apart from the space of everyday life – and a performance occasion – a period of time structured for the purposes of performance. But, Thom stresses, it is the performance that establishes something as its setting and occasion, rather than – as on an institutional theory – something's counting as a performance in virtue of its being staged in a particular institutional context such as a theater. He cites, as an example, Trisha Brown's *Roof Piece* (1973) which, in being presented on a mile of rooftops in Manhattan, established this location as its performance setting. We have performance institutions when we have the *concepts* of a performance setting and a performance occasion. Given these concepts, we can find novel ways of instantiating them, as in Brown's case. Thom also rejects the suggestion that something becomes a performance by being the object of "playful attention." His target here is the view implicit in John Cage's definition of theater, as "something that engages both the eye and the ear," which would permit everyday life to count as theater if beheld in the right way. Citing Arthur Danto's example of a riot that we can attend to *as if* it were a ballet, Thom argues that we need to preserve a distinction between something's *being* a performance and our treating it *as if* it were a performance. The essence of performance, he insists, lies no more in our manner of attending to actions than it does in the institutional context in which actions are performed. It lies, rather, in the particular relationship that obtains between the performers and the audience, whereby the former address the latter in a particular way.

Thus far, however, we have seen nothing to demonstrate that, in being *directed towards* an audience, a performance requires an *actual* audience. But Thom thinks that this follows from the distinctive nature of the address that partly constitutes a performance. This, he thinks, undermines Goodman's analogy between an audienceless performance and a readerless novel, for a novel does not involve the same kind of address as a performance:

> In doing something that has the force of saying, "Attend to me," I am not just making a hypothetical address, as the author of a work does, to whoever happens to be an addressee, rather, I make a categorical address to the audience, whom I assume to exist. In performing, I believe myself to be referring to present persons, to whom I am in effect saying, "You, attend to me." If no one is present at the performance, there is a failure of reference. By contrast, if the novel remains unpublished or the painting unexhibited, then there is no failure of reference because the work did not refer to anyone in the first place, even though it was made for a public to behold. The audience is not a mere dispensable accessory to performance ... All performance needs an audience if its reference is to succeed and if its assumption of audience attention and demand is to be warranted. (Thom 1993, 192)

Thom relies here on an analogy between the address issued by those participating in a performance, and an ordinary linguistic utterance that contains a term that purports, but fails, to refer, such as "the present king of France" as uttered in 2010. Just as such an utterance fails to make a statement if its purportedly referring term fails to actually refer, so a "performance" whose address fails to refer to an actual audience is not really a performance at all.

The correct analysis of utterances containing non-referring terms like "the present King of France" as their grammatical subjects is a matter of some dispute in the philosophy of language, and it is by no means uncontroversial to claim, as Thom does, that such an utterance fails to make a statement.[2] However, we need not take a stand on this matter in order to see that there is something suspect in Thom's attempt to draw an analogy between the question "Does an utterance of a sentence containing a non-referring singular term make a genuine statement?" and the question at hand, "Does an attempt to stage a performance whose 'address' fails to refer to an actual audience count as a genuine performance?" For it is obvious that we can perform various speech acts other than making statements – issuing directives or expressing intentions, for example – by means of sentences that contain non-referring expressions. Consider, for example, "The next person to talk in this class will get a detention," uttered by a teacher. Her intention is precisely that no one should satisfy the subject expression, but her success in bringing about this state of affairs does not entail that she failed to issue a directive. Or consider the following prescription by a composer whose work remains sadly unperformed: "Performers of my work must produce the following sound sequence." The lack of performers does not entail that the composer failed to issue a prescription.

Is it nonetheless necessary for a speech act having the form of an *address* of the sort contained in Thom's analysis of performance to have an actual addressee? As Thom sets it out, the address has the form of an *imperative* addressed to a particular subject. The suggestion, then, must be that one can issue such an imperative only if the addressed subject exists. But why think this is so? Should we say that the nervous sentry who hallucinates the sound of an intruder and utters the words "You there, stop or I'll shoot!" has failed to issue an order? Of course, it is difficult to make sense of someone uttering such an imperative if they don't *believe* that the addressee of the imperative exists. So we might think it is not possible for actors in an empty hall to issue the address necessary if what they do is to count as a performance, for how can they issue an address to a subject they know does not exist? But this assumes that Thom's way of characterizing what it is for an action to be "for an audience" – in terms of an address directed at an identified or a presumed audience – is correct. Is this preferable, however, to the account proposed in Chapter 1, in terms of the performer's actions being guided by the expected responses of an intended audience?

To answer this question, we must clarify certain aspects of this account that have thus far gone unelucidated. This will also allow us to identify certain implications of the account. Consider first the notion of an "intended audience" whose anticipated assessments consciously guide a performer in her actions. The performer's intended audience is composed of those *for whom* the performance is done. This audience must be in some way identifiable by the performer – either by acquaintance or under some description[3] – and she must have certain beliefs or expectations as to how this audience will respond to various things that she might do. Only under these conditions does it make sense to think of the performer as *guided* in her actions by expectations about *this* audience. But a performer can be so guided whether or not her intended audience is actually paying attention, and indeed whether or not her intended audience actually exists. In fact, the performer doesn't even need to *believe* her intended audience exists in order to be so guided. Consider a dancer whose dance tutor has recently died. She can surely perform a particular dance *for* her late tutor in the sense we have identified. She pays attention to certain details that she knows were of particular concern to him; she obtains pleasure from executing a particular movement in the way that she knows would have given him pleasure, etc.

This brings out a second feature of the proposed account of performing. To characterize an agent as performing is to place her actions within a particular kind of *explanatory space*. We assume that certain details of those actions are to be explained by reference to the agent's expectations as to their reception by an intended audience. While we explain such an agent's actions in terms of various goals she is pursuing, we assume that a principal motivation is the conscious desire to affect her intended audience in a particular way through their attention to her actions.

But if the difference between performing and mere acting resides in the kinds of considerations that guide the agent and in terms of which her actions are to be explained, this implies a number of things that might initially strike one as counterintuitive. First, there is no reason why one cannot perform *for oneself*, that is, be one's own intended audience. A musician who plays in an otherwise deserted room may do this. Thus a performance need not be open in practice to the appraisal of others. What is crucial is that an agent be rightly describable as guided in how she selects or executes a given course of actions by her expectations as to how these actions will affect an intended audience. The musician who plays for herself meets this condition to the extent that a principal constraint on how she plays is her expectation as to how she herself will judge what she does. A performer who performs for herself is as open to disappointment as one who performs for others, and for the same kinds of reasons. On the one hand, she may be dissatisfied with her playing because she fails to play in the way her expectations guide her to do. On the other hand, she may play what she intended but discover that she was wrong in her expectations as to how she would respond. It is important to stress, however, that when a musician plays or a dancer dances for pleasure, she does not usually consciously shape her actions in light of such expectations. She simply gives herself up to the activity. Thus, while one *can* perform for oneself, only some self-directed activity by performing artists counts as performance.

Second, much of what performing artists do in preparing for public performances also counts as performing. For it is consciously guided by expectations about the responses of an intended audience – in this cases, the audience that is expected to attend the public performance of the piece. This may sound odd, given that we are used to drawing a distinction between rehearsal and performance. But this oddness is easily dispelled. For the distinction in question is more accurately described as one between rehearsing and *giving a performance*. Performing artists perform both during rehearsals and when on stage, but only in the latter case do we describe them as giving a performance. The latter requires the establishment of a performance setting and performance location in Thom's sense. The important point, however, as noted above, is that to treat an agent as performing is to place her actions in a particular kind of explanatory space, a space as pertinent to what is done in rehearsal as to what is done on stage.

One final point needs clarification. A performer is guided in her actions by the ways in which she expects those *actions* to affect an intended audience.

Dancers, for example, perform whereas painters do not because, while each is guided in their actions by expectations about the evaluations of an intended audience, it is the *product* of the painter's actions – the finished canvas – that he expects the audience to evaluate, and not the actions themselves. But what about the musician? Is it not the product of her actions – an acoustic manifold – that she expects her intended audience to assess? So why is she a performer when the painter is not? Primarily, I think, because the audible results of a musician's playing are directly correlated with and intimately linked to the actions she performs. It is therefore natural to think of the instrument as an extension of the performer through which she acts and of the sounds produced as her actions. Recall here Levinson's claim that expressive properties of musical works are partly dependent on the actions needed to elicit particular sounds from given instruments. Furthermore, the performing musician's actions generate the music in real time, without the possibility of revisions. The acoustic manifold we appreciate is contemporaneous with the actions of the musician. It therefore can be, and usually is, experienced and evaluated through one's attentive engagement with those actions. Only in the case of certain "action" painters might painters satisfy these conditions, and it is only in such cases that we might classify painters as performers.

Having clarified the account of performance sketched in Chapter 1, we can return to Thom's contrasting account of the role of the audience in performance. In addition to his argument based on the kind of address made by a performer, Thom offers a further argument in support of his claim that we have a performance only where we have an actual audience. This argument is based on the *causal* interaction between performers and an audience. The act of performing, he maintains, "assumes the existence of a gaze that is making a certain demand of it, and it supplies what that demand seeks" (Thom 1993, 192). The suggestion here seems to be that the performer must tailor her performance to an audience that makes particular demands upon her. But why does this require that the audience be actual rather than intended in the above sense? Of course, there are certain kinds of artistic performances that do require an actual audience because the audience plays a role in realizing the work. Thom mentions the simple example of a children's pantomime, which relies on the audience saying such things as "He's behind you," or responding "yes" to the question whether they believe in fairies. He also mentions the more complex example of La Monte Young's *Drift Study* which requires certain movements on the part of the audience. But these cases don't justify the more general claim that *all* performances need an actual audience.

A related argument starts from the fact that, where there is an actual audience, performers may respond to it, so that the performance may change when the audience changes. In Chapter 6, we noted David Osipovich's remarks to this effect in defense of the "liveness" model of *theatrical* performance. Our concern there was with Osipovich's claim that the "unscriptability" of theatrical performances defeats the attempt to subsume them under the classical paradigm. But, we may recall, the reason why theatrical performances are unscriptable, according to Osipovich, is that theater requires the co-occurrence at a given time of an act of showing and an act of watching what is shown. Unscriptability is a consequence of the fact that the performers – those who are doing the showing – must always be sensitive to, and willing to respond to, the responses of those who are watching. Osipovich talks here of audience and performers having to "contend" with each other: "Each affects the other and is affected by the other. Noting that audience and performers have to contend with each other in shared space and time is just another way of saying that theatre is live" (Osipovich 2006, 466). It is only the liveness of theater, so construed, that differentiates it from live television, he maintains. To deny the liveness of theater is, then, to mask one of its important distinctive aesthetic features.

The role that Osipovich assigns to an actual audience cannot be played by a non-actual intended audience, or at least this would call for challenging psychological gymnastics on the part of the performers who would have to somehow "contend" with their own intendings. But Osipovich's claim that "contending" between performers and audience members is a defining condition of theater seems to beg the question at issue. This is certainly an essential feature of *live* theater if we define the latter in terms of the presence of an actual audience. But why should we assume that all theater must be live in this sense? Why, indeed, assume that we no longer have theater if the audience is viewing the performers live – in the different sense of "simultaneously with the performance" – on a television screen? Or, indeed, why assume that the status of what is being done by the performers as theater is further compromised if it is transmitted to the same audience with a short time delay? In both cases, why should we deny that the audience is seeing a televised transmission of a theatrical performance? A televised broadcast of a football match played in a closed stadium is still a broadcast of a football match, after all.

Osipovich's argument rests on the assumption that the liveness – in his sense – of theatrical performances is a source of aesthetic features that distinguish theater from live television and cinema. But this runs together two different questions. First, what grounds the relevant aesthetic differences between theatrical performances and films? The answer is that the former are live in a third sense – they unfold in real time without the possibility of revisions. Second, what distinguishes theatrical performances from live television broadcasts of theatrical performances? The answer is that the latter provide a less than optimal way of conveying the distinctive aesthetic features of the former. In this case, we don't have two distinct artistic entities that differ in their aesthetic properties: we have a single artistic entity and two ways of gaining access to its aesthetic properties.

We might also ask how Thom or Osipovich can explain a work like *Roof Piece*, where, fairly obviously, no audience could watch the entire performance. Thom claims that, in this case, "the performers collectively were an audience of their performance. Maybe nobody saw everything that was done to produce this performance, but the performers collectively saw it" (1993, 193). But this is puzzling. For it would need to be the case that the performers were each other's *intended* audience. It seems very implausible, however, to think that this was Brown's intention, or the way in which the performers thought of their actions. As Thom admits, part of the point of holding the performance on the rooftops of Manhattan was to exclude the possibility of an actual external audience addressed by the piece. Furthermore, if we do allow this account of *Roof Piece*, why cannot the actors on stage in the empty hall also count as the intended audience for their own performance? The answer, again, is that while they are a possible audience for this performance, they are not the intended audience whose anticipated responses shape the performance.

While Thom's and Osipovich's arguments do not, I think, establish that there can be a performance only in the presence of an actual audience, the relationship between artistic performers and audiences is clearly more subtle and intimate than the one between, say, athletes and spectators, and much that they say on this question is insightful. We find complementary insights in James Hamilton's attempts to clarify what is distinctive not only about the relationship between performing artists and an audience, but also about this relationship as it exists in theater (2007, 50–53). Hamilton agrees with Thom and Osipovich that interactions between performers and members of an audience are a central element in theater, and he further agrees with Osipovich that this distinguishes theater from the other performing arts. What he terms "audience practice" – skill in presenting something to an audience gathered for that purpose – is paradigmatic in theater but not in dance and music: "Whereas playing music and dancing commonly can have both audience and non-audience forms of practice, theatrical playing has no common non-audience form of practice" (J. Hamilton 2007, 51). While we find nothing strange in the idea of individuals dancing or making music purely for their own enjoyment, it is difficult (though not impossible) to envisage individuals doing this in the case of theater. In these respects, theater is inherently social. As such, it also generally seeks to engage the audience in distinctively complex ways: "Audiences watch, listen, and react to theatrical performers. Performers shape what they do with a view to the fact that audiences will observe them. Performers are also disposed to modify what they do in response to the reactions of an observing audience" (52). Hamilton is not denying that one can find parallel phenomena in the other performing arts. His claim is, rather, that the ability to engage in this way with an audience is an essential part of doing theater, whereas it is not, in the same way, an essential part of performing music or dance.

Unlike Thom and Osipovich, however, Hamilton doesn't think that the presence of an actual audience is necessary if there is to be theatrical performance. This is because, as the first of the quoted passages indicates, he understands the distinctively social character of theater in terms of how theatrical performances are generally presented and received, and the kinds of goals they generally have. As just noted, theatrical performers take their craft to involve the ability to engage with an audience, but the craft can still be exercised even if no actual audience is attending. What matters, we might say, is whether expectations about an intended audience guide the actions of the actors. But theatrical performers' expectations as to how their actions will be received by their intended audience reflect their understanding of the distinctive kinds of interactions between performers and audience characteristic of theater. It is the nature of these interactions that distinguishes the very idea of engaging in theater "for an audience" from the very idea of engaging in music and dance "for an audience."

2   Audience Response

We asked in the previous section whether performance requires an attending audience. But "attending" here is ambiguous. On the one hand, it can refer to the physical presence of an audience in the location where the performance is taking place. In this sense, Berthold and Magda are an attending audience at the performance-event taking place on stage in the provincial theater – they are "in attendance" at that event. But for an audience to play its part *as* an audience, it must not only attend but also attend *to* what is being presented. It is reasonable to assume that members of an audience for an artistic performance who are there of their own choosing – rather than, say, being dragged there by friends interested in their cultural education! – have a predisposition to attend to what is presented. For they are presumably interested in getting from the performance whatever the performers have to offer, and this requires attending to it. Thus performers can usually expect that the audience will take an interest in what they do, and, indeed, an interest informed by some understanding of the kind of thing they are doing. But this expectation does not absolve them from a responsibility to present to the audience something that will engage this interest and thereby *sustain* the predisposition to attend to the performance. Berthold would obviously say that the performers in the provincial theater failed to live up to this responsibility, although the performers might respond that visiting aesthetes like Berthold were not their intended audience!

Philosophers have reflected upon the nature of the attention that is demanded by an artistic performance. James Hamilton, for example, offers a general analysis of what it is to attend to someone or something (2007, ch. 4). Attention requires a sensitivity to particular events involving, or particular features manifested by, the focus of one's attention. *Which* events or features these are is determined by the nature of the situation calling for such attention. One must also be prepared to respond in different ways if particular events or features of the relevant kind occur. To what range of events and features, then, should we be sensitive if we are members of the audience for an artistic performance, and how should we respond to these events and features if they transpire? And what must performers do if they are to *sustain* an audience's attention?

A traditional answer to these questions, as they apply to theatrical performance, is implicit in Paul Woodruff's account of theater. Woodruff, we may recall, holds that there is no theater without a watching audience: "If no one is watching, it's not theater, though it may truly be a performance" (2008, 42). But watching, Woodruff argues, requires something worth watching, something we can care about, something to which we can emotionally respond: "Theater depends on watching, watching depends on caring, and caring depends on emotion" (154). The objects of our caring and the focus of our emotions in a theatrical performance are generally the characters. To care for the characters means, at least, that we want to know what happens to them, and usually that we feel with and for them (148). To eliminate altogether the audience's empathetic responses to the characters would be to fail in the art of theater (170). When an audience is not emotionally engaged by any of the main characters, we have what Woodruff terms "bad watching" which is really a failure to watch in the relevant sense (179). "The nature of theater," he maintains, "is to be watched; when it cannot be watched it cannot be theater in the full sense; you must be fully capable of empathy with the chief characters" (184). He acknowledges, however, that a performance where we cannot emotionally engage with the characters might still be "worth watching" and thus qualify as theater in virtue of its plot alone. While "theatrical reasons for watching a performance to the end belong mainly to plot and characterization, and these are almost always reasons for caring," good plots can be reasons for watching theater even if we don't care about the characters: "A plot can keep us caring about events, by stringing our emotions onto what happens next, as the plot works steadily through complication toward resolution" (154).

In according emotional engagement a central role in audience response to theater, Woodruff might seem to be endorsing what is usually termed an "Aristotelean" conception of theatrical performance. This would then seem to commit him to opposing the alternative "epic" conception of theater defended by Bertolt Brecht. But Woodruff claims that the difference between Aristotelean and epic theater is in fact best accommodated within his own model of audience response, the difference lying in the ways in which emotions are enlisted for cognitive purposes.[4] To clarify what is at issue here and to assess Woodruff's claim, we must say something about the two conceptions of theater in question.

The Aristotelean conception is so named because it informs the discussion of tragedy in Aristotle's *Poetics* (1941b). The aim of the tragic work, Aristotle maintains, is to produce a particular kind of emotional response in the spectator. The performers' task is to present events that arouse pity and fear, but in such a way as to produce a *catharsis* of these emotions. There is some dispute as to how catharsis is to be understood. Some view it as a purging of the emotions, where the latter are conceived as harmful to one's moral health, while others take it to be a purifying of the emotions to bring them into harmony with a rational assessment of things. What is clear is that catharsis is supposed to be a good thing, and that dramatic works are socially valuable in virtue of their capacity to produce such an effect. This supports the "purification" reading of catharsis, given Aristotle's more general views about the proper place of the emotions in human agency (see Aristotle 1941a). Thus read, the *Poetics* can be seen as in part an answer to Plato's (1941) charge that theater is morally harmful because it leads us to mimic the flawed characters that are presented to us on stage.

Aristotle holds that if a play is to both arouse pity and fear *and* produce a catharsis of those emotions, it must meet certain conditions. First, the central character – the "tragic hero" – must be a person with whom we can both identify and empathize, otherwise the emotions of pity and fear will not be elicited. This means that the central character must be a fully developed individual, psychologically speaking, whom we can come to understand through the dialogue and the action. The central character must therefore be a person who is basically good, but with some failing of character that explains why a bad fate befalls him or her. For, Aristotle argues, we would be repulsed, rather than moved to pity and fear, by evil happening to a completely good person. And we would rejoice, rather than feel pity or fear, at the prospect of a thoroughly evil individual coming to a bad end.

In order to produce a catharsis of the emotions of pity and fear, the plot must proceed with a certain inevitability, given our understanding of the laws that govern the world of the play and the psychological profiles of the characters. The fate that befalls the central character must strike us as a probable consequence of his or her fatally flawed judgment. This presupposes a measure of intellectual involvement on our part, as audience, if we are to determine that events are indeed unfolding in the way we would have expected. We must be moved in the relevant ways by what we take to be an intelligible fate that befalls one who deserves our pity and/or fear. Only in this way can our experience in watching the tragic drama help to bring our emotional dispositions into line with our rational assessment of situations. This enables the emotions to support reason in shaping our conduct, as Aristotle thinks they should. But the tragic effect does not require that we respond critically to what is *represented*. Rather, we must be carried along by the narrative in order for the tragic effect to occur. Thus, in an important sense, the task of the playwright is to emotionally manipulate the audience, via their involvement with the fate of the characters. The theatrical medium is then the means whereby such manipulation takes place. For this reason, it is important that the medium not interfere with the spectator's emotional engagement with the narrative, otherwise catharsis will not occur.

Theater, then, must meet a number of conditions if it is to realize its proper Aristotelean purpose. Characters must be psychologically rich, fully drawn individuals, whose experience the viewer seeks to understand, thereby becoming emotionally engaged by the narrative. The play must present a self-contained narrative universe, where events can be understood in terms of the laws of that universe and the motivation of the characters. This leads us to relate the represented events to other things within the universe of the play, and to experience a sense of narrative and moral closure when the curtain falls. The medium strives to be *transparent*, so that viewers attend to what is going on, rather than to the technical devices being used in the narrative.

The Aristotelean model of theatrical performance faces at least two kinds of challenge, only the second of which will concern us here. The first challenge is to explain how Aristotelean theater is *possible* in the face of two famous "paradoxes." First, the paradox of fiction asks, of fictional narratives in general, how we can be emotionally moved by something we take to be fictional. Normally, it seems, our emotions presuppose certain beliefs about the reality of the things that move us. This is obviously a serious matter for the Aristotelean account, since the "proper pleasure" of tragedy – catharsis – can occur only if the play has already elicited pity and fear in the audience. The second paradox – the paradox of tragedy – asks why, if tragedy arouses in us the unpleasant emotions of pity and fear, we would choose to subject ourselves to the experiences associated with tragic drama. Philosophers have offered a number of solutions to these two paradoxes, but we need not pursue them further here.[5]

The challenge that does concern us relates not to the possibility but to the *desirability* of theatrical performances that fit the Aristotelean model. The figure most commonly associated with this kind of challenge is the German playwright and theorist Bertolt Brecht.[6] Brecht's "epic" conception of drama conceives both the aim and the proper methodology of theater differently from the Aristotelean view. The aim of theater, Brecht argues, should be to critically engage the audience in an attempt to understand the *point* of the play, and its bearing on the world outside the theater. The question that the viewer should ask herself is not merely "Why did that happen?" or "What is going to happen next?" but also "What is this play for?" To put this in the terms introduced in Chapter 6, the Brechtian audience is intended to take both an internal and an external interrogative interest in what is being presented, with the predominant focus upon the external interest.

What is distinctive about Brecht's conception of epic theater, however, is his account of how this critical aim of dramatic performance is to be achieved. Brecht proposes that, in order to elicit the desired response, we replace the individualist conception of characters, as psychologically rich individuals, with a generic conception, where characters are presented as psychologically thin representatives of their classes or socio-economic roles. This prevents the spectator from emotionally identifying with the characters, and forces her to relate the presented events to the world outside the theater where real individuals occupy the kinds of roles represented by the characters. In order to bring the viewer to interrogate the play externally as well as internally, Brecht urges performers to stress the *representational* nature of what the viewer is looking at. This involves various kinds of "distanciation" techniques, such as direct address by the actors to the audience, the use of songs, "gestic acting" which accentuates bodily movements in a quasi-mechanical way, and the projection of a film backdrop as a commentary on the action. All of these techniques remind the viewer that she is watching a theatrical performance that has been organized with some point in mind. Brecht also argues that a play should resist narrative closure. This can be done by making the represented events more open-ended and by avoiding the tight plotting entailed by the Aristotelean requirement that events in the drama be related to one another in a probable or necessary fashion.

As Woodruff correctly maintains, it is important to separate Brecht's claims about the proper aims of theater from his concrete proposals as to how those aims should be achieved. Critics have argued that we do not need to reject the narrative structure of Aristotelean theater in order to use dramatic art for critical purposes.[7] They argue that Brecht's conception of epic theater rests on a number of questionable claims about the effects of traditional dramatic narratives on the audience. For example, Brecht is ascribed the view that such narratives numb the critical faculties of spectators by putting them under the illusion that they are watching actual events, and that the tight narrative structure of Aristotelean theater conveys to viewers a sense of the inevitability of existing social structures. While Brecht's writings provide some support for these readings, it isn't clear that the overall case for epic theater requires such dubious hypotheses about the nature of the viewer's experience of Aristotelean theater. All the Brechtian needs to argue is that standard Aristotelean theater fosters an emotional engagement with the characters and an internal interrogative interest in the unfolding of the plot, and discourages the sort of critical engagement with the dramatic presentation that requires an external interrogative interest in what is being presented. The company that seeks to elicit the latter kind of interest therefore has reason to try to counter the kind of purely internal engagement to which Aristotelean drama is conducive. But, having defended the general Brechtian argument in this way, we must acknowledge the weakness of the case for the further claim that such an internal engagement can be countered only by completely abandoning the central elements in Aristotelean drama – psychologically rich characters and a tightly crafted plot – and by the utilization of the kinds of distanciation techniques proposed by Brecht.

Our interest here, however, is in the dispute between the Aristotelean and the Brechtian over the proper *aims* of theater and the kind of *response* that the dramatic work should seek to elicit. Should this be a predominantly emotional response grounded in an internal interrogative interest in the presented action, or a predominantly critical response grounded in both an internal and an external interrogative interest in that action? If we view these as alternative conceptions of the proper aim of theatrical performance, this presents a problem for Woodruff's general model. For that model seems ill-equipped to recognize performances utilizing Brechtian distanciation techniques as theater, let alone as theatrical performances that could be, as Woodruff admits, "electrifying" (2008, 169). How are we to account for this if "generally, a play fails when the watchers do not engage emotionally with the characters and action of the play itself" (Woodruff 2008, 152).

As noted earlier. Woodruff thinks that his account of theater *can* accommodate epic theater by bringing it under a more general model that distinguishes between dramatic performances in terms of *how* they emotionally engage the audience. He argues that the success of Brecht's pieces as theater depends upon their ability to produce an empathetic response in the audience, contrary to Brecht's protestations. First, audiences do feel empathy for characters like Mother Courage, for example, in spite of Brecht's efforts to the contrary, and this in part accounts for the success of the play. Second, while Brecht's epic theater may not aim to produce empathy with the characters, it does aim to elicit outrage on the part of the viewer.

The problem with this second claim, however, is that the feelings of outrage Brecht seeks to elicit are directed not at the actions presented on stage, but at real world circumstances upon which the events on stage are taken to bear. For us to be moved to the intended state of outrage therefore seems to require that we determine that the point of doing *this* on stage is to get us to reflect upon things that are not present. This would involve the recognition that the actors are presenting to us not characters about whose individual fate we can care, but social roles that exemplify features of the society in which we live. Thus, it seems, the emotional response at which Brecht aims requires that the audience first takes an external interrogative interest in the performance.

But it appears that Woodruff wants to exclude such an external interrogative interest from our proper engagement with a dramatic performance as presented to us in a theater. He claims that any reflection concerning the intentions of the author (or, presumably, the director or the company) has "nothing to do with theater as such" (Woodruff 2008, 200). And he rejects "reflective identification" during a theatrical performance – reflection on what it would be like to be a character presented on stage so as to know what she felt – on the grounds that "the art of theater does not seek to engage an audience through reflection, because this belongs not to watching but to thought" (179). The place for reflection is in understanding the script of a play, or after the curtain falls, he maintains. Reflection occurs only insofar as our emotions are not engaged, and thus only insofar as we are not "watching." "The purpose of theater," he maintains, "is watching" (37).

But why take this to be the *purpose* of theatrical art, rather than the means whereby its purposes are achieved? It seems that these purposes, even if Aristotelean, may *require* reflection, since reflective attempts to work out what is going on inside a character seem crucial in some cases to understanding what one is watching. Indeed, this is part of our internal interrogative interest in a dramatic performance. Furthermore, a general proscription on reflection while watching a dramatic performance would prohibit an external interrogative interest in a drama one is watching. If, as I suggested in Chapter 1, such an interrogative interest is integral to our engagement with an artistic manifold *as* an artistic manifold, then to accept Woodruff's's account seems to entail that a receiver's having an artistic interest in a dramatic performance is incompatible with its functioning for that receiver as theater. Also, if the outrage that is an aim of Brechtian theater presupposes the adoption of an external interrogative interest, then a proscription on reflection will exclude such emotional responses from the operations of theater on Woodruff's account.

How might Woodruff respond to these charges? We noted earlier that he wishes to bring both Aristotelean and epic theater within the scope of a model that locates their differences not in the presence or absence of a role for emotional response, but in the ways in which the emotions play a cognitive role. In both cases, he argues, we have "theater that seeks to engage emotions in ways that are themselves instructive, so that in arriving at an appropriate emotional attitude towards what she sees the spectator arrives at a greater understanding of it as well" (Woodruff 1988, 250). In the case of Aristotelean drama, our understanding of the characters is in part a matter of being moved by them in the appropriate ways. In pitying a certain character, we understand that she is worthy of pity, for example. In the case of Brechtian theater that aims to elicit a critical response from the spectator, it is, so Woodruff maintains, our emotional responses to the characters – responses that may alternate between attraction and repulsion – that lead us to adopt such an attitude to social realities outside the world of the play (251–252). This suggests that Woodruff accords to emotional engagement the role that he denies to thinking in theatrical experience. It is through the emotions engendered in the watching spectator that she is led to an understanding of the characters in the Aristotelean drama, and to an understanding of the point of the Brechtian play.

But, if this is Woodruff's view, it is not clear that it can accommodate epic theater in its Brechtian form. For, even if we reject the idea that a critical theater must take such a form – must employ the kinds of techniques advocated by Brecht – it surely *can* take this form, as Brecht's own productions testify. And it is difficult to see how a drama that employs devices such as generic characters and gestic acting can elicit in the spectator the kind of internally focused emotional responses of which Woodruff speaks.[8] Can we really be appalled at the characters in such a drama? Woodruff, as noted earlier, thinks that, in spite of Brecht's best efforts, we can: "In *Mother Courage* a mother is driven by mother-love to set profits above her children's lives and this at once repels and attracts an audience" (Woodruff 1988, 252). But, to the extent that Brechtian theater aims to produce indignation at real social injustices generically related to the events enacted on stage, is this really mediated by indignation at those events themselves? Or is it more plausible to assign the mediating role to reflective engagement with those events as part of our external interrogative interest in the play, as I have suggested?

I have questioned whether Woodruff's account of the role of emotions in audience response to theater can accommodate, as theater, dramatic performances employing Brechtian devices. But should we not simply conclude that Aristotle and Brecht offer us two incompatible views about the nature of theater? A Brechtian account of the role of the audience in theater, it might be said, will face a parallel problem to Woodruff's account: it will not be able to accommodate as theater the kinds of dramatic performances directed by *Aristoteleans*! But this response misses the point of the objection against Woodruff's account. Brechtian theater puts to political use the audience's external interrogative interest in what is presented. When the viewer asks why she is being presented with the kinds of generic characters and distanciation techniques in a Brechtian production, the reflections to which she is moved are intended to lead her to view as outrageous certain features of the social and political world outside the theater. But the external interrogative interest upon which the Brechtian relies is, we have said, crucial to our taking an *artistic* interest in a presented manifold. The Brechtian, then, puts our artistic interest to political use. But an artistic interest in a performance of Aristotelean theater will also require that we take an external interrogative interest in *that* performance, even though the Aristotelean production is not putting the latter interest to any political use. To simply respond to the Aristotelean performance emotionally in the way intended is not to take an artistic interest in it, any more than someone who simply wallows in the visual experience elicited by an "op art" painting is taking an artistic interest in the painting.

The objection to Woodruff's account, then, is that it excludes from our experience of theatrical performances something central to our interest in these performances as *art*, whether the performance be Aristotelean, Brechtian, or, indeed, Hamilton's hypothetical *Something to Tell You* (discussed in Chapter 6). As Thom stresses, the audience of an artistic performance is required to respond not only by being affected in certain ways by the performance, but also by *interpreting* what is going on (1993, 196–199). And interpretation is an activity on the part of the audience that requires an external interrogative interest, as we have termed it, in what the performers are doing.

3 The Embodied Performer and the Mirroring Receiver

When the Irish poet W. B. Yeats asked, "How can we know the dancer from the dance?"[9] he traded for metaphorical effect upon a distinctive feature of dance as an art form. He could not have inquired, to similar effect, how we could know the painter from the painting, or the musician from the music, or even, for traditional theater, the actors from the play. It is most common to characterize this distinctive feature of dance by saying that in the latter the performer uses her own body as the vehicle through which an artistic content is articulated. Martha Graham, for example, wrote that the solitary aim of dance training has always been "so to train the body as to make possible any demand made upon it by that inner self which has the vision of what needs to be said" (1974, 139). It is because a dance seems to just be the movements executed by the dancer's body that we can raise the question posed by Yeats.

It is not only in dance that the artistic content of a work can be in part a function of what the artist does with her body. We have already encountered

Jerrold Levinson's contention that some of the expressive qualities of musical works depend upon the kinds of movements required to generate the designated sequence of sounds on the prescribed instruments. And the notion of "facture" in the visual arts — visible indications in the artistic vehicle of how it was produced by the artist — may provide the basis for something similar in abstract expressionist canvases by painters like Jackson Pollock. In these cases, however, it might be said that the expressive properties in question derive from the ways in which the artist uses instruments to manipulate a vehicular medium distinct from herself.[10] In dance, on the other hand, it seems that the artist's own body serves as the vehicular medium through which the artistic content of her performance is articulated. The musical analogue of dance is not the playing of instruments by musicians but the singer's use of her own voice.

This distinctive role played by the artist's body means that dance is an art form naturally fitted for the artistic exploration of issues relating to our embodied nature. We encountered in Chapter 1 a striking example of this. In "task dances" like Yvonne Rainer's *Room Service*, the dancers exemplify in their movements the practical intelligence of the body in the pursuit of everyday goals. Dance has also attracted feminist artists wishing to explore themes relating to embodiment.[11] However, Graham's way of characterizing the distinctive role of the body in dance carries with it certain philosophical preconceptions that are open to challenge. To suggest, as Graham does, that the dancer uses her body as an *instrument* is to subscribe implicitly to a dualistic conception of the "mindedness" of the human agent. On such a conception, the agent — in the present case, the dancer — is identified with the "inner self" who is distinct from her body but able to act in virtue of her ability to make demands upon and control it. The dualism here is not Cartesian — that is, it doesn't require that the "inner self" be something non-physical. It holds just as clearly if we identify the "inner self" with something definable in neurological terms. It consists in the idea that the self, however construed, stands in an instrumentalistic relation to the body. Such a dualism actually provides us with an easy answer to Yeats's question. The dancer, we can say, is the person responsible for those bodily movements that constitute the dance. And, in another sense of "know," we can know the dancer from *observing* the dance by reading off from the movements of the body the states of the "inner self" that are directing those movements.

The instrumentalistic way of putting things seems very natural if, as Graham is doing, we consider what is involved in dance training and rehearsal. For, as she points out, dance training aims at providing the dancer with the ability to use her body in ways that are unavailable to those lacking such training, and this seems to require an instrumental conception of the relationship between the dancer and her body. The dance educator Margery J. Turner, for example, writes that "the human body, as the instrument of communication, has to transcend its personal limitations; it must be trained ... to make neuromuscular discriminations; to sense degrees of action, textures, qualities ... It must respond sensitively to the dancer's feelings and needs and to the demands of the choreographer" (1971, 23). And a text on dance technique states that through such technique "you learn how to control your body and make it your instrument" (Minton 1984, 3).

However, writers on dance influenced by the French phenomenologist Maurice Merleau-Ponty reject such a dualistic conception of human agency in general, and its application to dance in particular.[12] Phenomenologists counter the idea of the human body as an instrument for the use of the mind in two ways, which effectively provide two perspectives on the same phenomenon. First, they maintain that the body itself is a "lived body" whose engagements with the world are always inflected by the "intentionality" – the purposes, projects, and perspectives – of the agent. The human body encounters objects in its world in ways that reflect both its capacities for embodied agency and the agent's intentionality. When I reach to pick up a glass in front of me, my hand shapes itself to grasp the glass without any explicit awareness on my part of its so doing, for example. This is what Merleau-Ponty termed "primary consciousness," our embodied ability to negotiate our lived world successfully without the need for explicit awareness of relevant features of that world. When we walk across a room to greet someone, we are conscious of what we are doing in terms of this purpose, with no explicit awareness of the ways in which we navigate around the furniture of the room. The lived body relies upon what can be termed a "body schema," a system of sensory-motor capacities that function without conscious awareness or the need for perceptual monitoring. These capacities operate in ways that can be precisely shaped by our intentionality, as in the preceding examples.[13] The psychologist J. J. Gibson (1979) talks here of the "affordances" in terms of which creatures like us perceive and interact with their environments, an "affordance" being a way in which something fits with our projects and purposes given our physical capacities.

Complementing such talk of the lived body is talk of the "embodied mind," whose cognitive and practical activities are structured by the intelligence of the lived body. In How the Body Shapes the Mind, Shaun Gallagher (2005) reworks the Merleau-Pontian project by drawing upon recent work in psychology and cognitive neuroscience. He argues that our conscious apprehension and understanding of the world depends on experiences that are informed in their very structure by a body with various perceptual and motor capacities. To understand our cognitive engagement with the world, Gallagher argues, we must focus not merely on the brain but also on the body understood as embedded within physical and social environments and situations

that motivate thought and action. Relatedly, Richard Shusterman characterizes what he terms "body consciousness" as "the embodied consciousness that
a living sentient body directs at the world."

On such a phenomenological picture of human cognition and agency,
what sense can we make of the idea – central, as we have seen, to writings
on dance training and dance technique – that the dancer trains her body as
an instrument to be used to execute her artistic intentions in the dance?
Writers sympathetic to the phenomenological picture have addressed
this question in different ways. Sondra Fraleigh, for example, argues that,
while there is an indissoluble lived unity of body and mind, it is possible,
either in states of personal disintegration or through deliberate effort, for
a person to take her physical body as an object, abstracting, in so doing,
from its lived nature. She cites Merleau-Ponty, who writes of the body as
"the bearer of a dialectic" which can lead to a rupture in the lived unity of
embodied agency:

> Our body does not always have meaning, and our thoughts, on the other
> hand – in timidity, for example – do not always find in it the plenitude of
> their vital expression. In these cases of disintegration, the soul and the body
> are apparently distinct; and this is the truth of dualism. (Merleau-Ponty
> 1963, 209)

The dancer who wishes to train her body to perform must bring about such
an objectification voluntarily. As she learns the dance, such a dualism

> grows of necessity from an objectification of the body in rehearsal and per-
> formance through creative experiment with, and critical observation of, the
> body in motion. A psychic distance from the body is necessitated in the dialec-
> tical creative process of dance. It is significant, though, that such a phenomenal
> (or lived) duality is formulated upon a basic unity and according to intent, as
> existential phenomenology has held. (Fraleigh 1987, 13)

Gallagher's work, and work on dance that falls within the broadly Merleau-
Pontian tradition, suggests how empirical work in psychology and neuroscience
can bear indirectly upon our most fundamental assumptions about dance and
the terms in which we describe what is going on in dance performance. As
noted above, both Merleau-Ponty and Gallagher ground their claims about
the lived body and the embodied mind in the empirical studies of their time in
various areas of cognitive science. Gallagher, for example, draws upon a broad
range of research in developmental psychology and cognitive neuroscience,
including extended studies of pathological conditions. If our philosophical
interest in dance comprises questions about the nature of the artistic vehicle
and the ways in which the dancer is able to articulate an artistic content

through her performance, where this involves an interest in her achievement in so doing, the bearing of this kind of empirical work on the philosophy of dance seems clear.

More controversial, however, are recent philosophical explorations within this tradition that draw upon a particular strand in contemporary research in cognitive neuroscience. Richard Shusterman (2009), for example, raises questions similar to the ones canvassed above about how the phenomenological picture of the lived body can accommodate the kinds of demands made upon the performing artist both in training and in actual performance. He acknowledges that, in our everyday dealings with the world, it is the spontaneous bodily intentionality of the lived body that enables us to successful negotiate our way around. In such contexts, explicit attention to our movements can get in the way of ordinary functioning, as when the bike rider thinks about exactly how she is propelling her vehicle and promptly loses her balance. But, Shusterman insists, while the habits comprised by the lived body play an essential part in human agency, these habits sometimes need to be corrected or refined if we are to flourish in our projects. The golf player, for example, needs to relearn his swing when his spontaneous activity leads him to shank the ball to the left. In the same way, the dancer needs to train her body so that its spontaneous activity achieves what she desires. This requires that she explicitly attend to the movements that her body is making in order to *change* the bodily intentionality that enables her to spontaneously generate such movements. Then, once she has retrained her body, she can once again rely on spontaneous agency.

Shusterman raises an interesting question, however. Is it possible to achieve such an explicit awareness of what one's body is doing – to in this sense treat one's body as an object – at the very same time that one *exercises* the sort of embodied skill involved in the performing arts? Merleau-Ponty thought that such explicit awareness would hamper the exercise of the skill in question. Shusterman disputes this, however. He looks at the kind of training given both to dancers and to performers in Japanese Noh theater. He argues that, for the skilled performer who trains herself properly, the best performances may involve both the exercise of a spontaneous embodied skill and a simultaneous explicit awareness of what one is doing.

His argument however, as he acknowledges, draws speculatively on recent work in cognitive neuroscience on so-called "mirror neurons." We should briefly say something about the latter before sketching Shusterman's argument.[14] Mirror neurons are neurons, primarily in the pre-motor cortex, that are activated both by my execution of certain types of movement and by my observing another person executing the same types of movement. They play a crucial role in the explanations that some have offered of puzzling phenomena, such as the neonate's apparent ability to mimic facial expressions without visually observing its own face.[15] Mirror neurons, it is claimed, are involved in certain kinds of cross-modal neurological connections which "translate" between our visual apprehension of the world and our acting on the world through our motor systems.

Shusterman appeals to mirror neurons in defending the possibility, proposed by Zeami Motokiyo, a renowned teacher of Noh theater, that an actor, while acting, should not only "look ahead" to see the other actors, the audience, and his place in the full theatrical performance, but also "look behind." To "look behind" is to "see" how one appears to those spectators who are behind one, and to modify one's performance accordingly. Shusterman considers three hypothetical accounts of how such looking behind might be possible. First, an actor might use literal mirrors, properly configured, to view his back in various postures, and note through proprioception how the different postures feel. By associating different postures with their different feels, the actor could then infer how he looked from the back from how his posture felt. Second, an actor A could enlist another actor B to adopt various postures and could observe these postures from behind. The mirror-neuronal system would produce a firing of the same neurons in the observing A as are firing in the posturing B, and this could generate in A "a proprioceptive feel of that action, a felt understanding that the actor could confirm perhaps by then imitating the posture and seeing whether his taking this postural attitude indeed produces this kind of proprioceptive feelings" (Shusterman 2009, 142). The third possibility attempts, via a "highly speculative and improbable" strategy, to make literal sense of Zeami's talk about the actor *seeing* himself as the audience views him from behind:

> If proprioceptive feelings of posture could generate through mirror-neuron systems a corresponding visual input of that posture, then in principle someone very skilled in vivid proprioceptive awareness might be able to generate a visual image in his mind of how his posture would look ... from his own proprioceptive self-observation of his posture or movement. (Shusterman 2009, 142)

We need to say something briefly about proprioception, which plays a role in all three of Shusterman's scenarios. We noted above that Merleau-Ponty and Gallagher share a conception of the "body schema," as the unconscious basis of spontaneous bodily intentionality. This is to be contrasted with what Gallagher terms the "body image," a system of perceptions, attitudes, and beliefs pertaining to one's own body that are accessible to consciousness. In the case of both body schema and body image, a crucial role is played by proprioception, the means by which we obtain information about, and awareness of, the positions and movements of our own bodies.

Proprioception operates by means of receptors situated throughout the body – in the tendons and ligaments, for example – which provide information to the brain as to how the body is disposed at any given moment. It is this information that enables the body schema to direct our actions in a monitored way without our being consciously aware of how this is being accomplished. More significantly in the present context, empirical research has established that the same receptors that provide the *information* necessary for the operation of the body schema ("proprioceptive information") are also responsible for our *awareness* of how our bodies are positioned, or how we are moving our bodies, at a given time ("proprioceptive awareness"). This awareness is usually only at the periphery of consciousness, but it can be brought into focus when we deliberately attend to our bodies.

Barbara Montero (2006) has argued that proprioceptive awareness plays a crucial role in both dance performance itself and the appreciation of dance performance. She argues, first, that proprioception can function as an aesthetic sense – a sense whereby we are able to grasp aesthetic properties of things. What we are able to grasp through proprioception are aesthetic properties such as the grace or beauty of a bodily movement. Proprioceptive beauty is a felt property of the movement not reducible to the ways in which, qua visible movement, it would aesthetically affect an observer. But our judgments of visual beauty and our judgments of proprioceptive beauty are related in complex ways:

> In some cases, one might proprioceptively judge that a movement is beautiful because one knows that the movement, if seen, would look beautiful. But in other cases one might visually judge that a movement is beautiful because one knows that, if proprioceived, this movement would feel beautiful. (Montero 2006, 236)

There are two possible readings of the relationship between proprioceptive beauty and visual beauty. On the first reading, they are closely related but *distinct* aesthetic properties. On the second reading, beauty is a *uniform* property of bodily movement that applies to certain movements on the basis of both their look and their feel: if we are aware of only one of these things, then our aesthetic judgments may be mistaken. While the passage just cited suggests that Montero subscribes to the second reading, the first reading fits better with her claim that dancers can sense directly whether their movements possess certain aesthetic qualities by the way those movements feel, without having to see, or imagine seeing, them.

The claim that proprioception can be an aesthetic sense goes against a long tradition that has restricted experiential access to the aesthetic properties of things, including artworks, to those senses that most obviously provide us with access to objects distant from us, namely vision and audition.[16] Hegel (1975), for example, claimed that "art is related only to the two theoretical senses of sight and hearing, while smell, taste, and touch remain excluded from the enjoyment of art." Montero argues, however, that proprioception, insofar as it can *mis*represent the disposition of my body – as, for example, in the case of "phantom limb" experiences – has the power to represent its object as being a certain way, and thus does not differ from vision and audition in this respect.

However, if proprioception were to be an aesthetic sense, this seems to imply – at least on the first reading rehearsed above – that there are aesthetic properties of some artworks – dance performances – that are accessible only to a single individual – the performer herself. Montero argues, however, that proprioception gives the *spectator* the ability to experience proprioceptive aesthetic properties[17] of the movements of others. Like Shusterman, she appeals here to mirror neurons. Her claim is that, when an appropriately qualified spectator observes a dancer executing a particular sequence of movements, the neurological activity in the spectator will mirror the relevant neurological activity in the dancer. Thus, she argues, they can share a proprioceptive awareness of what it is to perform that sequence of movements, and thus a proprioceptive awareness of its aesthetic properties. An appropriately qualified spectator, Montero suggests, must have had training in dance in order for the relevant mirror neurons to be activated in response to the dancer's movements.[18]

Both Montero and Shusterman admit that their theses are speculative extensions of the relevant current literature in neuroscience. But what constraints are there on such speculations if they are to advance our philosophical understanding of the performing arts? How far do they transcend what has been established in the relevant neurological research, and how does this bear on the explanatory force of the accounts? There are at least four kinds of concern.

First, the work on visuo-motor mirror neurons was done on macaque monkeys and has not been verified on human subjects. What has been verified in humans is another kind of mirroring that links engaging in a given activity and imagining that one is engaging in that activity. But the relationship between this work and the work on mirror neurons remains to be established. Nonetheless, those scientists who work on mirror neurons generally agree that mirror neurons operate in humans much in the way that they do in macaques, so we can set aside this concern in the present context.

Second, and more significantly, mirror-neuronal activity in macaques has been verified only for certain types of movements of the face and arms – in particular, certain types of grasping behavior. This makes sense in evolutionary terms given the importance of being able to mimic certain kinds of arm and facial movements, especially for the neonate. But many of the most significant movements bearing upon the aesthetic qualities of dance are leg movements. Here no parallel evolutionary story is likely to be forthcoming. This is not to say that there are not other kinds of mirror systems that are more generally operative – for example, the system that relates action to the imagining of action. If imagining is a neural activity, it seems plausible that imagining performing a particular activity would activate those motor areas of the brain enlisted in the performance of that activity. But this isn't evidence for a broader range of visuo-motor mirrorings.

Third, and crucially, both Montero and Shusterman assume that the firing of mirror neurons provides the observer of a given action with propriocep-tive *awareness* of that action, and not merely proprioceptive *information*. For Montero, this is essential to her argument for third-person knowledge of proprioceptive aesthetic properties. It is only if I am aware of those proprio-ceptively given qualities of the movement that form the supervenience base for the proprioceptive aesthetic properties that I can experience the beauty of the movement. And for Shusterman, this is an explicit assumption in his second strategy for explaining "looking behind." In watching another person adopt a posture, he maintains, I am proprioceptively aware of how the pos-ture feels. But experimental work on mirror neurons provides no basis for these assumptions. First, we have no way to tell whether the macaques whose motor areas fire when given visual input of grasping behavior feel what it is like to grasp. Gallagher himself notes that there is no evidence linking mirror neuron activity to awareness: "studies of mirror neurons are clearly studies of *non-conscious*, automatic processes that may or may not be experienced at a conscious level, although they surely shape conscious behaviour" (Gallagher 2005, 221; emphasis in original). Second, given the role that mirror neurons play in coordinating visual input and motor activity as part of "primary con-sciousness," it isn't clear what purpose would be served by proprioceptive awareness, since the relevant coordination proceeds at the level of the body schema rather than the body image.[19]

Fourth, as we saw, Shusterman's third account of looking behind requires that an actor's proprioceptive awareness of the particular posture that he adopts can stimulate his visual system to produce the (virtual) visual experi-ence of seeing himself from behind adopting that posture. However, all of the empirical evidence on mirror neurons runs in the opposite direction – from seeing someone perform a given action to activation of the motor circuits involved in the performance of that action. This is not a problem for Montero, for whom the claimed mirror-neuronal connections at least run in the right direction. But it is a serious problem for Shusterman.

To be fair, he acknowledges this anomaly in his explanation, granting that there are no experimental studies that deal with proprioceptive generation of visual stimulation. He cites, however, an e-mail correspondence with Gallese where the latter grants the possibility in principle of proprioceptive stimulation producing stimulation in the visual areas of the brain. But, as Shusterman also concedes, this doesn't give us any basis for ascribing visual *awareness*, let alone clear visualization of a particular posture. Nor, indeed, does this deal with the need for the visual image to be perspectival, of the actor viewed from the back. The firing of the mirror neurons involved in observing an action is presumably not perspectivally coded, but reflects a classification of the bodily motions under some goal.[20]

In support of Montero's claims, it might be thought that dance training does, or should, make an aesthetic difference to one's ability to appreciate dance. This would fit with our judgments in other areas of art. For example, we assume that painters are able to see facture in paintings that escapes the eye of the untrained viewer, however aesthetically sensitive that eye, and that only a trained musician can properly appreciate the virtuosity of certain performers. But we can remain skeptical about the idea of proprioception as an aesthetic sense, yet still acknowledge that only one with the relevant dance training can properly appreciate certain aspects of dance performance. For such training may be necessary to appreciate *what the performer has achieved*. If we think that the artistic achievement of the artist is one element entering into the artistic value of the artwork, then, just as a knowledge of the practice of painting is necessary to appreciate a painter's achievement, so a knowledge of dance technique may be necessary to appreciate the artistry demonstrated by the dancer in executing a given sequence of movements.

This line of reasoning will be challenged by those who think that an artist's achievement has no bearing on the artistic value of her work. The argument, here, would be that, as appreciators of dance, our concern is only with the realized artistic spectacle, not with the messy mechanics that go into producing that spectacle. But if there are reasons to reject such an "empiricist" conception of artistic appreciation and artistic value,[21] then we may agree with Montero that an experiential acquaintance with techniques and practices in the performing arts may be necessary if we are to fully appreciate at least some artistic performances as the works that they are.

Notes

1. John Milton, *Paradise Lost* Book VII, ıı, 30–31.
2. Indeed, the principal objective in Russell's classic 1905 is to show how such utterances do make genuine statements.
3. This requirement corresponds to Thom's requirement that a performance involve an address to an identified audience. But one can identify an audience without the latter being present.

4. This idea is spelled out more clearly in Woodruff 1988. See especially 250–253.

5. For a critical survey of these paradoxes and their proposed solutions, see D. Davies 2007a, ch. 7.

6. See Kuhn and Giles 2003.

7. See, for example, Carroll 1988, 90–106.

8. The example he cites in support of his view of Brechtian theater – Wallace Shawn's *Auntie Dan and Lemon* (New York, 1985) – did not, as far as I can tell, employ such devices.

9. W. B. Yeats, "Among School Children," in Allt and Alspach 1965, 443–446.

10. As noted in the previous chapter, however, the status of the musician as performer suggests that her relationship with her instruments is not purely "instrumental." If so, the issues about embodiment discussed in this section will arise in performing arts other than dance.

11. For discussions of these issues, see Kozel 1997; Banes 1998, ch. 6; and Desmond 1999.

12. See, for example, Sheets-Johnstone 1984; Fraleigh 1987; Shusterman 2008. All of these texts draw upon Merleau-Ponty 1962.

13. See Merleau-Ponty 1962; and Gallagher 2005, ch. 1.

14. Mirror neurons are discussed in a number of places in Gallagher 2005, especially 220–223. For recent critical reviews of work on mirror neurons by principal researchers in the field, see Gallese 2009; Rizolatti and Sinigaglia 2010.

15. See Gallagher 2005, ch. 3, for an argument to this effect.

16. Based, presumably, on the assumption that aesthetic properties themselves are such that they can be accessed only by these sensory modalities.

17. Or, on the second reading, to experience aesthetic properties proprioceptively.

18. See Gallese 2009, 7, for a survey of research on the bearing of past motor experience on the operation of mirror neurons.

19. Another problem for Shusterman's second scenario is that, according to the mirror neuron research, it is goal-oriented activities such as grasping that trigger such neurons. It isn't clear that posture by itself will trigger mirror-neuronal activity. See Gallese 2009.

20. See again Gallese 2009.

21. See, for example, Dutton 1979; Currie 1989; D. Davies 2004.

10

Performance Art and the Performing Arts

1 Introduction

In Chapter 1, I began by distinguishing a performance from a mere action. In the case of a performance, the agent is consciously guided in her actions by her expectations as to how these actions would be judged by an intended audience who would apply certain kinds of evaluative criteria. In this sense, a performance is "for an audience" and "directed towards an audience." As we saw in the previous chapter, however, there are no compelling reasons to think that there can be a performance only when the agent's actions are observed by an actual audience of the sort intended. I then distinguished artistic performances from other performances. Something counts as an artistic performance if it makes perceptually manifest to receivers qualities that bear upon the appreciation of a work of art in certain ways to be specified. I fleshed this out in two ways. First, I explained what it is to appreciate something as a work of art in terms of the kind of regard required to determine a work's artistic content. This kind of regard, I claimed, is necessary in virtue of the distinctive ways in which artworks articulate their contents. Second, I distinguished two ways in which a performance can qualify as an *artistic* performance by manifesting qualities that bear in this way upon the appreciation of a work of art. First, the performance may itself be an artwork, the actions of the performer(s) being the artistic vehicle through which the artistic content of the work is articulated. A performance that is itself an artwork is a performance-work. In Chapter 7, we looked at Keith Jarrett's *Köln Concert* as an example of such a work. Second, the performance may be *of* something else that is an artwork.[1] In this case, the performance is a work-performance, and the thing it is *of* is a performable work. I argued in Chapter

Philosophy of the Performing Arts, First Edition. David Davies.
© 2011 David Davies. Published 2011 by Blackwell Publishing Ltd.

7 that at least some work-performances are themselves performance-works. I also looked at the conditions that must be satisfied for this to be the case.

In this chapter, we shall consider some performances that occur in artistic contexts but whose status as *artistic* in either of the above senses is moot. Some performances in artistic contexts are obviously not artistic in either sense because they play no part in articulating the artistic content of an artwork. The stage hands who entertained Berthold and Magda in the provincial theater clearly put on a performance. They were consciously guided in their actions by expectations as to how these actions would be judged by their intended audience. But they presumably lacked any intention that their actions articulate a content in the way that artworks do, and they were not soliciting from their audience the kind of regard that artworks demand. Similar considerations would apply to the performance of a gallery guide who prides himself on his ability to "put on a show" for the punters, liberally interlacing information about the paintings with anecdotes, theatrical asides, and similar devices.

In other cases, however, there is clearly both a performance, or a prescription for a performance, *and* a clear intent to articulate, through that performance or prescription, an artistic content of some kind, yet the status of the performance as artistic in either of our senses is unclear. These performances are usually classified as "performance art," and are exemplified in the works of artists like Vito Acconci, Laurie Anderson, and Joseph Beuys. We need to clarify how such performances are to be understood and whether they are rightly viewed as falling within the performing arts. It will be helpful, here, to consider a range of examples, and then to ask how they stand in relation to one another.

2   Some Puzzling Cases

We can begin with an example of a kind familiar to us from the discussion of improvisation in Chapter 8:

(1)   "A series of five scales, each to be played as long as the soloist wishes until he has completed the series."[2]

This description, by Bill Evans, of Miles Davis's piece "All Blues," obviously requires further elaboration (*which* series of five scales?) in order to fully identify the piece. As argued in Chapter 8, it seems most plausible to view this as a thin performable work designed to be a framework for improvisation. A canonical recorded performance of this piece by the Miles Davis Quintet is on the album *Kind of Blue*.

(2)   A B and an F sharp tone – a perfect fifth – "to be held for a long time."

This description captures what is prescribed to performers of La Monte Young's *Composition 1960 #7*. We might think this is simply a variant on (1), differing in that the element of improvisation or interpretation on the part of the performer relates to the manner in which the tones are generated and the length of time for which they are sustained. But we might be more cautious when we learn that the other works making up Young's *Compositions 1960* include prescriptions to release a butterfly in the auditorium, to "draw a straight line and follow it," and to attempt to push a piano through the wall of the auditorium![3]

(3) "Tacet. For any instrument or instruments." The piece is in three movements, lengths of the movements being 30″, 2′ 23″, and 1′ 40″.

This is one account[4] of what is prescribed to players of John Cage's notorious *4′ 33″*. David Tudor gave the initial "performance" of this piece at Maverick Concert Hall, Woodstock, New York, in August 1952. He elected to punctuate the piece by closing and opening the piano lid to mark the beginning and end of each "movement." He also followed assiduously the "score" for the piece, which, naturally, was devoid of musical notation save for bar lines. Cage determined the length of the movements by a chance device, reputed to have been the I Ching. When we learn that the principal influences on the development of La Monte Young's music prior to his *Compositions 1960* were his encounter with Cage and his familiarity with the white canvases produced by his friend, the painter Robert Rauschenberg, our initial reading of (2) as a thin performable musical work becomes less secure.

(4) "Colour ink wash: the background is grey, blue, grey, blue; left pyramid: the apex is left – four sides: 1 – red, blue, blue, red, blue; 2 – yellow, blue, grey, blue; 3 – grey, grey, blue, red, red; 4 – red, grey, red; right pyramid: the apex is centre – four sides: 1 – grey, grey; 2 – grey, red, yellow; 3 – yellow, grey, blue, blue; 4 – grey, blue, red, red."

This description identifies *Wall Drawing No. 623 Double asymmetrical pyramids with colour ink washes superimposed*, a piece by the visual artist Sol LeWitt. It was executed on November 14 to 17, 1989 in the National Gallery of Canada in Ottawa, and is displayed together with the above description. It is one of over a thousand "wall drawings," all of which are specified in a similar manner. Murals generated in compliance with LeWitt's specifications are not painted by LeWitt, but by other artists who "execute" his plan.

(5) "Activity, 23 days, varying durations. New York City. Choosing a person at random, in the street, any location, each day. Following him wherever he goes, however long or far he travels. (The activity ends when he enters a private place – his home, office, etc.)"

This description identifies *Following Piece* by Vito Acconci. The execution of this piece by Acconci in 1969 is documented by photographs that accompany the description of the piece in galleries where the work is presented (see Acconci 2004).

(6) "Drill a hole into the heart of a large tree and insert a microphone. Mount the amplifier and speaker in an empty room and adjust the volume to make audible any sound that might come from the tree."

This description identifies a September 1969 piece by Bruce Naumann, which featured in a 1970 exhibition entitled *Art in the Mind* (see Lippard 1973, 162–163). The described action was not, as far as I know, actually performed, by Naumann or anyone else.

(7) "Draw an imaginary map ... Go walking on an actual street according to the map."

This piece was one of Yoko Ono's contributions to the exhibition *Information* staged at MOMA in New York in summer 1970 (see Goldberg 2001, 154). It differs from earlier examples in at least two respects. First, it proposes that the visitor to the exhibition herself be the executor of the piece, rather than its being executed by the artist herself, as in Acconci's case, or by others assigned to the task, as with LeWitt's wall drawings. In this respect, it resembles Janet Cardiff's "Walks." Visitors to exhibitions of Cardiff's work are given headphones and (for video "Walks") a small video camera. The headphones provide instructions for walking a specific route, but intercut into these instructions is a fiction by Cardiff involving things encountered on the route. In the video "Walks," the video screen illustrates the fictional narrative by presenting scenarios enacted at the very location occupied by the person who executes the work by following the prescriptions given on the headphones. Second, and more significantly, it is questionable whether it is possible to perform Yoko Ono's work. The prescriptions seem impossible to fulfill if one understands walking "according to" a map as a matter of *following* it. For how can one *follow* an imaginary map on an actual street? At best, one can come up with some way of reinterpreting the details of the map to make them apply to the street in question.

The examples thus far have taken the *form* of performable works, whether or not these works have, or can have, actual instances and whether or not they are really the performable works they seem to be. In each case, we began with what looks like a set of prescriptions for actors or performers, and then we noted what seem to be salient features — the kind of thing prescribed, the kinds of individuals to whom such things are prescribed, and the extent to which the prescriptions have been realized in actual performance. But many of the more notorious performances given by those characterized as "performance artists" are not prefigured by a prescription of this kind. Consider, for example,

(8)   Joseph Beuys's *Coyote: I Like America and America Likes Me*, which RoseLee Goldberg describes as:

a dramatic one-week event which began on the journey from Düsseldorf to New York in May 1974. Beuys arrived at Kennedy Airport wrapped from head to toe in felt, the material that was for him an insulator, both physically and metaphorically. Loaded into an ambulance, he was driven to the space which he would share with a wild coyote for seven days. During that time he conversed privately with the animal, only a chainlink fence separating them from the visitors to the gallery. His daily rituals included a series of interactions with the coyote, introducing it to objects — felt, walking stick, gloves, electric torch, and the *Wall Street Journal* (delivered daily) — which it pawed and urinated on, as if acknowledging in its own way the man's presence. (Goldberg 2001, 150–151)

Beuys's later verbal reflections on the piece indicate his intention that the artistic content of the performance relate to the persecution of the American Indians, whose perspective on America, represented by the coyote, Beuys sought to acquire through his actions: "I wanted to isolate myself, insulate myself, see nothing of America other than the coyote … and exchange roles with it" (Goldberg 2001, 151).

Another politically pointed performance work is Mona Hatoum's *The Negotiating Table* (1983) (Goldberg 2001, 151). Hatoum lay on a table, her body covered in animal blood and entrails and encased in a transparent plastic bag, illuminated by a single light. The performance was intended to exemplify the situation of people who have to live in war zones. Political readings have also been offered of the early performances by Chris Burden, such as *Shoot* (1971) — where he had himself shot in the left arm by an assistant — and *Trans-Fixed* (1974) — where he had himself nailed to the back of a Volkswagen Beetle. These performances were "documented" through photographs and/or video footage.

In each of our examples, the description refers us to an artwork, and does so either by (1) offering what appears to be a prescription for a class of performances, or (2) providing a description of an individual perform-ance. In the first case – as with the pieces by Miles Davis, John Cage, and Yoko Ono – it would appear that we have a performable work, appreciable through its performances. In the second case – as with Beuys's *Coyote* or Hatoum's *The Negotiating Table* – we presumably have the articulation of an artistic content through a single performance, similar in principle to Jarrett's *Köln Concert*. What Beuys and Hatoum generated through their actions would thus be pure performance-works, no more re-performable than Jarrett's work. In the case of Beuys and Hatoum, however, this is not because the per-formance is intended to be an improvisation. Hatoum, at least, and probably Beuys predetermined most if not all of the artistically relevant properties of their performances (how many depends upon which properties we take to be artistically relevant). If we treat these performances as performance-works rather than as work-performances, it must be because they are partly constituted by their particular occasions of performance or by the intentions and identity of the person carrying out the performance.

Acconci's *Following Piece*, however, seems to lie between these two models. On the one hand, in line with the first model, the work is identified through a prescription that pre-exists any performances that might conform to it. On the other hand, in line with the second model, the context of performance and the identity of the artist seem to be partly constitutive of the artistic content ascribable to its single actual performance. Would it be possible for another individual to "re-perform" Acconci's *Following Piece*? Or for Acconci himself to do so? Or would this be as misguided as attempts to re-perform the *Köln Concert*?

Acconci's piece is puzzling in another respect. In the case of Jarrett's *Köln Concert*, we noted that, if we allow the particular event in Köln to count as an artwork, this commits us to artworks only properly appreciable on a single given occasion. We reconciled ourselves to this possibility. But in the case of Acconci's performance, no opportunity was offered to potential apprecia-tors to watch the performance as it was taking place. Our only access to the manifest properties of his actions is through a small set of photographs that were actually posed after the original event. (In the case of other perform-ances by Acconci, we usually possess a video or Super 8 record of what he did, although we may still ask as to the significance of such records to the appreciation of the work.) Does this call into question whether Acconci was actually *performing* at all? In what ways, we might ask, was he guided in his actions by the anticipated evaluations of an intended audience?

Even more radical are some of the cited works by Young, Naumann, and Yoko Ono. Suppose that no one has ever performed Naumann's piece, or Young's piece calling for the performer to attempt to push a piano through a wall, or Yoko Ono's (arguably unperformable) piece that calls for following an imaginary map on a real street. Are these simply unperformed (or unperformable) performable works, analogous to the newly discovered Eighth Symphony of Sibelius hypothesised in Chapter 2? There is at least one reason to question whether this is the right way to view such pieces: it isn't clear in what ways an actual performance would bear upon their appreciation. Recall, here, that we defined a performable work in terms of the role that actual performances play in its proper appreciation.

Finally, Cage's work raises problems of a different kind. It seems fairly clear this is a performable work – indeed, it has been performed on a number of occasions. Some have questioned, however, whether it is a *musical* work, since the performer is not required to produce an ordered sequence of sounds.[5] He is, perhaps, prescribed to permit a series of ambient sounds to be audible, but that is a different matter.

3　What is Performance Art?

We shall return to these examples in the following section, where we shall try to determine which of them are rightly categorized as falling within the performing arts. First, however, we need to say something about the general idea of "performance art." Acconci, Beuys, and Burden are usually described as "performance artists," but this term is a very difficult one to pin down. In attempting to locate works of performance art in the more general context of the performing arts, the most obvious strategy would be to identify them with particular performance-events that are artworks in their own right but are not also performances of independent works. This certainly seems a plausible way in which to view Beuys's *Coyote* and Hatoum's *Negotiating Table*. If we wanted to argue that these performances should count as *artworks*, we might point to the ways in which they seek to articulate their contents, as specified above. The use of exemplification, relative repleteness in the range of properties playing a content-determining role, and the hierarchically ordered way in which content is articulated, meet the conditions laid down in Chapter 1 for a content to be articulated "artistically."

These kinds of criteria also seem relevant if we consider the possibility of performance "counterparts" analogous to the counterparts celebrated in writings on the visual arts. The latter are not themselves visual artworks but share with particular visual artworks all of their manifest properties. An example would be a snow shovel of ordinary mass manufacture that shares all the perceptible properties of Duchamp's "ready-made" *In Advance of the Broken Arm*. Consider the following example of such a counterpart in the realm of performance. In April–May 2007, the Chinese performance artist Hai Rong Tian Tian and a fellow performance artist sealed themselves in rooms behind glass walls for a month so as to expose their daily lives to those who visited the exhibit.[6] If this is a work of performance art, and not an amateurish attempt to replicate the television program *Big Brother*, this is not because of the different institutional contexts in which the events took place but because of the *point* of what the performance artists were doing and the way in which this point was articulated through the performance.

But the idea that works of performance art are simply particular performance-events that are artworks in their own right but not work-performances conflicts in at least two ways with our antecedent classification of artworks. First, it would make free jazz improvisations works of performance art. Second, it would exclude accepted works of performance art that are themselves performable works admitting of multiple performances – for example, works by Robert Wilson and Laurie Anderson – and foreclose in an arbitrary fashion on the status as performance art of many of the puzzling examples given above. The pieces by Young, Naumann, and Yoko Ono, for example, seem to be multiply performable at least in principle. Some, indeed, have sought to restrict works of performance art to non-repeatable events. Alan Kaprow, for example, so restricted the use of the term "happening" which he coined to describe performances carried out in the 1950s and 1960s. But artistic practice does not endorse this restriction, and neither should we.

Given these difficulties, it is perhaps better to identify works of performance art through their relation to certain historically situated traditions of artistic making, traditions from which they emerge or by reference to which they define themselves. This is the approach taken by two prominent writers on this issue, RoseLee Goldberg (2001), who has authored an authoritative history of performance art, and Noël Carroll (1986), who situates performance art in relation to theoretical and practical innovations in the visual and theatrical arts in the latter half of the twentieth century. Both authors resist the invitation to *define* "performance art," on the grounds that the phenomena we seek to capture under that label are too diverse. Goldberg stresses that much twentieth-century performance art stems from artists' dissatisfaction with more established artistic practices, and with working within the limitations of particular artistic media (2001, 9). Performance artists often draw in a single work upon different art forms and different media – literature, poetry, theater, music, dance, architecture, and painting, as well as video, film, slides, and narrative. They deploy these resources in ways that by their very novelty defeat any attempt at definition. All that can be said is that performance art is "live art by artists." But, as we have seen, this is at best a necessary condition for being performance art in the accepted sense. And it is by no means necessary that a performance by a performance artist be presented live *to an audience*. Acconci's *Following Piece*, if this is indeed a work of performance art, would demonstrate this, as would his other pieces that are available to us through film but that were performed privately. (They were performed privately partly because one of the issues that Acconci was exploring in these works was the boundary between the private and the public.[7]) And the works of one of the most famous contemporary performance artists, Matthew Barney, are made available to audiences in highly complex cinematic presentations.

Goldberg traces the roots of performance art in the second half of the twentieth century to such earlier movements as Italian Futurism, Russian Constructivism, Dada, Surrealism, and Bauhaus. In each case, she maintains, the "object" works customarily associated with these movements come out of an artistically revolutionary impulse whose initial, but now widely ignored, expressions were in performance. This often involved theatrical performances that stressed provocation, interaction with the audience, and the rejection of the traditional theatrical idea that performance is work-performance. Such performances drew upon such non-artistic practices as the circus, vaudeville, cabaret, and puppet shows, and sought to relocate art in public space rather than in galleries. The focus was not, as in theater traditionally conceived, on the representation of action and the rendering of a text, but upon the performers themselves and the visual aspects – the spectacle – of the performance. The conjoining of different traditional artistic media in such performances is well illustrated in the Bauhaus conception of the "total art work," something echoed in the "happenings" of the 1950s and 1960s and also in later works by artists such as Robert Wilson.

Carroll takes avant-garde theater, as represented in particular by Artaud, to be one of two sources of the interest in performance in the art of the 1970s and 1980s. He distinguishes between what he terms "art performance" and "performance art." The former originated in the 1960s as a reaction to perceived problems with the ways in which visual artworks were presented in galleries. The doctrine of "medium-purity," promoted most forcefully by Clement Greenberg, was seen as denying the relevance of the artist's "performance" in creating a work, as exemplified in the action painting of Jackson Pollock. "Art performance" manifested itself initially in "happenings" that rejected both the idea of the purity and autonomy of different artistic media, and the focusing of artistic interest on formal properties of objects divorced from the activities of artists. One of the most famous such performances took place at Black Mountain College in North Carolina in 1952, and involved collaborations, under the aegis of John Cage, between musicians, choreographers, poets, painters, and film-makers. Later exponents of "art performance" included individual artists such as Acconci, who used his body as a medium for exploring and expressing themes relating to human interaction, and Gilbert and George, who produced works of "live sculpture." While their artistic vehicles are actions, these works, like traditional visual artworks, are made accessible to audiences in art galleries, but through the visual or verbal records or documentations of the performances. Carroll, like Goldberg, stresses the awareness, on the part of those involved in the development of "art performance," of the earlier traditions of Futurism and Dada.

"Performance art," in Carroll's sense, developed out of traditional theater, as a reaction against the idea that dramatic performance should be a vehicle for a literary text. It stressed, rather, the performative aspects of group or individual activity on a stage, and the values, such as spectacle, realizable through such activity. The orientation of traditional theater towards representation, spectatorship, and fidelity to the text was replaced by a concern with the presentational, the participatory, and the visual and gestural. In dance, this manifested itself in the interest in the body in motion explored in the work of choreographers like Yvonne Rainer – something that echoes the interests of the Futurists in the body as mechanism. Rather than the performer mediating between the audience and a character that she represents, there is a focus on performativity, the unmediated interaction between the performer and her audience. Recent work in "performance art" in Carroll's sense has generated, and in turn been influenced by, philosophically inflected studies of performativity by those working in "performance studies."[8]

4   When Do Works of Performance Art Involve Artistic Performances?

Goldberg and Carroll are surely right in thinking that the category of performance art is to be understood in broadly art-historical and sociological terms, rather than in terms of a distinctive medium employed by artists. In this respect it resembles "street art" and differs from "cinematic art." But *our* interest in performance art *is* an interest in the ways in which at least some performance artists use a particular medium for expressive purposes. More specifically, we want to determine, with particular reference to the "puzzling cases" identified earlier, whether, and if so when, works of performance art fall within the scope of the performing arts as understood in the body of this book. In Chapter 1, we characterized the performing arts as those practices whose principal aim is the presentation of artistic performances. An artistic performance, in turn, is one that serves as an artistic vehicle through which an artistic content – the content of an artwork – is articulated. Whether that content belongs to the performance itself – qua performance-work – or to a performable work which it instantiates, it is the performance that serves as the vehicle whereby that content is articulated.

This principle holds however bizarre the nature of the content and however bizarre the nature of the performance. For this reason, we should have no problem identifying the performances by Beuys, Hatoum, and Burden as artistic performances in our first sense. The actions of the performers are the artistic vehicle of a performance-work. Nor should we have any problem identifying the performance by the Miles Davis Quintet as an artistic performance in the second sense. The actions of the performers serve to instantiate a performable work whose artistic content is thereby articulated. We can also enfranchise as artistic performances the kinds of events that fall under what Carroll terms "performance art." For these are simply more radical extensions of theater, which is indisputably a performing art whether we view the performances as falling under the classical paradigm, or under Hamilton's ingredients model. Indeed, we discussed some examples of Carroll's "performance art" in Chapter 6, where we considered the applicability of the classical paradigm to modern theater.

What of our remaining puzzling cases? We can begin by looking at LeWitt's wall drawings. While, for fairly obvious reasons, these will not turn out to involve artistic performances, exploration of possible ways of viewing the wall drawings will be helpful in determining the status of other more puzzling cases.

The wall drawings are puzzling pieces in a number of respects, something well brought out by Kirk Pillow (2003) in a paper on this subject. For example, in his comments on the pieces, LeWitt sometimes talks of the "same work" as being multiply "performable," much as musical works can be multiply performed (1984, 21). At other times, however, he maintains that each materialization of the constraints for a wall drawing is a *distinct* work (LeWitt 1971, 376). Again, there are what seem to be conflicting claims as to the bearing of the finished wall drawings on the being and being appreciated of LeWitt's pieces. On the one hand, in his *Paragraphs on Conceptual Art*, he says the following:

> I will refer to the kind of art in which I am involved as conceptual art. In conceptual art, the idea or concept is the most important aspect of the work. When an artist uses a conceptual form of art, it means that all of the planning and decisions are made beforehand and the execution is a perfunctory affair. This kind of art ... is usually free from dependence on the skill of the artist as a craftsman. (LeWitt 1967)

On the other hand, in "Doing Wall Drawings," he avers that "the explicit plan should accompany the finished wall drawing. They are of equal importance," and that "ideas of wall drawings alone are contradictions of the idea of wall drawings" (LeWitt 1971, 376).

What, then, is the artistic vehicle in the case of a work like LeWitt's *Wall Drawing No. 623*, and what bearing do our aesthetic responses to the manifest properties of the painted surface of its solitary realization – in the National Gallery of Canada – have upon the appreciation of this piece? At least three possible answers to these questions are suggested by LeWitt's various observations.

(1) *The "conceptual work" interpretation*: The vehicle is the *idea* of carrying out the actions characterized in the specifications. If enactment of the idea furthers our appreciation, it does so only by enlivening the idea as verbally specified. Or, more radically, the experiencing of the object together with the realization of the contingent nature of our aesthetic responses given LeWitt's plan, serves merely to bring home to us the purely conceptual nature of the piece. This fits well with the account of conceptual art in the "Paragraphs," but fits much less well with LeWitt's insistence on the importance of there being executions of his plans.

(2) *The "multiple work" interpretation*: This suggests a second answer to our questions, which supplements the first answer by developing LeWitt's "music" analogy. The vehicle, on this view, is an abstractly specified design-structure, or perhaps an "indicated" design structure in Levinson's sense,[9] which has executions as "performances" through which various aesthetic possibilities permitted by that design-structure can be realized. On this reading, an encounter with a particular executed product of a LeWitt plan is essential if we are to properly appreciate the work, just as properties bearing essentially on the appreciation of musical works are given only through performances of those works. Where the executed wall drawing complies with the plan, we can refer appreciable properties of the mural to the piece itself in determining the artistic statement thereby articulated. Pillow rejects the music analogy, however, as a confusion on LeWitt's part, and as incompatible with what Pillow views as the most philosophically interesting feature of the wall drawings, namely, LeWitt's "remarkable stipulation that each execution of a particular plan makes for a distinct work rather than an instance of one work" (Pillow 2003, 378).

(3) *The "two-stage work" interpretation*: Pillow's own reading focuses on the latter claim. A LeWitt wall drawing, or a LeWitt as he terms it, is a two-stage art form "consisting of instructions and their execution on some wall" (Pillow 2003, 370). The artistic vehicle, then, is the particular materialization that one confronts in the gallery, taken together with the plan with which it complies. The plan might be thought to function rather like the title for a standard work of visual art, providing a weighting for the manifest properties whereby the piece articulates its artistic statement.

LeWitt's wall drawings exemplify something symptomatic of late modern visual art, namely, genuine puzzlement as to the nature of a work's artistic vehicle, and, consequently, puzzlement as to what the work is *about* – what artistic statement is articulated through the vehicle. But, whichever option we favor of the three canvassed above, the wall drawings will not fall under the performing arts because the actions prescribed by LeWitt are neither the artistic vehicle of an artwork nor the artistic vehicle of a performance of a performable artwork. Thus the wall drawings do not involve an artistic performance in our sense.[10] On the "multiple work" interpretation, the artistic vehicle of an instance of the artwork is the physical design on the gallery wall that results from an execution of the prescribed actions. On the "two-stage work" interpretation, the vehicle is still the product of an executionary action, but in this case it has to be taken in association with the prescription for that action. Details of the particular actions that brought the physical design into existence, however, play no part in articulating the artistic content of a LeWitt.

Most interesting for our purposes is the "conceptual work" interpretation. While it is the nature of the prescribed *actions* rather than the product that is used to articulate the artistic content of the wall drawings on this interpretation, it is the *idea* of carrying out such actions that serves as the artistic vehicle. This is why this interpretation classifies the wall drawings as *conceptual* works. We can define a conceptual artwork as one whose artistic vehicle is a concept or an idea – this is what Peter Goldie and Elisabeth Schellekens (2010) term the "idea idea" central to conceptual art.[11] Since the prescribed actions themselves play no role in the articulation of the artistic content of a conceptual artwork, save perhaps by enlivening the idea that is its artistic vehicle, it fails to qualify as an artistic performance in either of our senses, even on the "conceptual work" interpretation.

We should be struck by certain similarities between LeWitt's wall drawings viewed as conceptual pieces and some of our other puzzling cases, such as the works by Naumann, Young, and Ono. In the latter cases, it is clear that what matters for the articulation of an artistic content is the nature of the prescribed performance, rather than the product of such a performance. But, as with the "conceptual work" interpretation of the wall drawings, what matters is not the details of an actual performance or action conforming to what is prescribed, but the *idea* of such a performance or action. This applies particularly where it is unclear whether the prescribed action *can* be executed. But, even where the possibility of executing the action is not an issue – as, for example, with the Naumann piece and the Young pieces that prescribe releasing a butterfly or attempting to push a piano through a wall – we must ask whether the artistic content of the work depends in any way upon the details of an *actual* performance fitting those prescriptions. Does it matter, for example, for our appreciation of Naumann's piece, or the Young pieces, whether anyone ever did what was prescribed and, if so, what the manifest properties of the resulting performance were like? If a negative answer to these questions seems appropriate, the pieces in question will turn out to be conceptual works. They will not, appearances to the contrary, be performable works with performances that belong to the performing arts, since their appreciation as the works they are does not depend upon qualities realized in performances that would enact their prescriptions.

This leaves us with three puzzling cases whose status has still to be determined: Young's *Composition 1960 #7*, which seems to be a performable work and which can be, and indeed has been, performed on different occasions; Acconci's *Following Piece*, which seems to be a performable work that has been performed once, and Cage's *4' 33"* which again seems to be a performable work that has been performed many times, but which seems to lack properties that we expect a performable *musical* work to possess. Let us consider these three examples in turn.

As we have seen, we face a general problem in our attempts to appreciate many contemporary works of art. We seek to identify a work's artistic vehicle in order to determine the work's artistic content. But this requires that we establish the relationship between the work and the *documentation* or other material presented in a gallery or theater that plays a role in making the work accessible to receivers. If we had some independent idea as to the point of the work, this would help us to distinguish between a work's artistic vehicle and its documentation. And if we had some independent idea as to the artistic vehicle of the work this would help us to determine what the point of the work is. Given this dilemma, we can best proceed by exploring different ways of reading a work that would ascribe to it particular artistic contents articulated through particular artistic vehicles. In judging between these readings, we can appeal not only to their coherence and intrinsic plausibility, but also to clues to be found in other works by the artist, perhaps in her pronouncements on her works, and in more general features of the art-historical context in which she was working.[12]

In the case of Young's *Composition 1960 #7*, we can be guided in this exercise by something that is perhaps clearer in the case of the other pieces making up the larger collection *Compositions 1960*. The point of these other pieces seems to be to subject to critical scrutiny certain presuppositions about the nature of music and of art. If we assume a common thematic meaning to the pieces making up the collection, this suggests that the point of #7 depends upon the *kind* of thing that is prescribed, rather than on qualities that would be realized in actual performances meeting those prescriptions. On this reading, #7 would be no less a conceptual piece than the piece prescribing that one draw a straight line and then follow it. On the other hand, the musical qualities that are manifest when #7 is performed prefigure the sound structures in Young's later pieces, which are indisputably performable musical works. This reading would make #7 a performable work and its playings artistic performances. It is an interesting question whether, in such a case, we must choose between these readings, or whether there can be works that are intended to be appreciated both as conceptual pieces and for certain manifest properties of their physical realizations.

Turning to the Acconci piece, there is no doubt that much of his work falls within the performing arts. His actions in such pieces are artistic performances in the first of our senses – they are the vehicles of performance-works appreciable in virtue of qualities that they possess as performances. Consider, for example, his *Conversions I, II, and III* (1971), described in an exhibition catalogue as follows: "Acconci attempts to alter his sexual boundaries and, by implication, his sexual identity by turning himself into the image of a woman."[13] One of these attempts involves using a candle to burn the hair off his chest, something that was recorded without sound on Super 8 film. This is one example of Acconci's work as a "body artist," where he uses his body to explore various themes relating to our embodied interactions with one another. In another such piece, he deliberately stood "too close" to strangers in public places. We appreciate these works by watching the filmic records of what Acconci did, which give us a mediated access to his performance.

Following Piece, however, is significantly different. Our access to what Acconci did is limited to a few photographs which, as noted earlier, were staged after the completion of the performance. Here the performance-event in question arguably enters, as vehicle, into the identity of the work only by instantiating the *type* of performance characterized in the performative constraints set out by Acconci. The photographic record serves only to imaginatively enliven the performance for the receiver, to help her to imagine what the performance was like in virtue of satisfying those constraints. The use of photography in such a minimal documentary role is understood by the receiver as indicating that visible features of the actual performance not preserved on film are not important for the appreciation of the work. The photographs serve to isolate those features of the performance-event, as vehicle, which bear upon the articulation of an artistic content.

This speaks to our earlier observation that *Following Piece* has a curiously ambiguous status. In the terms introduced a few paragraphs ago, we can say that the piece has an essentially conceptual dimension – what matters is the *idea* of doing the *type* of thing that Acconci did – and an essentially performative dimension – what matters is that he actually *did* something of this sort. Unlike Young's *Composition 1960 #7*, however, this doesn't yield two distinct ways of interpreting the piece, as either a conceptual work or a performance-work.

Rather, the artistic vehicle is a performance-event which articulates an artistic content solely in virtue of being of the type in question. Although Acconci provided no opportunity for his intended audience to directly observe what he did, his actions qualify as an artistic *performance* because he elected to do the kind of thing that he did in the way that he did it in light of his expectations as to how his intended audience would respond to these actions. There was no need for the intended audience to view the actual performance, however. The relevant manifest aspects of what was done are conveyed to his intended audience through the photographic documentation.

We can turn, finally, to Cage's *4′ 33″*. We have, again, a number of options. First, we might read it as a purely conceptual piece, where the artistic content is articulated simply by the idea of such a performance. That the work has received numerous actual performances would be, in a sense, part of the joke. However, there are good reasons not to favor such a reading. Part of Cage's point, it seems, relates to the nature of the ambient sounds that occur during a performance of the piece. Cage aims to undermine in the mind of the audience the standard distinction between music and non-musical sounds. Thus the work can properly make its point only if performed – it is not enough for the receiver to apprehend the work at a purely conceptual level.

If we decide that the piece is indeed a performable work, however, we can still ask what kind of performable work it is. In a very interesting discussion of Cage's piece, Stephen Davies (1997) argues that *4′ 33″* is indeed a work for performance, and is written for musical instruments, even if they are not to be used to produce sounds. He further argues that the work is performed by the individual who follows the prescriptions in the score, not by the audience whose responses to what is done (or not done!) provide some of the ambient sounds through which the work makes its point. However, Davies argues, it should not be regarded as a performable *musical* work, since it fails to satisfy a necessary condition for being such a work: that it prescribe to its performers that they bring into being "*organized sound*." While the noises that occur during a performance of *4′ 33″* may have some structure, the nature of this structure is not due to the actions of the musician.[14]

According to Davies, *4′ 33″* is "an artistic happening, a conceptual piece that reflects on the world of music without itself being a musical work." As such, it is properly classified as a *theatrical* work: "It is not a work of musical theater, such as opera, but a performance piece about music" (S. Davies 1997, 26). He cites Kendall Walton as another philosopher attracted by this kind of approach (Walton 1987, 76–77). While Davies refers to *4′ 33″* as a "conceptual piece," it should be apparent from our earlier discussion of LeWitt that it is not a conceptual *work* in the proper sense. It is not the idea of doing what is prescribed that articulates the artistic content of the piece. Rather, what is articulated through the actual performances, as artistic vehicles, is a conceptual point about our appreciation of certain kinds of sounds as music.

5   Performance as Art: A Final Case

I have spoken of the task that faces the consumer of contemporary art in identifying the artistic vehicle of a work when the work is made accessible through documentation. Echoing the question that introduced the final section of Chapter 9, we may wonder at times how we are to know the work from the documentation! I have also stressed throughout this book the ways in which an interrogative interest in the artistic vehicle of an artwork is required if we are to determine the artistic content of the work that is thereby articulated. Sometimes, however, such an interrogative interest is required to determine what the artistic vehicle of a work is. I close with a cautionary example of this phenomenon.

Francis Alÿs's 1997 work *Patriotic Tales* is described in the catalogue of a recent retrospective exhibition as "video documentation of an action." The "action" in question is described as follows: "Alÿs first leads a line of sheep around the Zócalo flagpole [in Mexico city], then follows them, as if forecasting a hypothetical moment when the leader would become the follower" (Godfrey et al 2010, 85). The catalogue also provides necessary background for the viewer to appreciate the political resonance of the work. In the 1968 student protests against the then Mexican government, civil servants were brought to the main Zócalo square in Mexico City under orders to protest in support of the government. Instead, they rebelled by turning away from the government representatives and bleating like a flock of sheep. Alÿs's *oeuvre* contains many performance-works in which the artist is documented walking and acting in a context where this has a political resonance. His 2004 piece *The Green Line*, for example, involved walking through Jerusalem with a leaking can of green paint retracing the "green line" that originally partitioned the city between Israelis and Palestinians when the state of Israel was established.

What is interesting about *Patriotic Tales*, however, is that, as one watches the 24-minute "documentation," it becomes apparent that it is *not* what it claims to be. The initially baffling obedience of the sheep circling the flagpole is revealed to the observant viewer to be a feat of digital manipulation. The "clue" is that the light on the back of the sheep as they leave the circle fails to match the patterns of light in the rest of the image. This is "disguised" by the grainy nature of the black and white image, and is nowhere explained in the presentation of the work. But it is apparent to the interrogative regard of the suitably observant viewer.

Is *Patriotic Tales* a performance-work? The answer, I think, is that it is not. For the vehicle that articulates the content of the work is the digitally altered image. The content of the work depends crucially upon the obedience of the sheep in entering and leaving the circle around the flagpole at their appointed time. But this did not in fact happen, nor did it happen, as the film shows, under the ministrations of Alÿs himself. Thus what Alÿs himself did – his actions as captured on video – is not the work's artistic vehicle. Rather, the original video of what he did is an ingredient in the work, manipulated to generate the work's artistic vehicle, which is a moving image. Thus the interrogative interest that we take in what is presented as the documentation of a work of performance art reveals that the "documentation" is in fact itself the work's artistic vehicle. Constant vigilance is the price of artistic appreciation when we encounter an art that revels in being, as the title of the Alÿs exhibition warns us, "a story of deception"! Alÿs's complex work is a final testimony to the richness and diversity of performance in the arts that we have explored in this book.

Notes

1. Or, as we have seen, of a *production* or *interpretation* of an artwork. Or, on the ingredients model, of a production that is itself an artwork. I ignore this complication here.
2. See the liner notes to Miles Davis's *Kind of Blue* (Columbia WPC-8163).
3. For discussion of these works, see Nyman 1999.
4. For an account of the different versions of the "score" for *4′ 33″*, including the lost original, see Solomon 2002.
5. See S. Davies 1997.
6. *China Daily*, August 30, 2009, www.chinadaily.com.cn/. . ./25/content_860008. htm, accessed August 30, 2009.
7. See Linker 1994.
8. See, for example, the papers collected in Parker and Sedgwick 1995.
9. See Chapter 2 for Levinson's conception of performable musical works as "indicated structures."
10. Indeed, they do not involve a *performance* in our sense for reasons given in Chapter 9, section 1.
11. To say that the artistic vehicle of a conceptual work is an idea may sound mysterious. How can an idea serve as a work's artistic vehicle? A couple of remarks may be helpful here. First, if an idea serves as a work's artistic vehicle, then it must be through the idea that the work articulates its artistic content. But, as with any other work, the content is not to be *identified* with the artistic vehicle.

So the idea that serves as the artistic vehicle of a conceptual work is not to be identified with the work's artistic content. It is, rather, the means whereby that content is articulated. Second, if an idea is to serve as an artistic vehicle, then it must articulate the content of a work in the distinctive manner sketched in Chapter 1. Appreciation of a conceptual work requires that the idea be subjected to the kind of interrogative attention whereby we determine any artwork's artistic content. So, for example, it may be significant to reflect on what the idea exemplifies, to scrutinize in careful detail how the idea is embodied in what the artist does or prescribes, or to explore how it performs a number of hierarchically related roles in relation to the overall point of the work.

12. For more on the problems that arise in constructing what I have termed an "identifying narrative," see D. Davies 2007b.

13. I draw here on the booklet for an exhibition including this piece at the Duke Street Gallery, London, 2001.

14. Andrew Kania (2010) argues, against Davies, that Cage's piece does qualify as organized sound. But Kania also argues that it fails to be music because it does not satisfy a further necessary condition for being music, namely, being intended to either have some basic musical feature, such as pitch or rhythm, or to be listened to for such features.

References

Acconci, V. (2004) *Vito Hannibal Acconci Studio*. Museu d'Art Contemporani Barcelona, Barcelona.

Allt, P., and Alspach, R. K. (eds) (1965) *The Variorum Edition of the Poems of William Butler Yeats*. Macmillan, New York.

Alperson, P. (1984) On musical improvisation. *Journal of Aesthetics and Art Criticism*, 43, 17–29.

Alperson, P., Chíbén, N., and Thanh, T. N. (2007) The sounding of the word: reflections on traditional gong music of Vietnam. *Journal of Aesthetics and Art Criticism*, 65, 11–20.

Anderson, J. (1975) Idealists, materialists, and the 32 fouettes. *Ballet Review*, 6.

Archer, K., and Hodgson, M. (2000) Confronting oblivion. In S. Jordan (ed.), *Preservation Politics: Dance Revived / Reconstructed / Remade*. Dance Books, London.

Aristotle (1941a) *Nicomachean Ethics*, trans. W. D. Ross. In R. McKeon (ed.), *The Basic Works of Aristotle*. Random House, New York, pp. 935–1112.

Aristotle (1941b) *Poetics (De Poetica)*, trans. I. Bywater. In R. McKeon (ed.), *The Basic Works of Aristotle*. Random House, New York, pp. 1455–1487.

Banes, S. (1998) *Dancing Women: Female Bodies on Stage*. Routledge, New York.

Baugh, B. (1988) Authenticity revisited. *Journal of Aesthetics and Art Criticism*, 46, 477–487.

Baxandall, M. (1985) *Patterns of Intention*. Yale University Press, New Haven, CT.

Beardsley, M. C. (1982) What is going on in a dance? *Dance Research Journal*, 15, 31–37. Reprinted in part in D. Goldblatt and L. B. Brown (eds) (2005), *Aesthetics: A Reader in Philosophy of the Arts*, 2nd edn. Pearson Prentice Hall, Upper Saddle River, NJ, pp. 241–249. Page references are to this version.

Beardsley, M. C. (1983) An aesthetic definition of art. In H. Curtler (ed.), *What is Art?* Haven, New York, pp. 15–29.

Bell, C. (1914) *Art*. Chatto & Windus, London.

Borges, J. L. (1970) Pierre Menard, author of the *Quixote*, trans. J. E. Irby. In *Labyrinths*. Penguin Books, Harmondsworth, pp. 62–71.

Philosophy of the Performing Arts, First Edition. David Davies.
© 2011 David Davies. Published 2011 by Blackwell Publishing Ltd.

Bowers, F. (1955) *On Editing Shakespeare and the Elizabethan Dramatists*. University of Pennsylvania Press, Philadelphia.

Brook, P. (1988) *The Shifting Point*. Methuen, London.

Brown, L. B. (1996) Musical works, improvisation, and the principle of continuity. *Journal of Aesthetics and Art Criticism*, 54, 353–369.

Brown, L. B. (2000) Phonography, repetition and spontaneity. *Philosophy and Literature*, 24, 111–125.

Burgess, J. P. (1983) Why I am not a nominalist. *Notre Dame Journal of Formal Logic*, 24, 93–105.

Caplan, B., and Matheson, C. (2006) Defending musical perdurantism. *British Journal of Aesthetics*, 46, 59–69.

Carroll, N. (1986) Performance. *Formations*, 3, 63–79. Reprinted in part in D. Goldblatt and L. B. Brown (eds) (1997), *Aesthetics: A Reader in Philosophy of the Arts*. Prentice Hall, Upper Saddle River, NJ, pp. 389–397.

Carroll, N. (1988) *Mystifying Movies*. Columbia University Press, New York.

Carroll, N. (1998) *A Philosophy of Mass Art*. Clarendon Press, Oxford.

Carroll, N. (2003) Dance. In J. Levinson (ed.), *The Oxford Handbook of Aesthetics*. Oxford University Press, Oxford, pp. 583–593.

Carroll, N., and Banes, S. (1982) Working and dancing. *Dance Research Journal*, 15, 37–42. Reprinted in part in D. Goldblatt and L. B. Brown (eds) (2005), *Aesthetics: A Reader in Philosophy of the Arts*, 2nd edn. Pearson Prentice Hall, Upper Saddle River, NJ, pp. 249–255. Page references are to this version.

Cochrane, R. (2000) Playing by the rules. *Journal of Aesthetics and Art Criticism*, 58, 135–142.

Cohen, S. J. (1982) *Next Week, Swan Lake: Reflections on Dance and Dances*. Wesleyan University Press, Middletown, CT.

Conroy, R. (2006) The identity conditions of danceworks. Unpublished paper presented at the American Society for Aesthetics Pacific Division meetings, Asilomar, CA, March 2006.

Conroy, R. (2007) Dancework reconstruction. Unpublished paper presented at the American Society for Aesthetics Pacific Division meetings, Asilomar, CA, March 2007.

Currie, G. (1989) *An Ontology of Art*. St. Martin's, New York.

Da Fonseca-Wollheim, C. (2008) A jazz night to remember. *Wall Street Journal*, October 11.

Danto, A. (1981) *The Transfiguration of the Commonplace*. Harvard University Press, Cambridge, MA.

Davies, D. (2003) Medium. In J. Levinson (ed.), *The Oxford Handbook of Aesthetics*. Oxford University Press, Oxford, pp. 181–191.

Davies, D. (2004) *Art as Performance*. Blackwell, Oxford.

Davies, D. (2007a) *Aesthetics and Literature*. Continuum Press, London.

Davies, D. (2007b) Telling pictures: the place of narrative in late-modern visual art. In P. Goldie and E. Schellekens (eds), *Philosophy and Conceptual Art*. Oxford University Press, Oxford, pp. 138–156.

Davies, D. (2009a) Dodd on the "audibility" of musical works. *British Journal of Aesthetics*, 49, 99–108.

Davies, D. (2009b) The primacy of practice in the ontology of art. *Journal of Aesthetics and Art Criticism*, 67, 159–171.

Davies, D. (2010) Multiple instances and multiple "instances." *British Journal of Aesthetics*, 50, 411–426.

Davies, S. (1987) Authenticity in musical performance. *British Journal of Aesthetics*, 27, 39–51.

Davies, S. (1988) Authenticity in performance: a reply to Young. *British Journal of Aesthetics*, 28, 373–376.

Davies, S. (1991) *Definitions of Art*. Cornell University Press, Ithaca, NY.

Davies, S. (1994) *Musical Meaning and Expression*. Cornell University Press, Ithaca, NY.

Davies, S. (1997) John Cage's *4′ 33″*: is it music? *Australasian Journal of Philosophy*, 75, 448–462.

Davies, S. (2001) *Musical Works and Performances*. Oxford University Press, Oxford.

Davies, S. (2003) Ontology of art. In J. Levinson (ed.), *Oxford Handbook of Aesthetics*. Oxford University Press, Oxford, pp. 155–180.

Davies, S. (2007) Balinese aesthetics. *Journal of Aesthetics and Art Criticism*, 65, 21–29.

Davies, S. (2008) Musical works and orchestral colour. *British Journal of Aesthetics*, 48, 363–375.

Desmond, J. (1999) Engendering dance: feminist inquiry and dance research. In S. H. Fraleigh and P. Hanstein (eds), *Researching Dance: Evolving Modes of Inquiry*. University of Pittsburgh Press, Pittsburgh, PA, pp. 309–333.

Dickie, G. (1974) *Art and the Aesthetic: An Institutional Analysis*. Cornell University Press, Ithaca, NY.

Dipert, R. (1980) The composer's intentions: an examination of their relevance for performance. *Musical Quarterly*, 66, 205–218.

Dodd, J. (2000) Musical works as eternal types. *British Journal of Aesthetics*, 40, 424–440.

Dodd, J. (2005) Critical notice of *Art as Performance*. *British Journal of Aesthetics*, 45, 69–87.

Dodd, J. (2007) *Works of Music*. Oxford University Press, Oxford.

Dutton, D. (1979) Artistic crimes: the problem of forgery in the arts. *British Journal of Aesthetics*, 19, 304–314.

Edidin, A. (1991) Look what they've done to my song: "historical authenticity" and the aesthetics of musical performance. In P. French, T. Uehling, Jr., and H. Wettstein (eds), *Midwest Studies in Philosophy*, 16, pp. 394–420.

Fraleigh, S. H. (1987) *Dance and the Lived Body*. University of Pittsburgh Press, Pittsburgh, PA.

Franco, M. (1989) Repeatability, reconstruction, and beyond. *Theatre Journal*, 41, 56–74.

Gallagher, S. (2005) *How the Body Shapes the Mind*. Oxford University Press, Oxford.

Gallese, V. (2009) Motor abstraction: a neuroscientific account of how action goals and intentions are mapped and understood. *Psychological Research*, 73, 486–498.

Gaut, B. (1997) Film authorship and collaboration. In R. Allen and M. Smith (eds), *Film Theory and Philosophy*. Clarendon Press, Oxford, pp. 149–172.

Gibson, J. J. (1979) *The Ecological Approach to Visual Perception*. Houghton Mifflin, Boston.

Godfrey, M., Biesenbach, K., and Greenberg, K. (eds) (2010) *Francis Alÿs: A Story of Deception*. Tate Publishing, London.

Goehr, L. (1989) Being true to the work. *Journal of Aesthetics and Art Criticism*, 47, 55–67.

Goehr, L. (2007) *The Imaginary Museum of Musical Works*, rev. edn. Oxford University Press, Oxford.

Goldberg, R. (2001) *Performance Art*, rev. and expanded edn. Thames and Hudson, London.

Goldie, P., and Schellekens, E. (2010) *Who's Afraid of Conceptual Art?* Routledge, London.

Goodman, N. (1976) *Languages of Art*, 2nd edn. Hackett, Indianapolis.

Goodman, N. (1978) *Ways of Worldmaking*. Hackett, Indianapolis.

Goodman, N. (1984) *Of Mind and Other Matters*. Harvard University Press, Cambridge, MA.

Gould, C. S., and Keaton, K. (2000) The essential role of improvisation in musical performances. *Journal of Aesthetics and Art Criticism*, 58, 143–148.

Gracyk, T. (1996) *Rhythm and Noise: An Aesthetics of Rock*. Duke University Press, Durham, NC.

Graham, M. (1974) A modern dancer's primer for action. In S. J. Cohen (ed.), *Dance as a Theatre Art*. Dodd, Mead, New York.

Grotowski, J. (1988) *Towards a Poor Theatre*, preface by Peter Brook. Simon & Schuster, New York.

Hamilton, A. (2007) *Aesthetics and Music*. Continuum Press, London.

Hamilton, J. (2007) *The Art of Theater*. Wiley-Blackwell, Oxford.

Hamilton, J. (2009a) *The Art of Theater*: A précis. *Journal of Aesthetic Education*, 43, 4–14.

Hamilton, J. (2009b) Replies to criticisms. *Journal of Aesthetic Education*, 43, 80–106.

Hegel, G. W. F. (1975) *Aesthetics: Lectures on Fine Art*, 2 vols, trans. T. Knox. Clarendon Press, Oxford.

Jacobs, J. E. (1990) Identifying musical works of art. *Journal of Aesthetic Education*, 24, 75–85.

Kalderon, M. E. (ed.) (2005) *Fictionalism in Metaphysics*. Oxford University Press, Oxford.

Kania, A. (2005) Review of *Art as Performance*. *Mind*, 114, 137–141.

Kania, A. (2006) Making tracks: the ontology of rock music. *Journal of Aesthetics and Art Criticism*, 64, 402–414.

Kania, A. (2008) The methodology of musical ontology: descriptivism and its implications. *British Journal of Aesthetics*, 48, 426–445.

Kania, A. (2010) Silent music. *Journal of Aesthetics and Art Criticism*, 68, 343–353.

Kania, A. (forthcoming) All play and no work. *Journal of Aesthetics and Art Criticism*, 69.

Kaplan, D. (1990) Words. *Proceedings of the Aristotelian Society Supplementary*, 64, 93–119.

Kenyon, N. (1988) *Authenticity and Early Music*. Oxford University Press, Oxford.

Kivy, P. (1983) Platonism in music: a kind of defense. *Grazer Philsophische Studien*, 19, 109–129.

Kivy, P. (1988) Orchestrating Platonism. In T. Anderberg, T. T. Nilstun, and I. Persson (eds), *Aesthetic Distinction*. Lund University Press, Lund, Sweden, pp. 42–55.

Kivy, P. (1995) *Authenticities*. Cornell University Press, Ithaca, NY.

Kivy, P. (2006) *The Performance of Reading: An Essay in the Philosophy of Literature*. Blackwell, Oxford.

Kozel, S. (1997) "The story is told as a history of the body": strategies of mimesis in the work of Irigaray and Bausch. In J. Desmond (ed.), *Meaning in Motion: New Cultural Studies of Dance*. Duke University Press, Durham, NC, pp. 101–109.

Kuhn, T., and Giles, S. (eds) (2003) *Brecht on Art and Politics*. Methuen, London.

Leppard, R. (1988) *Authenticity in Music*. Faber, London.

Levinson, J. (1979) Defining art historically. *British Journal of Aesthetics*, 19, 232–250.

Levinson, J. (1980) What a musical work is. *Journal of Philosophy*, 77, 5–28. Reprinted in J. Levinson (1990), *Music, Art, and Metaphysics*. Cornell University Press, Ithaca, NY, pp. 63–88. Page references are to this version.

Levinson, J. (1990a) Authentic performance and performance means. In *Music, Art, and Metaphysics*. Cornell University Press, Ithaca, NY, pp. 393–408.

Levinson, J. (1990b) What a musical work is, again. In *Music, Art, and Metaphysics*. Cornell University Press, Ithaca, NY, pp. 215–263.

Levinson, J. (2005) Musical expressiveness as hearability as expression. In M. Kieran (ed.), *Contemporary Debates in Aesthetics and the Philosophy of Art*. Blackwell, Oxford, pp. 192–204.

LeWitt, S. (1967) Paragraphs on conceptual art. *Artforum*, 5(10), 79–81.

LeWitt, S. (1971) Doing wall drawings. Reprinted in G. Garrels (ed.) (2000), *Sol LeWitt: A Retrospective*. Yale University Press, New Haven, CT.

LeWitt, S. (1984) *Sol LeWitt: Wall Drawings, 1968–1984*. Stedelijk Museum, Amsterdam.

Linker, K. (1994) *Vito Acconci*. Rizzoli, New York.

Lippard, L. R. (1973) *Six Years: The Dematerialization of the Art Object from 1966 to 1972*. Praeger, New York.

Mackie, J. L. (1977) *Ethics: Inventing Right and Wrong*. Penguin, New York.

Mark, T. C. (1981) The philosophy of piano playing: reflections on the concept of performance. *Philosophy and Phenomenological Research*, 41, 299–324.

Matravers, D. (1998) *Art and Emotion*. Oxford University Press, Oxford.

McFee, G. (1992) *Understanding Dance*. Routledge, London.

McFee, G. (2000) Dance. In B. Gaut and D. M. Lopes (eds), *The Routledge Companion to Aesthetics*. Routledge, London, pp. 545–556.

McFee, G. (2007) Performing danceworks: some conceptual concerns. Unpublished paper presented at the American Society for Aesthetics Pacific Division meetings, Asilomar, CA, March 2007.

Merleau-Ponty, M. (1962) *Phenomenology of Perception*, trans. C. Smith. Routledge & Kegan Paul, London.

Merleau-Ponty, M. (1963) The relation of the soul and the body and the problem of perceptual consciousness. In *The Structure of Behaviour*, trans. A. L. Fisher. Beacon Press, Boston.

Minton, S. (1984) *Modern Dance: Body and Mind*. Morton Press, Englewood, CO.

Montero, B. (2006) Proprioception as an aesthetic sense. *Journal of Aesthetics and Art Criticism*, 64, 231–242.

Nyman, M. (1999) *Experimental Music: Cage and Beyond*, 2nd edn. Cambridge University Press, Cambridge.

Osipovich, D. (2006) What is a theatrical performance? *Journal of Aesthetics and Art Criticism*, 64, 461–470.

Parker, A., and Sedgwick, E. (eds) (1995) *Performativity and Performance*. Routledge, London.

Pillow, K. (2003) Did Goodman's distinction survive LeWitt? *Journal of Aesthetics and Art Criticism*, 63, 365–381.

Plato (1941) *The Republic of Plato*, trans. F. M. Cornford. Oxford University Press, Oxford.

Quine, W. v. O. (1969) Ontological relativity. In *Ontological Relativity and Other Essays*. Columbia University Press, New York, pp. 26–68.

Raffman, D. (1993) *Language. Music, and Mind*. MIT Press, Cambridge, MA.

Rizolatti, G., and Sinigaglia, C. (2010) The functional role of the parieto-frontal mirror circuit: interpretations and misinterpretations. *Nature Reviews*, 11, 265–274.

Rohrbaugh, G. (2003) Artworks as historical individuals. *European Journal of Philosophy*, 11, 177–205.

Rubidge, S. (1996) Does authenticity matter? In P. Campbell (ed.), *Analysing Performance*. St. Martin's Press, New York, pp. 219–233.

Russell, B. (1905) On denoting. *Mind New Series*, 14, 479–493.

Saltz, D. (2001) What theatrical performance is (not): the interpretative fallacy. *Journal of Aesthetics and Art Criticism*, 59, 299–306.

Sarlòs, R. K. (1989) Performance reconstruction: the vital link between past and future. In B. A. McConachie and T. Postlewait (eds), *Interpreting the Theatrical Past*. University of Iowa Press, Iowa City, pp. 198–229.

Scruton, R. (1997) *The Aesthetics of Music*. Oxford University Press, Oxford.

Sessions, R. (1950) *The Musical Experience of Composer, Performer, Listener*. Princeton University Press, Princeton, NJ.

Sheets-Johnstone, M. (1984) Phenomenology as a way of illuminating dance. In M. Sheets-Johnstone (ed.), *Illuminating Dance: Philosophical Explorations*. Bucknell University Press, Lewisburg, PA, pp. 124–145.

Shusterman, R. (2008) *Body Consciousness: A Philosophy of Mindfulness and Somaesthetics*. Cambridge University Press, Cambridge.

Shusterman, R. (2009) Body consciousness and performance: somaesthetics East and West. *Journal of Aesthetics and Art Criticism*, 67, 133–145.

Solomon, L. J. (2002) *The Sounds of Silence: John Cage and 4′ 33″*, rev. edn. Available online at http://solomonsmusic.net/4min33se.htm, accessed August 30, 2009.

Sparshott, F. (1982) *The Theory of the Arts*. Princeton University Press, Princeton, NJ.

Sparshott, F. (1988) *Off the Ground: First Steps to a Philosophical Consideration of the Dance*. Princeton University Press, Princeton, NJ.

Sparshott, F. (1995) *A Measured Pace: Towards a Philosophical Understanding of the Art of Dance*. University of Toronto Press, Toronto.

Sparshott, F. (2004) The philosophy of dance: bodies in motion, bodies at rest. In P. Kivy (ed.), *The Blackwell Guide to Aesthetics*. Blackwell, Oxford, pp. 276–290.

Stecker, R., and Dilworth, J. (2005) Double review of *Art as Performance*. *Journal of Aesthetics and Art Criticism*, 63, 75–80.

Stern, T. (2000) *Rehearsal from Shakespeare to Sheridan*. Oxford University Press, Oxford.

Stern, T. (2004) *Making Shakespeare*. Routledge, London.

Storey, I. C., and Allan, A. (2005) *A Guide to Ancient Greek Drama*. Blackwell, Oxford.

Taylor, G. (1989) *Reinventing Shakespeare*. Vintage Press, London.

Thacker, D. (1992) Contributions to panel discussions. In J. Elsom (ed.), *Is Shakespeare Still Our Contemporary?* Routledge, London, passim.

Thom, P. (1993) *For an Audience: A Philosophy of the Performing Arts*. Temple University Press, Philadelphia.

Turner, M. J. (1971) *New Dance: Approaches to Nonliteral Choreography*. Pittsburgh University Press, Pittsburgh, PA.

Van Camp, J. (2009) Dance. In S. Davies, K. Higgins, R. Hopkins, and R. Stecker (eds), *A Companion to Aesthetics*. Blackwell, Oxford, pp. 76–78.

Walton, K. (1987) Style and the products and processes of art. In B. Lang (ed.), *The Concept of Style*, rev. and expanded edn. University of Pennsylvania Press, Philadelphia, pp. 72–103.

Wollheim, R. (1980) *Art and Its Objects*, 2nd edn. Cambridge University Press, Cambridge.

Wolterstorff, N. (1975) Towards an ontology of art works. *Nous*, 9, 105–142. Reprinted in J. W. Bender and H. G. Blocker (eds) (1993), *Contemporary Philosophy of Art*. Prentice Hall, Englewood Cliffs, NJ, pp. 322–338.

Wolterstorff, N. (1980) *Works and Worlds of Art*. Clarendon Press, Oxford.

Wolterstorff, N. (1991) Review of Gregory Currie, *An Ontology of Art*. *Journal of Aesthetics and Art Criticism*, 49, 79–81.

Woodruff, P. (1988) Engaging emotion in theater: a Brechtian model in theater history. *Monist*, 71, 235–257.

Woodruff, P. (2008) *The Necessity of Theater*. Oxford University Press, Oxford.

Wreen, M. J., and Callen, D. M. (eds) (1982) *The Aesthetic Point of View*. Cornell University Press, Ithaca, NY.

Young, J. O. (1988) The concept of authentic performance. *British Journal of Aesthetics*, 28, 228–238.

Young, J. O., and Matheson, C. (2000) The Metaphysics of Jazz. *Journal of Aesthetics and Art Criticism*, 58, 125–133.

Index

Acconci, V. 201, 206, 208
  Conversions I, II, and III 214
  Following Piece 8, 9, 18, 203, 205,
    207, 213, 214–15
Alperson, P. 102n6, 151, 152–4, 158,
    170n5
  on jazz improvisations as artworks
    139–41, 142, 146–7, 160–1
Alÿs, F.
  The Green Line 216
  Patriotic Tales 216–17
Anderson, J. 132n15
Anderson, L. 201, 207
Arbus, D. 43
Archer, K., and Hodgson, M. 127
Aristotle
  Poetics 183–5, 186, 187, 188
Artaud, A. 113, 115, 208
artistic performance
  aesthetic theories of 10–13
  and artistic regard 14–17
  institutional theories of 7–10
  two kinds of 18–19
artistic regard
  and Levinson's historical definition
    of art 17
  nature of 14–16
  and performance-works as
    artworks 142

Ashcroft, P. 117
audience
  response of, to theatrical
    performance 181–9
  role in defining theatrical
    performance 172–81
Austen, J.
  Pride and Prejudice 26
authenticity
  and dance reconstruction 127–8
  historical, in the arts 72–3
  historical, three notions of *see*
    historical authenticity
  kinds of, in musical
    performance 73–4
  personal 74, 83–5
  in theatrical performance 107–12,
    169

Bach, J. S. 151, 152, 153
  Goldberg Variations 91
  The Musical Offering 158–9, 160–1,
    162, 165, 170n8
Balanchine, G.
  production of *The Nutcracker* 121,
    123
Banes, S. 199n11
  see also Carroll, N., and Banes, S.
Barney, M. 208

Philosophy of the Performing Arts, First Edition. David Davies.
© 2011 David Davies. Published 2011 by Blackwell Publishing Ltd.

Bartok, B.
  First String Quartet 55–6
Baryshnikov, M.
  production of *The Nutcracker* 123
Baugh, B. 86n4, 86n11
Baxandall, M. 49n22
Beardsley, M. 4
  on dance performance 10–12, 13,
    14, 21n4, 21n5
Beatles, The 97
  "All You Need Is Love" 97
  "A Day In the Life" 98
  "With a Little Help from My Friends" 99
Beethoven, L. v. 37, 151
  First Symphony 79, 81, 83
  Hammerklavier Sonata 34, 48n13
Bell, C. 47n1
Beuys, J. 201, 206
  Coyote 204, 205, 206, 209
Borges, J. L.
  "Pierre Menard, author of the
    Quixote" 64
Bourne, M.
  production of *Swan Lake* 124
Bowers, F. 165
Brahms, J.
  Hungarian Dances 96
  Second Piano Sonata 37
  Sextet in G major 96
Brecht, B. 113, 183
  epic conception of theater 185–7,
    188–9
Brook, P.
  production of *King Lear* 106, 113,
    121, 131n3, 144, 147
Brown, L. B. 162–4, 170n9, 170n10,
    170n11
Brown, T.
  Roof Piece 174, 180
Budd, H.
  "Gypsy Violins" 124
Burden, C. 206
  Shoot 204, 209
  Trans-Fixed 204, 209
Burgess, J. 50n37

Cage, J. 174, 208
  4' 33" 21n5, 202, 205, 206, 213,
    215–16, 218n14
  *Concert for Piano and Orchestra, Solo for
    Piano* 89
Caplan, B., and Matheson, C. 41,
    50n27, 50n30
Cardiff, J. 203
Carroll, N. 48n4, 48n5, 105, 115,
    121, 132n10, 132n14, 199n7
  on the nature of performance
    art 207, 208–9
Carroll, N., and Banes, S.
  on dance performance 12–13, 15,
    16, 18, 120
Cervantes, M.
  Don Quixote 64
Chopin, F. 138, 143
Citizen Kane 26
classical paradigm
  applicability to classical music
    pre-1800 91–4
  applicability to dance 120–8
  applicability to jazz 95, 155–7
  applicability to non-Western
    music 101–2
  applicability to rock 95–101
  applicability to theater 105–20,
    164–70
  defined 24
Cochrane, R. 153, 170n7
Cocker, J. 99
Cohen, S. J. 124
Coltrane, J.
  "My Favorite Things" 96, 136,
    155, 161
Conroy, R. 125, 128, 132n13,
    132n17
Cunningham, M. 125
Currie, G. 21n6, 39, 49n18, 49n22,
    199n21

Da Fonseca-Wollheim, C. 140,
    142, 148n1
Danto, A. 21n6, 49n18, 49n19, 174

Davies, D. 48n3, 49n13, 49n18,
    50n32, 67n9, 67n10, 70n20,
    70n23, 86n13, 123, 199n5,
    199n21, 218n12
Davies, S. 18, 21n4, 33, 48n4, 48n5,
    48n10, 67n3, 67n11, 68n14,
    85n1, 132n18, 162, 163,
    170n9, 170n11, 170n12,
    171n18
  on authenticity in musical
    performance 77–80, 82, 83,
    85n2, 86n4, 86n7, 86n8, 86n10,
    86n12, 89, 132n19
  on Balinese music 20n3, 101–2
  on Cage's *4′ 33″* 21n5, 215, 217n5,
    218n14
  on Goehr on the "work-concept"
    93–4
  on improvisational
    composition 158–9, 170n5,
    170n6
  on jazz standards 95, 96, 156–7,
    170n2, 170n4
  on the nature of improvisation 151,
    152–4
  on rock works as works for studio
    performance 97–100
  on thick and thin musical works 91
Davis, M.
  "All Blues" 201, 205, 210
  "Blue in Green" 136, 155, 157
  Kind of Blue 201, 217n2
  "My Funny Valentine" 95
Day, T. 51–3, 54, 55
Desmond, J. 199n11
Dibbs, M. 148n1
Dickens, C.
  David Copperfield 129
Dickie, G. 4
  on the institutional theory of
    art 7–10, 14, 16, 20n1
Dilworth, J. 50n32
Dipert, R. 75–6, 86n7, 111
Dodd. J. 36, 39, 43, 49n21, 50n27,
    50n30

  on identity conditions for
    types 48n9, 49n15, 49n16,
    49n17, 50n29, 67n4
  on musical works as norm-types 42,
    48n8, 49n24
  on sonicism 32, 33, 48n10, 48n12,
    48n13
Duchamp, M. 21n5
  In Advance of the Broken Arm 206
Dürer, A. 73
Dutton, D. 49n18, 148n5, 199n21

Edidin, A. 76, 81–2, 86n3, 86n4,
    86n5, 86n6, 86n7, 111
Eicher, M. 135
Eimert, H. 98
Eliot, T. S.
  "The Love Song of J. Alfred
    Prufrock" 144, 145
  The Wasteland 31
embodiment of the performer 189–98
Evans, B. 201

fictionalism 44–7
Fraleigh, S. 192, 199n12
Franko, M. 128

Gabrieli, G. 82
Gallagher, S. 191–2, 194, 197,
    199n13, 199n14, 199n15
Gallese, S. 198, 199n14, 199n18,
    199n19, 199n20
Garrick, D. 166, 168
Gaut, B. 171n21
Gibson, J. J. 191
Gilbert and George 208
Gluck, C. W. 75, 76, 78
Godard, J.-L.
  One Plus One 102n3
Goehr, L. 86n4, 151
  on the "work-concept" 91–4
Goldberg, R. 203, 204
  on the nature of performance
    art 207–8, 209
Goldie, P., and Schellekens, E. 212

Goodman, N. 48n7, 173, 175
  on forgery 59, 63–4, 66
  on the role of the score in
    individuating musical
    works 58–65, 68n12, 68n14,
    68n15, 68n16, 71, 89, 125, 159
  on symptoms of the aesthetic 21n8
Gould, C. S., and Keaton, K. 151–4
Gould, G. 144
Gracyk, T. 96, 162, 170n9
  on rock works as
    recordings 96–100, 101
Graham, M. 126, 127, 189, 190
Greenberg, C. 208
Greene, G.
  The Heart of the Matter 129
Grotowski, J. 113, 115
  production of The Constant
    Prince 114, 119
  production of The Tragical History of
    Doctor Faustus 113

Hai Rong Tian Tian 206–7
Hamilton, A. 148n3, 170n1
Hamilton, J. 113, 155, 165, 166, 167, 189
  on attention 182
  on "audience practice" in
    theater 180–1
  on the ingredients model of
    theatrical performance 114–19,
    128, 131n7, 148, 210
Harrell, L. 152, 153–4
Hatoum, M.
  The Negotiating Table 204, 205,
    206, 209
Haydn, J. 81, 152
Hegel, G. 196
Heifetz, J. 96
historical authenticity
  defined in terms of composer's
    intentions 75–7
  defined in terms of performance
    practice 80–3
  defined in terms of sound
    sequence 77–80

Ibsen, H.
  Hedda Gabler 115–17, 118, 155–6
improvisation
  in classical music 93, 151–2
  as composition 158–60, 164–5,
    171n20
  in jazz 94–5, 136
  pure 160
  and recording 162–4
  and spontaneity 150–4
  on a theme 155–7
ingredients model of
    performance 102n4, 114–19,
    164–70
  see also Hamilton, J.
institutional theory of art see artistic
    performance

Jacobs, J. 88
Jarrett, K.
  The Köln Concert 135–43, 148n4,
    154, 156, 160, 161, 200, 205

Kalderon, M. 50n37
Kania, A. 21n5, 67n2, 95, 131n6,
    170n8, 170n13, 218n14
  on fictionalism 46, 50n32, 50n38,
    50n40
  on rock works as tracks 97,
    100–1
Kaplan, D. 50n28
Kaprow, A. 207
Kenyon, N. 86n4
Kingsmen, The
  "Louie Louie" 162
Kivy, P. 48n11, 90
  on authenticity in musical
    performance 74, 76–7, 78–81,
    82, 83–4, 86n4, 86n5, 86n6,
    86n7, 86n9, 87, 88
  on Goehr on the "work concept" 93
  on improvisational
    composition 158–9, 160, 165
  on the novel as performable
    work 129–31

Kivy, P. (*cont'd*)
  on performance-works as
    artworks 139, 143
  on work-performances as
    artworks 143–4, 145
Kozel, S. 199n11

Led Zeppelin 97
Leonardo da Vinci 73
  Mona Lisa 59, 64
Leppard, R. 76, 86n4
Levinson, J. 21n6, 49n15, 67n3
  on authentic performance and
    expression 70n19, 82–3,
    178, 190
  and contextualism 36–7, 60
  historical definition of art and
    artistic regard 17
  and instrumentalism 33, 34, 90,
    48n12
  on musical works as indicated
    types 38–40, 43, 44, 49n14,
    49n25, 53, 66, 68n13, 211
LeWitt, S.
  Wall Drawing No. 623 202, 203, 210
  wall drawings 210–12
Linker, K. 217n7
Lippard, L. 203

Mackie, J. 50n33
Mark, T. C. 143–4, 147
Marlowe, C. 113
Martin, G. 97
Massine, L. 127
Matravers, D. 67n3
McFee, G. 121, 131n10, 132n11,
    132n12
  thesis of notationality applied to
    dance 122–4, 125–7
medium
  physical and artistic 11, 123
Merleau-Ponty, M. 191–2, 193, 194,
    199n12, 199n13
methodology in the ontology of art 58
Milton, J. 173

Minton, S. 191
mirror-neurons 193–4, 196–8
Monk, T.
  "Straight, No Chaser" 155
Montero, B. 195–8
Motikiyo, Z. 194
Mozart, W. A. 81, 151, 152, 153
  Divertimento in D 91
multiple art forms 48n3
  defined 27
  three kinds of 27–8

Naumann, B. 203, 205–6, 207, 212
Nijinsky, V. 127
Nyman, M. 217

Ono, Y. 203, 205–6, 207, 212
Osipovich, D.
  on the constitutive role of the
    audience in theater 178–80, 181
  liveness model of theatrical
    performance 119–20, 137, 179

Pepys, S. 167
performable works
  as continuants 40–2
  creatability of 34–6
  defined 18
  as fictions 44–7
  as indicated types 38–40
  as indicatings of types 42–4
  multiple nature of 24–8
  as norm-types 29–37; *see also* type
    theories of performable works
  as only perceivable
    analogically 56–7
  as sharing properties analogically
    with their performances 55–6
performance
  and the actual presence of an
    audience 172–6, 178–81
  distinguished from mere action 5–7
  and the expected responses of an
    audience 5–7, 176–8
  see also artistic performance

performance art
  nature of 206–9
performance-works
  as artworks 137, 138–43
  defined 19
performed art
  defined 18
Pillow, K. 210–11
Plato 183
Pollock, J. 190, 208
Presley, E. 97
proprioception 194–5
  as an aesthetic sense 195–6

Quine, W. v. O. 67n8

Raffman, D. 162
Rainer, Y. 209
  Room Service 12–13, 14–16, 18,
    21n5, 24, 110, 120, 126, 190
Rauschenberg, R. 202
recordings 160–4
rehearsal 164–8
Renoir, J.
  La règle du jeu 30
Rizolatti, G., and Sinigaglia, C.
    199n14
Rodin, A.
  The Thinker 26
Rohrbaugh, G. 40–2
Rolling Stones, The 97
  Beggars Banquet 102n3
  "Sympathy for the Devil" 102n3
Rubidge, S. 86n4, 110, 126, 128,
    131n2, 132n13, 132n16
Russell, B. 198n2

Salz, D. 119
Sarlòs, R. K. 107
Scarlatti, D. 92
Schaeffer, P. 98
Scruton, R. 32, 48n11
Sessions, R. 161–2
Shakespeare, W. 112, 113, 165
  Hamlet 106, 109–10

King Lear 24, 34, 56, 57, 103–4,
    105, 106, 108, 109–10, 111,
    112, 169
  Measure for Measure 111
Sheets-Johnstone, M. 199n12
Shusterman, R. 192, 193–4, 196–8,
    199n12, 199n19
Sibelius, J. 58
  Second Symphony 23–30 passim,
    33, 34, 38, 43, 44, 49n25, 51–3,
    55, 56, 57, 62, 88, 90
singular art forms 27
Smith, B. 96
Solomon, L. J. 217n4
Sparshott, F. 122–3, 126, 131n10, 141
Springsteen, B. 97
  Born to Run 100
Stecker, R. 50n32
Stelarc 8, 9
Stern, T. 131n1, 131n4, 131n9,
    165–8, 170n15, 170n16,
    171n17
Stieglitz, A.
  The Steerage 26, 73
Stoppard, T.
  Jumpers 117, 131n5
Stravinsky, I.
  The Rite of Spring 91

Tate, N. 109, 110
Taylor, G. 165
Tchaikovsky, P.
  Swan Lake 56, 124
  The Nutcracker 121, 123–4
Thacker, D. 110, 120
Thom, P. 20n2, 145, 148n5, 189
  on the classical paradigm 89–90,
    105
  on the constitutive role of the
    audience in performance 172–6,
    177, 178, 180, 181, 198n3
  on improvisational
    composition 158–9
  on performance-works as
    artworks 138–9, 141–3

Tudor, D. 202
Turner, M. J. 190–1
type theories of performable works
  contextualism 36–7
  instrumentalism 33–6
  pure and timbral sonicism
    distinguished 32
  sonicism 32–3

Van Camp, J. 132n10
Vermeer, J.
  View of Delft 22n11, 27
Vivaldi, A. 92

Walton, K. 215
Weston, E. 43
Wilson, R. 207, 208
  Medea 10
Wollheim, R. 48n4
  on artistic regard 14, 21n7
  on multiple works as types 48n6,
    54–5, 105, 115, 121
Wolterstorff, N. 28, 30, 48n4, 48n8,
  49n15, 49n23, 159
  on analogical predication 55–6

on requirements for work-
    performance 71–2, 89
Woodruff, P.
  on audience response 182–3,
    186–9, 199n4
  on authenticity in theatrical
    performance 108–10
  on Brecht 185, 186–9, 199n8
  on the constitutive role of the
    audience in theater 172, 173
work-instance
  defined 26–7
  distinguished from performance 31,
    65–6, 68n13
work-performances
  as artworks 84, 143–8
  defined 18

Yeats, W. B. 189, 190
Young, J. 78–80, 83, 86n4, 86n6
Young, J., and Matheson, C. 170n3
Young, L. M.
  Compositions 1960 89, 202, 205–6,
    207, 212, 213–14
  Drift Study 178